Chicken Soup
for the Soul®

Grieving and Recovery

Chicken Soup for the Soul: Grieving and Recovery
101 Inspirational and Comforting Stories about Surviving the Loss of a Loved One
Jack Canfield, Mark Victor Hansen, Amy Newmark

The publisher gratefully acknowledges the many publishers and individuals who granted Chicken Soup for the Soul permission to reprint the cited material.

Front cover photos courtesy of iStockphoto.com/Iakov Kalinin (© Iakov Kalinin) and /Coldimages (© Jan Will). Back cover photos and Interior photo courtesy of iStockphoto.com/duckycards (© Jill Fromer)

Cover and Interior Design & Layout by Pneuma Books, LLC
For more info on Pneuma Books, visit www.pneumabooks.com

Distributed to the booktrade by Simon & Schuster. SAN: 200-2442

Publisher's Cataloging-in-Publication Data
(Prepared by The Donohue Group)

Chicken soup for the soul : grieving and recovery : 101 inspirational and
   comforting stories about surviving the loss of a loved one / [compiled by]
   Jack Canfield, Mark Victor Hansen, [and] Amy Newmark.

      p. ; cm.

   Summary: A collection of 101 true personal stories from regular people about losing
loved ones, covering all the phases of mourning and recovery, with emphasis on how
to accept the loss and move forward.
   ISBN: 978-1-935096-62-7

   1. Death--Literary collections. 2. Bereavement--Literary collections. 3. Death--
Anecdotes. 4. Bereavement--Anecdotes. 5. Loss (Psychology) I. Canfield, Jack, 1944-
II. Hansen, Mark Victor. III. Newmark, Amy. IV. Title: Grieving and recovery

PN6071.D4 C45 2011
810.8/02/03548   2010938808

Chicken Soup for the Soul®

Grieving and Recovery

101 Inspirational and Comforting
Stories about Surviving the
Loss of a Loved One

Jack Canfield
Mark Victor Hansen
Amy Newmark

CSS

Chicken Soup for the Soul Publishing, LLC
Cos Cob, CT

www.chickensoup.com

Contents

❶

~Making the Most of Memories~

❷

~Finding Comfort~

❸
~Helping Hands~

❹
~Attitude Adjustments~

❺
~At the End~

❻
~Moving Forward~

❼
~Across the Generations~

❽

~New Beginnings~

❾

~Healing in Time~

⑩
~Signs from Beyond~

Chapter 1

Grieving and Recovery

Making the Most of Memories

Bean Soup

Enjoy the little things, for one day
you may look back and realize they were the big things.
~Robert Brault, www.robertbrault.com

On the last real night of my marriage I made a pot of bean soup. At about 11 o'clock, the soup was ready, scents of garlic and bay leaf wafting through the apartment. I went into the den, where he was watching the Yankees play the Toronto Blue Jays, and invited him to have some.

We sat at the kitchen table, not talking much, or at least, not talking about anything that I remember. "That was great," he said, when he was finished. I probably said, "Thank you." He stood to go back to the game and I said, "Well, I have to get up early tomorrow. Goodnight." And I went to sleep. I didn't say, "I love you." I didn't say, "I bless the day I met you," or "I am so glad that we married each other." I just went to sleep.

The next time I saw him, he was face down on the bed, not breathing, and although he was in a coma for two weeks, and I believed he would recover for most of that time, in essence, I now know, he was dead.

When something like that happens there are so many regrets, and among the greatest is each and every time that you could have verbally or by action said "I love you." I regretted not learning to care about every thing he cared about. I grieved for every time I got upset over something inconsequential—and trust me, most of it seems inconsequential when the love of your life is in a coma.

For the first week he was unconscious I promised him the moon. I told him that if he would just open those big brown eyes I would never get mad about anything ever again. He could leave his socks two inches from the hamper and I would thank God that they were there. I would dress up more and take time out for lunch whenever he asked. We would watch football games together and talk about politics. I promised him prime rib in wild mushrooms and red wine, and tuna au poivre perfectly rare, on the Royal Doulton with candles every night.

The second week, I came back to earth. I stopped promising him the perfect wife. Instead I promised him Me. I promised that I would at times be impatient or scared, and that he would still have to take out the garbage. I promised that I would not always like his jokes, and that I would still nag him to exercise. I promised him that we would have interests in common but not all of them, and that we would still have things to be tolerant of in each other. I promised him bean soup.

But as part of bean soup, I promised him that I would love him as much as before or maybe even more and that I would try never to forget what we had almost lost. I wish I had been given the chance.

Marriage is not always made of rose petals and moonlight and perfect understanding. Sometimes it is made of kids with the stomach flu, and flights that have been delayed, or even just made of work and dinner and running out of light bulbs. At times like that, sometimes the marriage goes on autopilot and love is subtext, an article of faith. Then, the dust clears and we remember. And as you have no way of knowing when you are young, but as you come to know when you've been married a while, that is more than fine.

Reasonable minds may differ, but for me, it is the dailyness that I love the most about being married. I liked the anniversary dinners and the romantic moments, but even more I loved the mundane work-ings of our daily lives, coming home to trust and commitment and inside jokes, and even the predictable irritations like those socks.

When a marriage is lost in the way that mine was, it is the every-day memories that mean the most. The time we both had bad colds and spent the day in sweatshirts, bringing each other tea. The way he took in the dry cleaning every Friday. Or the nights, like that last one, where we didn't really talk but shared the deep ordinariness of a quiet Sunday night with our daughter asleep and the Yankees playing for him and some music for me, and a great big pot of soup.

~Jacqueline Rivkin

Daffodil Month

The flowers of late winter and early spring
occupy places in our hearts well out of proportion to their size.
~Gertrude S. Wister

Mother opened her eyes and stared, unblinking, at the vase of daffodils on the table beside her hospital bed. "Who sent these beautiful flowers?" she asked in a barely audible voice.

"No one sent them, Mother." I squeezed her hand. "I picked them from your yard. It's March — Daffodil Month."

She gave me a weak smile. "Promise me something?"

I nodded. I'd promised a lot since we'd come to accept that the cancer in Mother's pancreas would soon take her life.

"Promise that before you sell my house, you'll dig up my daffodil bulbs to plant in your yard."

I tried without success to hold back my tears. "I'll do that, Mother. I promise." She smiled and closed her eyes, lapsing again into the twilight fog that characterized the last days of her life.

Before Daffodil Month ended, Mother was gone. And in the weeks that followed, weeks so grief-filled that my siblings and I resembled nothing so much as walking zombies, we emptied her house, painted, washed windows, cleaned carpets, and listed the home we'd grown up in with a real estate agency. We hired a neighborhood boy to take care of the yard.

And I gave the daffodils, which had long since quit blooming, not a single thought until a day in late autumn when the house was finally to be sold. My brother and sister and I were to meet the buyers to sign papers early on a morning that I knew would be filled with conflicting emotions. On the one hand, it was good to be out from under the burden of owning an empty house. On the other, we would soon be turning over the keys to our family home to strangers.

Strangers who, I was certain, could never love it as much as we did.

Would this new family cook Fourth-of-July hamburgers on the brick patio grill my dad had built so many summers ago? Would their children spend fall afternoons raking the leaves under the giant maple tree into a mile-high pile to jump in? Would they figure out that one corner of the family room was the perfect spot for a Christmas tree? And would they be amazed at what pushed its way out of the ground in Mother's yard every spring?

Crocuses. Flowering onions. Hyacinths. And hundreds and hundreds of daffodils.

Daffodils! Eight months later, I suddenly remembered the promise I had made my mother as she lay dying. I tossed a shovel and a cardboard box into the trunk of my car and headed for the house and yard that would, in just a couple of hours, belong to someone not related to me.

There was no sign of daffodils anywhere, of course. They had long since been mowed down and were now covered with leaves. But I knew exactly where they were. Ignoring the fact that I was overdressed for gardening, I plunged the shovel's point into the dirt, lifted out a clump of bulbs, and tossed them into the box. Working my way down the fence line, I harvested dozens of daffodil bulbs.

But I left more than I took, certain that the family who'd bought my mother's house would take delight in her lovely harbingers of spring.

As do I. It's been more than five years now since my mother passed away. But every March, I gather armloads of the bright yellow blooms from my own yard and put them into vases. Some I use to decorate my house. Others I take to the cancer wing at a nearby hospital.

"Who sent these beautiful flowers?" a dying patient might ask.

And I will squeeze his or her hand and look into eyes clouded by that all-too-familiar twilight fog and speak words that I believe with all my heart to be true. "My mother sent them, especially for you," I'll reply. "It's Daffodil Month, you know."

~Jennie Ivey

My Mother's Recipe Box

Let your tears come. Let them water your soul.
~Eileen Mayhew

My husband reached it for me. It was on the highest of our kitchen cabinet shelves, the one that remains out of sight/out of mind. My mother's no-nonsense green metal recipe box had been stashed there three years ago, after her death at 97. And there it had stayed.

So many of the other objects in her household had been carefully sorted out, distributed to family members, donated to charity. But this box—this humble, ancient box, remained with me, untouched. I couldn't have explained to anyone exactly why.

Somehow, that afternoon, I was ready.

My first thought, as I touched the box and pried open its lid, was a guilty one. Why hadn't I seen to it that Mom had a prettier recipe file? Why hadn't I found a cheerful one for her, something sweet in floral or gingham?

Guilt is a handmaiden of sorrow, and I'd had plenty of both since the December day three years ago when we stood at my mother's grave and said a last goodbye.

There had been those awful wrenching times when I'd reached for the phone at dusk for our usual pre-dinner conversation, and forgotten that the number I was calling was "…no longer in service," as that awful, disembodied announcement reminded me.

There had been the presence of that empty chair at the table for family milestones, the proof that we were no longer going to be graced by the sweet face of our matriarch, beaming because family was her taproot, her greatest source of joy.

And there had surely been those moments when I thought my heart would break from missing the tiny blond woman who had loved all of us so unconditionally, and had asked so little in return.

But opening that recipe box… that was a long-overdue marker on the journey to healing.

Mom was a legendary cook. The sort who didn't actually need a recipe to guide her. Instinct was her best teacher, and somehow, she could make a meatloaf taste like filet mignon, or raise a simple roasted chicken to lofty heights.

But over the years, Mom had fortunately reduced some of her recipes to writing. "Someday, you may want these," she had said prophetically.

"Someday" had come.

Sitting at the kitchen counter, I began my search for remembered pleasures… for the taste of my childhood, at least figuratively.

As I scanned the categories—main dishes, side dishes, holiday foods, cakes, cookies—there was Mom's familiar scrawl. Her loopy letters, the "t's" left uncrossed in her haste, the crowded script—all came rushing back. It had been so long since I'd seen that familiar handwriting, now that her anniversary and birthday cards signed "With all my love," no longer arrived in our mailbox.

Mom had no patience for fad diets. So I sifted through detailed instructions for making a rich lasagna, a brisket swimming in gravy, for meatballs and spaghetti with her own "secret" sauce ingredient—brown sugar.

There were recipes for everything from a simple egg salad with pimentos to a noodle pudding that she had learned from her own mother.

Mom's parents—my maternal grandparents—were Eastern European immigrants, part of that vast wave that had arrived on these shores in the early years of the 20th century. And in this golden land, food—lots of it—was their solace. It soothed the loneliness, bewilderment and fear of lives forever changed.

So much of my own history and heritage was in that green metal recipe box.

I spent one long afternoon with it, smiling, remembering, and yes, weeping. So much of Mom came flooding back. Decades later, I was back in her kitchen—and it was so clearly HER kitchen in the days when fathers seldom strayed into the inner sanctum. I was smelling her amazing pot roast, her sour cream/apple coffee cake, her split pea soup.

And I was wishing—how I was wishing—that she was back, too, in her aqua cobbler's apron with the white ruffle.

"Do NOT overcook, Sally," I found on one recipe card for pot roast. It made me laugh out loud, because that was, after all, my high culinary crime. And Mom knew it.

Hours later, when I'd rummaged through the last of the recipe cards and newspaper clippings stuffed in the back, I felt a kind of peace I hadn't in too long. It was the sense that somehow Mom was in my life again.

She was peering over my shoulder, checking, re-checking, scolding, advising, and yes, teaching. She was handing down her traditions in the most loving way—through food as love.

Mom-food. The best of all possible cuisines.

And I carefully, deliberately placed that green metal box with its stubborn lid on the kitchen counter. Front and center.

Exactly where it belongs.

~Sally Schwartz Friedman

Two Lives

I dream of giving birth to a child who will ask, "Mother, what was war?"
~Eve Merriam

It was August fourteenth and August fifteenth.
It was two families shattered, shocked.
It was 1,000 friends at the candlelight vigil.
It was the three teachers I haven't seen since high school.
It was the boy who never cried who made an eloquent speech while
    he wept.
It was the sweat that stretched down my back.
It was my friend falling apart next to me.
It was the bug that drowned and burned in the wax of my candle.
It was the entire town, brought together.
It was incomprehensible.

It was the way that suddenly I couldn't remember their faces.
It was online message boards carved with words of remembrance.
It was breaking the news to my brother.
It was the questions from coworkers—"Did you know them?"
It was the front page newspaper articles the whole week.
It was the tribute on the billboard outside the pizza parlor.
It was the flags at half-staff when they finally came home.
It was the 21-gun salute, the 50-foot American flag,
and the two dozen yellow roses.

It was two boys just out of high school, not even men yet.
It was Iraq the first day, Afghanistan the next.
It was a Boy Scout and a punk rocker who were never quite friends.
And it was the tall man on the hill during the vigil who put it all
    into words:
"God bless your boys, and be with them."

~Paige Cerulli

A Family Heirloom

Memory is a child walking along a seashore. You never can tell what small pebble it will pick up and store away among its treasured things.
~Pierce Harris, Atlanta Journal

As far back as I can remember, my mother had a black fur coat hanging in the hall closet. Since it wasn't really my mother's style to wear fur, I always wondered why we had the coat at all. I remember asking her what it was made of. She said it was made of muskrat. I loved animals and I tried to imagine how many muskrats gave up their lives to make this big, beautiful coat. Yet, I couldn't resist rubbing against the silky fur. When I snuggled it in the closet, it filled my nose with a distinctive fragrance.

I am sure all of us tried it on at one time or another. There were four girls, at least, who paraded around in it. I am not so sure about the boys. Even at that time, we wondered who would get the coat.

The coat belonged to my grandmother. She was the daughter of a doctor in Ridgetown, Ontario. She married a lawyer from the United States and her wedding made the society news of the day.

My great-grandfather, the doctor, had found a bride in Glasgow and brought her home to Ontario, where they raised five sons and two daughters. My grandmother died in 1976. My mother died in 1995.

One day, after my mother died, I decided to make a pilgrimage to my grandmother's hometown. I found the largest house in town easily. There were many photos of it at home, but since my great-grandfather's day it had been turned into a funeral home. I found that a little depressing. I stopped to have coffee in the small town restaurant that felt a lot like my own hometown in Forest, Ontario. It gave me an insight into my grandmother's decision to buy our cottage in Forest. They both had that warm small-town feeling.

On the way home, I felt a little lost. I would have liked to have shared the experience with my mother, but she had already passed away. As I drove down a side road, the kind that are unmarked and seem to last forever, I saw a flock of white geese. I stopped to watch them and they gave me a thrill, because I had never seen a field full of Snow Geese before.

My mother left the coat behind in the closet. My eldest sister, Janet, inherited it with the house. Many years passed and she kept thinking about what she might do with the coat. One day, in the summer of 2009, my sister sent a parcel for my three children. One package labeled "Allison" caught me by surprise. I let the children open their presents before I opened mine. They were equally excited for me to have a present.

I ripped open the wrapping and a familiar smell assailed my nose, although I couldn't place it at first. In front of me sat a beautiful black bear with a pattern on his paws that I recognized from long forgotten days of snuggling in the hall closet. The feelings they evoked were joyful. Pictures of four identical black bears spilled out on the floor. I could hardly grasp what my sister had done!

When I finally got her on the phone, she confessed her long kept secret. She told me that she didn't like the fact that the coat hung in the closet, useless and unused. Then she saw a program on how people turned old fur coats into bears. She decided that's exactly what she wanted to do.

When she looked into the cost of the service, she found that each bear would cost $250. Since this price was outside her budget, she decided that the best way to get bears would be to ask if someone did it as a hobby. She mentioned it to her teacher friends. Then her old principal asked the lunchroom lady if she knew anyone who did such a hobby. Confused, the lady asked him why he wanted to know, because that's what she did in her spare time.

So, four identical bears were born, works of art, in Calgary, Alberta. I feel so lucky to have a sister who would take the time to put her love into such a bear project only to share it with her sisters. All my children sense the love I have for this heirloom bear, a bear of memories that no one can buy for me from a store.

~Allison Knight-Khan

Learning to Soar Again

He who would learn to fly one day must first learn to stand and walk and run and climb and dance; one cannot fly into flying.
~Friedrich Nietzsche

I made my decision and finalized it by driving the stake into the ground. Big, bold, red letters read HOUSE FOR SALE. I went inside, washed my hands and sat at the kitchen table, anxiously clutching a glass of cold lemonade, while my eyes rested on a cardinal pecking away at the food tray on the birdfeeder outside my window.

I smiled as the memories of this table, the window and the birdfeeder blessed my soul. My husband had painstakingly measured from the ground to my eye level and placed the birdfeeder on top of the pole. He said he did it for me, and he did, but he enjoyed our bird watching almost as much as I did. We emptied many pots of coffee sitting here in the early mornings, watching yellow and black finches, blue birds, nuthatches and chickadees. But my favorite was the cardinal.

My feet propped on a stool, I breathed in the crisp, clean air and savored the taste of home-squeezed lemonade. My eyes fixed on a cocoon attached to the bottom side of a green clematis leaf winding around the trellis. Silky threads quivered, split apart. Brilliant yellow and black wings emerged, and the butterfly wriggled its way out of its safe place. Defying predators and collectors with nets, it dared to soar through open fields and sip sweet nectar from nature's bounty, spreading its majestic wings, golden pennants glistening in the sun.

The larva transitioned from a warm, safe, ugly worm to a free-flying beauty, ready to embark on life's adventures.

Since I was going to sell this house, I thought I might as well practice what I might do and say to a prospective buyer. "Hello," I said as I walked to the door. "Come on in. Come through the kitchen door. All my friends enter here."

Then I began the tour. I couldn't help but point to the birdfeeder my husband built, as I mentioned how he painted it white to contrast with my red birds.

"Do you see the woods behind the house?" I again motioned toward the open window. "We often drank our coffee in silence so as not to scare away the deer, rabbits, squirrels and chipmunks that wandered into the yard. The trees offer fine shade for family barbecues, too."

I fingered the cut glass crystal vase as I talked to my imaginary visitors. "This vase once stayed filled with flowers from hubby's flower garden, Kroger's flower shop, or wildflowers picked from the open fields over there. My friends used to tease me, saying I was still being courted after 45 years of marriage. I didn't argue with them."

I pointed to the window on the other side of the house. "You can see the garage through here. It's still full of tools, from woodworking to mechanical. Even when my late husband was sick, he liked to tinker in his workshop. His motorcycle is parked in one corner and our pontoon and fishing gear in the other. We spent many hours traveling around the country in that little motor home parked under the carport."

I took them into our family room where the family Bible lay open on the coffee table and my husband's portrait hung on the wall. I pointed to it. "He sure was a handsome one. When he was young, friends told me he looked like Elvis. He didn't want pictures taken after he became bald from chemotherapy."

Nodding toward the television, I said, "I bought him that big screen TV so he could watch his Kentucky Wildcats play basketball. He leaned back in that big brown recliner over there, watching the games or his favorite courtroom show."

I picked at a loose thread. "The recliner's arms have worn spots on them where the grandkids climbed onto their pappy's lap. And the springs are a bit saggy because sometimes that chair not only held my husband, but both of our adult daughters at the same time." The vision of the three of them all piled into that chair flitted through my head.

"Let's look at that chair again. Search closely and you'll probably find a cellophane-wrapped peppermint ball that fell from his pocket where he kept a stash to give to the ladies and children at church. They lovingly called him the Candy Man."

An unbidden smile crinkled my face. "In fact, a peppermint ball mysteriously appeared in his hand after one of the ladies from church viewed his body in the funeral home."

I swept my hand toward the opposite wall. "These are my grand-children." I ran my finger over the hand-carved trim on the wooden picture frame, letting it come to rest on my youngest. "In the trek from infancy to elderly, we encounter many phases of life. She turned two this spring. Plate and spoon replaced mother's milk, and panties replaced Pampers. She put on her backpack when school resumed and announced she was going to school also, throwing a teary tan-trum when the bus picked up her two siblings and left her behind. Her transition from babyhood to childhood was complete."

My finger brushed over the next one. "Her brother, off to pre-school this year, anxiously boarded the bus, then stopped, looked back and waved goodbye with a hint of an unshed tear lurking behind his lashes.

"And my namesake became a pre-teen this summer. Instead of children's programs, her favorite TV personality is the latest popular teenage idol and her little girl clothes don't fit anymore. Ten is a trying time, too young for boy-girl relationships, yet toys no longer captivate the imagination."

In another photo, three grandsons stood in a row. "This grandson both eagerly and reluctantly moves up to middle school. Elementary school teachers will no longer be there to comfort him when he loses his lunch money or is harassed by bullies. So he faces a new level of independence. This grandson here is bravely facing the frightful monster called high school, while this one becomes a teenager next month. His baby fat is melting and a few pimples dot his face." I spoke softly now.

"Before we go into the bedrooms, let me show you my children." I turned to the pictures on the wall on the other side of the room. "My younger daughter will be thirty in September. She gained a few gray hairs while transitioning from a stay-at-home mommy to a freshman in college. My other daughter, once a special needs student battling dyslexia, has begun her quest to teach other special needs children."

I picked up the filigree frame and the face of a beautiful young woman, who has left a void in our hearts, stares back at me. My eyes become misty as I look upon my son holding his granddaughter, my great-granddaughter, who helps to ease the pain in our lives and fill the vacant place in the family portraits where his only daughter once stood.

A tear slid down my cheek as I smiled wistfully. I looked at my pretend house shoppers and said, "I'm sorry I wasted your time, but I don't think we will finish the tour because this home is no longer for sale. This house holds many memories and, with God's help, I think I'll keep them just as they are."

A cool, healing breeze rippled through the window as I finished my lemonade and began planning for a new day. A black and yellow Monarch glided over the trellis, fluttering its wings as it perched on the clematis leaf. Last month I began my transition from a happily married wife to a confused, insecure widow, but, like the butterfly, I too will develop my own wings and soar.

~Jean Kinsey

7

Sharing the Journey

*Where you used to be, there is a hole in the world, which I find myself
constantly walking around in the daytime, and falling in at night.
I miss you like hell.*
~Edna St. Vincent Millay

One of my dearest friends died recently. Dolores had been battling cancer for more than eight years with strength and an unflagging optimism. She was a take-charge person. Each time cancer recurred she would accept, almost welcome, and at one time demanded, the next round of chemo. She knew what was coming—the nausea, neuropathy, the sleeplessness and pain—but she also knew the consequences if she refused. There would be two or three days a week of discomfort but she focused on the four days when she would feel "pretty good." If the regimen called for chemo every three weeks, she happily anticipated the two weeks of feeling decent. But the periods of remission before cancer popped up again became shorter and shorter.

Dolores said that she would know when her quality of life was too diminished, yet despite her trials she held on. The time eventually came when she was in and out of the hospital and her daily existence was ruled by pain. That was when she made the decision to stop the tests, the chemotherapy, the distress to herself and her family, and to let go. She went home on hospice care. Three weeks later we attended her funeral.

She and I had met 30 years ago, through an introduction by a mutual friend who thought we would get along because I was moving onto the same street and we both were writers. Our friend was right. We did get along—on many levels—and we discovered more about each other as the years progressed.

Our friendship began when I invited my new neighbor to a writers' group I had been attending. She wrote poetry and I wrote children's books, two very different genres, but the group was eclectic: one man wrote horror stories à la Stephen King, a woman wrote feature articles for newspapers, someone else wrote poetry for his own pleasure. The group was fun and helpful, but it was our carpooling back and forth that helped our friendship blossom. We learned a lot about each other on those trips. We talked about our hopes and philosophies, our families, our worlds.

One day I got the idea that we could write a children's book together using my stories and her poems. We sent out queries and got rejections, but one editor suggested that we fill out the book with crafts and activities. Neither of us had done that before. We looked at each other and said, "Why not?"

Each day I trundled down to her house, three doors away, and we created projects for kids using what we had handy—laundry baskets, milk cartons, bed sheets, yarn. Our days were spent laughing. We couldn't believe what we were able to produce from ordinary household things. We ended up coauthoring two Halloween activity books, four joke books, and one picture book.

People asked us if it was hard to write with another person. We never thought so, perhaps because we wrote every sentence together. Every poem had both our voices; every activity was a combination of ideas. We didn't see the projects as hers or mine but rather as ours. There was no competition, only fun.

We did more than write together. We attended classes, took up Chinese brush painting, practiced Qi Gong and Tai Chi in our front yards. I taught yoga and she became a feng shui consultant.

Through the years we set aside Friday afternoons for meditating, either in her house or mine, and invited a couple of friends to join us.

It was during one of those sessions that she suddenly realized she had cancer. Six months later she was diagnosed and everything changed.

I visited her each day as she slowly succumbed to the disease those last weeks. I could see that she was waiting to leave. We talked a little, but mostly I just held her hand. I knew that her philosophy embraced a broad understanding of energy, but I could tell how hard the process was. When she left, I was relieved as much as I grieved.

She is still in my heart—and in my files. Our joint work, both published and unpublished, is a connection between our worlds. When I think of her, I am grateful for our years together. I never suspected when we met that our relationship would be so profound. But then, do we ever know where life takes us and who will share the journey?

~Ferida Wolff

8

Butterfly Miracles

To live in hearts we leave behind
Is not to die.
~Thomas Campbell, "Hallowed Ground"

I rummaged through the small cardboard box that passed for my jewelry box. On a mission to get rid of anything unworn, I gasped as my hand touched the metal butterfly—no bigger than a half dollar. Clutching it to my aching chest, the tears streamed down my face as I remembered.

Vivid images of the day my eight-year-old son presented the butterfly pin he'd made for me—my Mother's Day gift—rushed to mind. I could picture Mark, round face, straight blond hair, as he smiled up at me. "Here, Mom, I made this for you in art class. I painted a design on it, but they baked it and the paint all ran together. I think it turned out neat!"

I prepared myself to receive a gift of love more than beauty as I unfolded the paper wrapped by childish fingers. A witty, personable, and fun-loving child, Mark did not seem to possess artistic talent. The butterfly, to my surprise, emerged a masterpiece of swirling copper, blue and beige hues.

"It's beautiful," I said with complete honesty. He accepted my hug with eyes rolling, as I murmured, "Thank you, honey. I love it." He beamed with pride. I wore the pin frequently for years, often receiving compliments on its artistry.

One day, the back fell from the butterfly as I rushed to pin it to my lapel. I dropped the butterfly into the box in my drawer as I hurried to my appointment. I'll have it repaired later, I thought.

Life was filled with family, school and work. The butterfly rested, forgotten, in the bottom of the box for more than ten years.

This day, the full force of the painful loss pressed into my chest. Eighteen months earlier, as I cradled my husband in my arms, I felt half of me slip away as he died. Now, the rest of my heart had been ripped from my chest as my 22-year-old son died while I held his hand—helpless again to keep cancer from taking one I loved. Mark had fought the disease with great courage and confidence. In the end his body betrayed him when his spirit would have kept on fighting. The deep, painful cavity inside me screamed for relief.

How I'd longed for a part of Mark to keep near. His cap, his keychain—none of his possessions had provided comfort—only more pain. But this butterfly, a gift made by his loving hands, held the promise of his continued presence with me. His life changed, like the caterpillar to the butterfly. He was no longer bound by ill health and earthly trials. The butterfly reminded me of this truth. The miracle of this gift, rediscovered after so many years, soothed my grieving heart.

The butterfly, coupled with a gold cross and attached to a delicate gold chain (a gift from my daughter), traveled the journey through grief with me. I wore it constantly, even in the shower. Along the way, sometimes the telling of the story brought comfort to another traveler. It also held the promise of change and healing for me, but in some irrational way, I felt to take it off would be to forget Mark and stall the healing.

One night, about a year after his death, I, who almost never remember a dream, had a startling and memorable one. I found myself standing on my front porch looking for someone. I saw a young man in the distance and as he trudged nearer, I recognized Mark—tired, sick and dirty—but Mark without a doubt. Stunned, unable to move at first, I threw my arms around him as he came up onto the porch.

Holding tight, I cried, "Mark, oh Mark, it is so good to see you.

You're not dead. I thought you were dead and you're not. Oh Mark, Mark, I love you son," I babbled.

He pulled back from me and said, "Mom, I love you. I have to go now and you must let me go. You must let me go, Mom. You can't keep hanging onto me. Let me go now." With that, for just a second, he appeared healthy and vigorous—almost glowing—then vanished.

I woke up feeling his embrace and hearing his words echo in my mind. I clutched the butterfly as tears streamed down my face. I raced to the front door to look for him and saw only an empty street. I started to grasp it was only a dream, but a strange peace crept into my darkness.

As I pondered the dream, I realized that in order to heal, to move on, I had to let Mark go—not forget, but refuse to cling to what might have been. The butterfly became the symbol. I started by taking it off to shower, then to sleep. Little by little I accepted my son's departure from my life, but never forgetting what we'd shared. The awful pain and emptiness declined as I persisted in enjoying the memories of the occasions we'd spent together—not dwelling on the times we'd never have.

As my journey continued, the butterfly reminded me of the new life that awaited me. But when would that lingering ache in my chest depart? Five years passed. I believed that as long as I lived, the ache would remain. After all, I'd shed tears with women who buried children 60 years before.

On a walk one day, as I mulled over this "fact," a butterfly fluttered toward me as if heaven-sent. Healing in his wings, I thought. And suddenly the ache was gone, replaced by joy for Mark reveling in all the glories of heaven.

Do I miss him? Yes. Is there sadness or a tear now and then? Yes. But there is a difference. The sadness no longer steals the joy away. Now when I wear the butterfly it is a symbol of victory over death and a new life not just for Mark, but for me as well. Clearly, more than one butterfly miracle came my way.

~Jeanne Wilhelm

9

The Red Pen

Sometimes, when one person is missing, the whole world seems depopulated.
~Alphonse de Lamartine

My thoughts turn to what has been with me for weeks. I am thinking about a past boyfriend whom I met again by chance. I cannot get him out of my mind.

He was not my boyfriend. He was the very special friend of my beloved sister Ivy when she was in high school. Ivy was 16 when she died in a plane crash with my father.

Ivy was sister number four, the baby, although in many ways she was probably the most mature within her short life. She was a very rare young woman who had the ability to empathize like few people I have ever known. She was stunning physically and within. She had long wavy brown hair, oval chocolate brown eyes and a smile that mesmerized. Her gentleness and insight were the foundation of a poise that was well beyond her age.

Seeing her friend David again was an overwhelming experience. I could only think of Ivy's description of how she first met him while walking down the hall of her high school. She had told me that she knew instantly that she had to find out who he was. It was a romantic and womanly moment in her life.

When I ran into this incredibly handsome man, then in his late thirties and still single, I hugged him and he returned the warmth and greeted me by the nickname Ivy called me. My heart ached in response and yet I was filled with an indescribable fulfillment. I was looking into the eyes of someone who shared so much of my sister's life in a way that belonged only to them. I am thankful that she had whatever they shared. She would sometimes ride on the back of his motorcycle, her long dark hair waving in the wind. I am glad that she rode on a motorcycle. I am grateful for every moment and experience she enjoyed in her life.

I told him that I was so happy that they shared a special relationship. He shook his head and smiled sweetly and shyly. He was a quiet man with an intensity that he also had as a boy. It was only to Ivy that he would open his heart. She would often listen to him for hours and advise him. She never told anyone what they talked about, but I know she reached him in a way no one else ever had. He needed her and she was there for him, as she always was when you needed her.

After the accident, David came to our home and sat in Ivy's room shaking. He looked at my mother, my sisters and me but he could not speak. His silence eloquently expressed the depth of his loss.

I often wondered how he was able to express his grief. I wrote about mine. My ability to express my feelings through my writing saved me after the accident.

For David it was in his smile and private memories that she lived on. They shared the same birthday. I would always love him for being part of her life.

In time, David chose to express his grief in a college English class. He was not sure that he wanted to go on to school, but he decided to try it and enrolled in a community college.

His teacher assigned a composition about "the most important memory or experience of your life." For whatever reason, David was ready to talk for the first time about the loss of his beloved friend. He opened his soul and poured his heart into his paper.

When David received his graded composition, it was covered with red ink marks. Spelling and grammar corrections were everywhere. There was not one comment about his subject. There was not one word about his feelings. There was not one phrase expressing condolence for his loss. David dropped out of college. He became a successful businessman.

Years after our chance meeting, I heard about David again and I was utterly shattered. In his early forties David learned he had cancer. His doctors had missed the diagnosis at first. He was in a wheelchair and his father had brought him home to die. Home was the house where he was raised, the house in which he and Ivy had spent time together.

I knew what I had to do. It took everything in me to do it. I pulled up in front of his house. His father had a wheelchair ramp constructed off the garage. Two full-time nurses shared shifts.

My heart was beating so fast and hard that it hurt. I knocked on the door and the nurse opened it. There he was. David was sitting in his chair. He raised his head as though it was a weight and his eyes met mine. That shy sweet smile was still there and as ill as he was, he was still that stunning young man.

He was very weak and I had to put my ear close to his mouth so I could hear him. "I talk to her every day," he whispered. I tried with all my strength to contain myself. I did not want to embarrass him in any way. My eyes, however, filled with tears.

"She is with you, David," I answered, smiling back at him. "She is with you."

Then we sat together, my hand on his, and I read him the story I had written about them.

I think of Ivy's favorite song, "Color My World," by the group Chicago. The melody is beautiful, the lyrics loving and embracing. Like her life, like their love, the song is brief yet hauntingly unforgettable.

~Elynne Chaplik-Aleskow

Grieving and *Recovery*

Finding Comfort

10

Beacon

We are each gifted in a unique and important way.
It is our privilege and our adventure to discover our own special light.
~Mary Dunbar

There is something graceful about a well-made hurricane lamp. Especially the antique ones. The kind that were made with all the love and pride a true artisan has for his work. Heavy, hand blown bowls to cradle the oil. Tightly woven braid wicks bridging the distance between fuel and flame. Tall tunnels of thin glass entrusted to guard the dancing light inside them. Such fragile glass to be so strong, to stand up against the elements, against the inevitable night. Mom had a great affection for the lamps. They were designed to keep their light lit through the harshest of moments, no matter how dark the night or windy the storm. She needed something like that in her life.

I can remember searching through countless flea markets, antique stores, and garage sales for them. She had a huge collection of hurricane lamps in every shape, size, and color. Heavy, cut crystal bowls with short hurricanes, squat and sturdy. Delicate cylindrical bowls with paper thin hurricanes, too fragile to be used but beautiful. Plain, round functional ones filled with red tinted oil. Mom tried very hard to buy the lamps in pairs but her favorite of all the lamps had no mate.

This one unmatched lamp was rather large, standing about two feet tall with the hurricane glass. Its bowl was octagonal and clear. A simple, elegant lamp, one that could stand on its own. It didn't need a partner to be spectacular. She found it just after we moved 3,000 miles away from everything we knew, after she left my stepfather. It was the first beautiful thing she bought for our new home without the fear that it would be smashed to pieces. On rough nights, when she was down or lonely or frightened, she would light her lamp and sit for hours until she could sleep.

Through the long, fearful nights at the height of a miserable divorce, she'd sit there until the sun came up, fear beating out her exhaustion. When she first found the two marble-sized lumps on her back, Mom found her comfort in the lights that danced untouchable behind glass, lights that would shine forever if she fed them. The night she got the official diagnosis of cancer, she let me help light them.

The spring after Mom's first battle with malignant melanoma, we went to a local craft fair to pass the time, to keep busy. We were still waiting to hear from the doctors on the results of her follow-up tests. She was feeling less than herself, and she wanted desperately to do something, anything, that would make her feel normal again. If not normal, then at least better.

Everything about the fair is a blur to me; I was so intent on seeing her smile, on not letting my brother see us panic, that I don't think I noticed anything. All I wanted was to make her smile. I hadn't seen her smile, heard her laugh, in months and I missed both.

Intent on my search, I bounded ahead of my mom and baby brother as they meandered along the tables and displays. I didn't make it far before something caught my eye. The recognition was immediate, a sizzle-snap-synapse moment, the kind that make the hair on your arms rise up to face the synchronicity. Standing proud on the display table sat a lamp. Not just a lamp — this was a tall hurricane lamp with an octagonal bowl.

I was excited, frantic, as I raced back through the crowd to my mom. She was inspecting a pair of small lamps at another vendor's table. Normally, I was not one to interrupt, but this was important.

Even at 12, I understood how much it would mean to her. "Mom! You have to see something!" I said.

"Hang on. I think I'm going to get these lamps. What do you think?" She held them up so I could see them but I didn't even look at them.

"You've got to see what I found first." I tugged on her jacket, unrelenting. She sighed, said something to the person behind the table and set the lamps down.

I dragged her through the fair, not letting her stop to look at anything else, not letting her waste time. She had to see that lamp. When she did, I knew I'd done well. She squeezed my hand and her eyes teared up. As she picked up the lamp, she ran her fingers over the bowl, over the hurricane glass, inspecting it closely. "See this?" She pointed at a very small mark in the glass on the bottom of the bowl. I nodded. "The one at home has the same mark." She smiled. It was the first time I had seen her truly smile since the doctors first found the melanoma.

When the lamp took its place on the mantle, next to its mate, she cried. After my brother and I were both in bed, she went back downstairs. I knew she went to light the lamps and sit in their glow until she could sleep. She'd done it before. I fell asleep knowing that I'd made her feel better—even if only for one night.

Years later, I understood her need for those lamps, those inextinguishable beacons through the darkest moments of her life. They didn't help her survive her last bout of cancer, nothing could have done that, but maybe they made those days less frightening. I love those lamps but I don't need them the way that she did. My memory of her is all I need. She was my hurricane lamp. She was inextinguishable—through the darkest moments, she lit my way without fail. She still does. In those hours when my life is storm-tossed and wind-battered, the light around me shines bright with hope shielded by her hurricane spirit.

~Sarah Wagner

11

Stork Stand

Love is missing someone whenever you're apart,
but somehow feeling warm inside because you're close in heart.
~Kay Knudsen

"We have to go, Mom," my young son had pleaded. "Dad needs to be there."

My husband had set up the trip to Kauai, Hawaii months ago. It was supposed to be for our 14th anniversary. Now, instead of a celebration, I was watching as my seven-year-old son Keefer spread part of my husband's ashes in the beautiful waves. It wasn't my idea. I didn't want to make the trip. I wanted to cancel it and try to make sense of what was left of my life. My son had different ideas.

Several months after we had returned from Kauai we were down on the Washington coast near our home when I watched my son step into the edge of the Pacific Ocean. He lifted his left leg, placed his foot against the inside of his right knee, drew his hands into a prayer position and bowed his head. I watched this for a couple of minutes, amazed at his balance and concentration. Finally I approached him and whispered, "What are you doing?"

He opened one eye and turned his head slightly toward me. "Talking to Dad," he said quietly.

"What?"

He placed his left leg back down on the ground, turned to me and took my hands in his. "I'm talking to Dad."

"How?" I questioned, confused.

"Mom," he said, shaking his head back and forth. "We placed Dad's ashes in the Pacific Ocean while we were in Hawaii."

"Yeah." I looked into his eyes a little deeper.

"Well Mom, anywhere there's an ocean, I can talk to Dad. He's everywhere now."

That statement took my breath away. He was right of course. All of the oceans connect, so anywhere there's an ocean, his dad, my husband will be there.

In that moment, I felt my husband's spirit touch my heart just as my son's had.

~Candace Carteen

12

Not Quite Unbearable

Baby let me be, your lovin' teddy bear.
~Elvis Presley

When we fell in love and married at the start of the millennium, each in our sixties with grown children, we anticipated endless years together. So even though he'd struggled with one debilitating illness after another in the nearly nine years of our marriage, even though I'd watched him wizen away, and even though we'd known since Valentine's Day that Ken couldn't survive... I still couldn't believe we wouldn't spend another cozy Christmas together. Ken was my big, tough, durable teddy bear.

He'd hinted at his own awareness in December 2008. "I'm asking the boys and the grandkids to write me stories this year for Christmas," he'd said. "I don't need more objects that I'll just have to give away. So don't go shopping for me. I have enough of everything to last me for the rest of my life."

I nodded, but secretly vowed that I'd find something he could use. I'd already written a couple of stories about our life together which were set to appear in a Chicken Soup for the Soul anthology, *Tough Times, Tough People*, in the late spring. So I settled on a couple of token gifts, a small bottle of Tuscany cologne and some sweat suits. Even if he didn't do much but lounge in his favorite chair, he'd still smell deliciously of oak moss and orange flower, just as he always had. And the fluffy fleece cardinal and azure sweats would replace the frayed and faded ones he'd been wearing daily.

By January he began to sort through his ties and tie tacks, deciding who would get what. I helped him box up his books on photography, poker and magic and lugged them to the post office. Still, I wrapped myself in denial.

By February he'd lost his appetite, even turning down my offers to prepare chicken fried steak or meatloaf, his favorite dishes. He lost nearly 40 pounds, became jaundiced and had to be hospitalized for tests, and then needed a stent procedure because there was a blockage in his common bile duct.

The surgeon who performed that procedure was frank. "What is causing the blockage is ampullary cancer. Because your husband's kidneys are so weak, we can't perform surgery or administer chemotherapy. All we can do is send him home to be comfortable."

He was approved for home hospice. Soon there were days when he couldn't manage more than a spoonful of chicken noodle soup or two or three grapes. The nurse confided that his time was growing short. Still, I simply couldn't imagine a future without him.

Ken knew the Chicken Soup books would arrive in June. In late May he'd dictated a list of the people he wanted me to send them to, as a final gift for relatives and friends. The books arrived on June 5th, the very morning of his death, shortly after I'd phoned the Neptune Society and the hospice agency. I already had the labels affixed to the envelopes. All I had to do was stuff them in the envelopes.

But now I had to phone his family and my friends. Then my things-to-do list burgeoned. In subsequent weeks I made trips to the county courthouse to take care of title deeds. I phoned and corresponded with banks and credit unions. Earlier I had agreed to participate as a reviewer in a federal grant program. The grants arrived two days after his death, and absorbed my time for a while. Since I serve on various boards and commissions, I had meetings to attend, material to review, reports to write. His sons visited in August and we planted a plum tree in his memory.

Then one late autumn morning, three months after Ken's death, I woke up with an urge to hurl things at the wall. Though I'd stayed busy, busy, busy, I felt empty, empty, empty. That afternoon I received an envelope from the Neptune Society chapter that had handled his cremation. I pulled out a certificate telling me a teddy bear had been named in memory of Kenneth D. Wilson and would be donated "to a child who may be alone, hurt or frightened."

A few days later I received an unexpected package from an old college friend who I hadn't seen in decades. It held a stuffed honey-hued bear. She'd included a note that suggested I could sob into its fur when woebegone, shake it when angry, or slam it on the floor when overwhelmed.

Just cuddling the bear calmed me considerably. Even now, some nights I tuck the bear into Ken's side of the bed. Ken had always liked bears.

Our first Christmas together, a Panda Wish Bear mysteriously had appeared under the tree. One not-long-ago Valentine's Day morning I discovered a hefty mulberry-hued heart-holding bear perched behind the wheel of my car. There'd been the evening I'd come home from a business trip to find a five-foot-high carved bear positioned in front of the house, with a sign proclaiming our names. Additionally, a bevy of ursine creatures line a shelf in the guest room: a British teddy that wears a Union Jack sweater, a lady brown bear in an elegant lacy lavender gown and granny glasses, a tiny polar bear that peeps out of a Christmas stocking. All Ken's picks. He had great taste in bears.

As the 2009 holiday season neared, my first in a decade without Ken, I realized that when my honey bear had arrived, I too, like the recipient of the Neptune Society's teddy, had been alone, hurt and frightened. After it had appeared, I'd felt less forlorn. Maybe I could soothe others' grief by providing bears in Ken's memory.

I immediately found several ways. I donated 15,000 of my frequent flyer miles to the American Cancer Society's Miles of Hugs and Smiles campaign, enough for two "Hugyou" bears to be given to children undergoing treatment. Then I discovered that the National Wildlife Federation sought people to symbolically adopt black bears. Small stuffed bears would be given to designees. I ordered one for Ken's youngest granddaughter and one for Toys for Tots. I visited the local Tree of Sharing and nabbed two tickets for toddlers who'd asked for teddy bears.

This year I couldn't quite bring myself to put up the Christmas tree. It's too soon yet to gaze at the ornaments we gathered on our trips together, the Pinocchio from Venice, the Alaska totem poles, the angels from St. Petersburg. But I did set out some of Ken's Santas, and… his Christmas bears. I sprayed a little of the remaining Tuscany onto their fur.

When I hit the local shops the day after Christmas, in search of next year's cards, I grinned to myself when I found a few boxes featuring teddies fashioning toys in Santa's workshop. Next December as I sign them, I'll be seeing Ken's smile.

I've no doubt now that Ken forever shall remain my tough and durable teddy bear.

~Terri Elders

13

Knit Together

While we are mourning the loss of our friend,
others are rejoicing to meet him behind the veil.
~John Taylor

I picked up Louisa almost every Friday morning on the way to our favorite hangout: a local yarn and coffee shop on the west side of town. Seated by the fireplace and surrounded by shelves of yarns in countless colors, we knitted chunky wool hats for our husbands, soft blankies for the newest additions to our families, and scarves, shawls, or mittens for ourselves. We dined on the shop's hearty sandwiches, creamy soups, and smooth homemade chocolates. And we talked for hours.

How quickly time passed in this warm environment and in the midst of our projects. How quickly it passed in the company of a good friend.

I would help Louisa with her coat. I picked up her knitting bag. I crooked my arm, and she took hold. It was a slow, careful walk to the car.

Louisa had been just two years old when her parents sensed something was wrong. She didn't play like other kids. Instead, Louisa was hesitant, wary, and visibly in pain on the playground. So began her lifelong struggle with rheumatoid arthritis, its crippling effects, and all the medical vulnerabilities that often come with the disease.

Despite constant aching, daily fistfuls of pills, and a rigorous regimen of physical therapy, Louisa was determined to live a "normal" life—and keep up with the high demand for her knittables. She seemed to have something prepared for almost every special occasion—baby showers, engagement parties, weddings, and the like—and countless friends, family, and mere acquaintances laid claim to Louisa's handmade creations.

The tradition came to a sudden end when, one gray afternoon in March, "pins and needles" penetrated and pricked the entire right side of Louisa's body. She could barely move once the paramedics arrived. Two months later, pneumonia set in, and I stood vigil at Louisa's bedside stroking her hand as my tears dropped in splotches on her bed sheets. The heart monitor's waves peaked, then rippled, then stilled. The doctor confirmed the grim news to those of us gathered around her.

Louisa was gone.

Though I saw it happen and heard the doctor's words, the reality seeped slowly into my consciousness. Though I knew I must one day face the pain of my own grief, I did what I could to help prepare for the funeral and to surround her husband, Joe, with the support he needed.

I offered my insight into her most treasured Bible verses and other passages and songs to include in her memorial service. I browsed her closet for potential burial clothes, remembering with others Louisa's favorite colors, patterns, and textures. I arranged for meals and rides and practicalities of all kinds, but it was with my best tender care that I searched Louisa's overflowing baskets and tote bags for her most impressive knittables to display at the funeral.

During my hunt, I found many completed projects. A sunshine-bright top-knotted baby hat. Dishcloths shaped like daisies, snowflakes, and stars. A scarf. But also among those treasures were even more projects waiting to take final form.

I took special notice of the earthy speckled socks she began for Joe last winter. Louisa had hoped to give them to him for Christmas last year, but the busyness of the holidays interrupted her plans. She had decided instead to give them to him for his birthday, but she didn't have time for that either. Louisa and I had made light of the delayed sock project just a few weeks before she died, my last memory of our knitting together.

With my mind caught up in bittersweet memories and my vision clouded by tears, I turned to Joe. "If you think it would be okay, I'd like to finish these for her someday."

That promise to Joe was a lifeline to which I clung every day thereafter. It's true that, in finishing those socks, I would eventually present Joe with a very special gift—and I felt good about that. But, deep inside me, I knew that finishing those socks would somehow help me cope with the loss of my friend—it would help me like nothing else could.

Several months passed before I gained the courage to make good on my promise. I dialed the number, cleared my throat, and hesitantly asked to stop by for Louisa's unfinished projects. A couple of days later, Joe greeted me at his door and pointed to the sofa, barely visible beneath Louisa's knitting supplies. After making sure I had all the necessary needles and notions, I loaded my trunk, headed home, and transferred the cargo to my own living room. My first assignment? To finish those socks.

I studied the pattern, arranged the needles just so, and fingered the coarse yarn. Louisa's work lay before me like a diary documenting both the celebrations and sorrows of her last months of life. As I twirled the one fully finished sock above my lap, I noticed its perfectly proportioned shape and the careful consistent stitches—how they reminded me of the harmonious and happy days that Louisa once enjoyed. But my attention then turned to the second sock, not only unfinished, but riddled with errors—signs of her increasing weariness toward the end.

Though reluctant, I knew I had no choice. I had to pick up the good where Louisa left off, no matter how devastating it might feel to undo evidence of some of our last memories together. I tore out hundreds of stitches to where the counting was right again. But any initial hesitation also unraveled as tiny hollow loops of yarn seemed to raise their arms in celebration of a new beginning.

A new beginning. Though I miss my friend every day, I embrace the countless opportunities I'm given to honor her memory—to honor our memories. I create pretty knitted gifts as Louisa once did. I extend her smile when those who are hurting need a lift. And I take delight in my other friends' dreams as revealed in the cozy warm corners of local coffee shops. Indeed, my new beginning—my new life without Louisa—proves that we're forever knit together.

~Barbara Farland

The Empty Table

He who has gone, so we but cherish his memory, abides with us, more potent,
nay, more present than the living man.
~Antoine de Saint-Exupery

W e were in Greece on holiday many years ago and drove into a small town, way off the tourist track. We wandered the narrow streets and began to get hungry. We decided to go into a little café to try the local Greek food. The floor and walls inside were made of stone, but there were modern chairs and tables. The tables and chairs were painted bright yellow, except for one old round wooden table and four wooden chairs that stood out amidst the brighter modern furniture.

There were shelves around the walls with various jars containing dried herbs, odd-looking pickles of some kind, fresh flowers, candles and many other things.

An old lady appeared through a glass-beaded curtain and asked us what we would like. We asked for a selection of their local dishes, some local wine and some coffee.

As it was just coming up to lunchtime, people began to drift in. I commented to the young girl bringing us our wine that they were busy. "On Fridays, many people come for lunch," she explained. They all sat down chatting and then an old man came in and shuffled his way over to the old wooden table.

He sat down and the young girl set down a glass of water in front of him and at the other three places round the table. She did the same with plates of bread and I realized he was expecting three others.

We ate the delicious food and chatted about where we would explore next. Nearly an hour later, I noticed the old man was still sitting there alone. Although he was eating something, the untouched glasses of water and plates of bread were still there. His hand shook as he took a drink and I was profoundly touched. Who would leave an old man to eat alone when he was expecting them?

As my husband went to pay the owner, and our children went off to the rest room, I studied the jars on the shelf, but my eyes lingered on the lonely old man. The old lady saw me and I commented, "Sad that his company did not arrive and he had to eat alone."

"He always eats alone. His company never turns up," she said.

I frowned at her and asked, "Does he just like to pretend they might?"

"No, he knows they will never turn up again. Many years ago, when he was a younger man, there were four of them who came here every day on their way home from work. They would have a glass of wine or two—four handsome, strong young men. Once a week they would sit at that table and have lunch together because it was Friday, and they did not work again until Monday. They laughed and told tales and planned their weekends. They had been friends since school days and were always together.

"Then the war came and first one and then another went off to fight. They were like brothers, you understand, and finally the war was over and we waited for all the boys to come home. Of the four who sat there, only Nikolas returned. He has come here every Friday since the day he limped out of the hospital and sat down to have lunch with his friends. In his mind he relives their happy childhood here as boys playing tricks on people, their lives as growing young men, and the farewell hugs as they all went off to war. The rest of the week, he lives a normal life with his wife and family around him. Nikolas needs these Fridays to cope with his grief, to spend happy times with his old friends."

It was so touching that I still get tears on my cheeks just thinking about the old man. I will never forget the final words of the old lady as I was turning to leave.

"The legacy of war isn't just about thousands of white crosses in a military cemetery; it's about empty chairs at a table, and the friends that can never meet again. As long as I am alive, Nikolas can always meet here with his friends."

~Joyce Stark

15

A Healing Gift

God gave us memories that we might have roses in December.
~J.M. Barrie

My dad was more than a father to me; he was my friend and confidant and one of the most amazing people in my life. So when he passed away suddenly from a stroke at the age of 51, my world fell apart. I was lost, along with my mother who had been with my father since age 16, two brothers, and everyone who knew him. We were thrown into a thick haze of anger, sadness, and shock.

I cried every night and tried to hold onto all my memories of him. I replayed every moment I could remember—jotting down thoughts, printing out old e-mails, reading old birthday cards—anything I could hang on to because I didn't want to forget. As I was going through all these old memories, I began to wonder about all the things I had missed. My dad was a quiet man who was known for his listening skills, his patience, his humor, and his smile. He was often the one listening instead of telling stories. I wanted to know what stories I had missed by losing him so soon. So I decided to compile a memory book as a surprise Christmas gift for my mom and brothers.

I started my project in November, contacting everyone I knew who was close to my dad or had been in the past. I sent e-mails and letters asking for friends and family of Gary Force to send me their thoughts and memories of him. I asked them specifically to share funny stories about my dad and the stories that maybe no one had ever heard or had long forgotten. I told them to respond no later than one week prior to Christmas.

I waited and waited and got very few responses by December. I began to wonder if this was a horrible idea or if anyone even cared. And then the responses started pouring in. About one week before Christmas I began to receive handwritten letters, old photographs, and e-mails by the dozens. I was amazed and awed by the response and even more moved by what people had written about my dad. Almost all the stories and memories were new to me. They were stories about my dad playing poker until 4 a.m. in high school, about pranks he pulled with his college roommates, about his first job after college, about how he met my mom and their life together, and stories involving his love for his family and friends. Every story was a precious gift.

In the end, my compilation included more than 50 entries and was 85 pages long. Family and friends poured out their hearts and souls about the man who was suddenly taken from them. They spoke of the things they had wished to say to him and the memories they would cherish forever. I compiled the book on the computer and had it printed at a local copy store. I gave it to my family as the last gift on Christmas Day. It was overwhelming. My mom was speechless, bawling her eyes out while looking at the thickness of the book. My brothers just stood up and hugged me without saying a word. My mom and brothers were both moved beyond words and it took them hours to go through the book. Through tear-filled eyes, my mom said it was the best gift she had ever received.

This book was more than just a book of memories. It was a healing process. I was not expecting to feel better about losing my dad through reading all of these stories, but I did. I felt happier knowing that he had led a great life and touched so many people. I am so proud to have him as my father. Making the book was my first step on the road to healing. Now whenever I am sad or missing him, I pick up the book and flip through it to laugh and smile. I know that he is looking down, reading it too, and hopefully laughing and smiling along with me.

~Jenny Force

16

The Chaplain's Prayer

Faith makes things possible, not easy.
~Author Unknown

My story of grief began with a phone call. The kind every mother dreads receiving. The call I found myself wishing I had never answered. The one that left me mourning for my baby boy—my son who had just turned 40.

It was still dark as I rode to work that May morning in 2008. I navigated the familiar route along Highway 40, headed for the Munroe Regional Medical Center in Ocala, Florida. A coworker had requested the weekend off and I was reporting to duty—prepared to work a tiring, 15-hour shift.

Arriving at the hospital, I went about business as usual. Parked my car and headed to the North Entrance. Walked a long hallway toward the kitchen. Made two left turns and arrived at my workstation. Listened to patient messages on the answering machine. Made personal menu changes for breakfast. Took a quick break. Came back to my computer and started working on lunch menus for every patient in the hospital.

In the middle of my routine, somewhere around 9:30 a.m., the outside phone line rang. On the other end was my youngest daughter, Nancy, calling from Michigan. She was crying and incoherent… and I was asking her what was wrong… and in between sobs she was trying to find a way to tell me… and I couldn't understand what she was saying and she was spilling out the words… and I was trying to find a way to step out of the nightmare and make sense of it all.

"Mom," she finally cried. "Michael is dead."

What happened next was a frightening blur of events. From the phone call, to the kitchen, to the dietician's office, I found myself screaming and out of control.

Did she say dead? I tried to grasp what was happening. I told myself to get a grip.

My only son couldn't possibly be gone. I struggled to make sense of it all. Did she say overdose?

Staff and fellow workers rushed to my side but I was inconsolable, confused, refusing to believe what I had heard, and yet the truth was slowly seeping into my soul. Two employees from the kitchen, concerned over my hysteria, insisted on taking me downstairs to the emergency room. To wait until I calmed down. To wait until a relative arrived. To wait until I could face reality. They called for a doctor and hovered near, offering words of comfort.

Later, as I sat in the ER—just waiting—without friend or family, without a hope in the world, without any way of knowing how I could possibly survive, I reached back in time to the God of my childhood and offered up a painful and desperate prayer.

I can't do this alone. I need Your help.

The chaplain on call that day was of the Catholic faith, casually dressed and soft spoken. Summoned to wait with me, he took me into a side room where we could be alone. He listened with genuine concern as I wept and told him—as best I could—about my only son, his overnight stay at his sister's house, his accidental overdose, his last hours before bedtime, and his silent death while everyone else was sleeping.

The chaplain reached out to take my hands. "May I pray with you?" he asked. I nodded, surrendering to the sorrow.

"Do you understand that we pray to Mary?"

"That's fine," I whispered.

The chaplain paused. "You know," he said, "Mary, too, lost a son."

And with that uncomplicated truth, my heartbreaking journey to recovery began.

I bowed my head and listened to the chaplain's prayer, amazed that God had sent help so quickly. That He had heard my insufficient plea for mercy and through the words of a total stranger, had reminded me of the suffering Mary must have endured, losing a son so young.

For two years, my rugged, mountainous road to recovery has been an uphill march. I continue to mourn my son's short life, but step by step, I find new comfort and strength knowing I am not alone. Knowing that another mother marched uphill, too, with a broken heart.

Each morning my cross seems easier to bear, and often when I pray, or meditate, or lift the cup, I embrace the chaplain's words, "Mary, too, lost a son." And I am comforted.

~Brenda Dawson as told to Charlotte A. Lanham

17

Cornell Sunflower

Oh heart, if one should say to you that the soul perishes like the body,
answer that the flower withers, but the seed remains.
~Kahlil Gibran

It was December 2002 when we held the memorial service for my beloved dad, Clarence Edward Gammon. A large display of sunflowers graced the pulpit in memory of the sunshine he brought into our lives and in commemoration of the gorgeous sunflowers he grew each year. They were the talk of the neighbourhood at their towering height as they kissed the eaves of our family home.

Each year since 2002, the seeds from these precious flowers have been replanted at my home in Cornell, in loving memory of my dad and respect for the care he showed these flowers. It was in 2006, as I began the process of seeding for the new season, that the wondrous story of these flowers came to a new height.

I entered the garage to retrieve the seeds that had been harvested the last fall, as I had done each year previously. It didn't register immediately as I viewed the tray of open shells but I soon realized that the seeds had been eaten by a hungry critter that took up winter residence in our garage. A terrible wave of dread and loss washed over me, as if I had lost my dad all over again.

My husband saw me crying through the kitchen window, opened the door and asked what the problem was. I explained what had happened. He looked at me with sympathy and stated, "It only takes one." I understood. For two hours I sifted through the shells and found a total of twelve remaining seeds. These seeds were planted in small pots and grew to seedlings in our kitchen window.

We returned from a weekend away to find that our cat had eaten the head off every flower! I could not believe these flowers were in jeopardy again. Once again, I cried—this time out of frustration and disbelief. And once again my husband said, "Don't give up... it only takes one." And one it was.

One seedling survived and was planted in our backyard garden. Over the next several weeks I watched it grow and gain strength until it was two feet tall. As I was weeding around the stalk, I could not believe what happened next—I heard a "snap," and sure enough, I had gotten too close and snapped the stem of the flower. This time there were no tears. I knew I was being sent some kind of message that I did not yet understand.

I could not bring myself to dig up the dying stalk, so it remained there for weeks. One day, while weeding, something caught my eye. The sunflower stalk had come back to life—from its down-sloped position it had reached up for the sky and was beginning to blossom. It was a miracle. This time the tears were for the message received instead of what had previously been lost. It only takes one to make a difference—one person or one sunflower.

No matter how beaten up, this flower had a purpose and was going to fulfill it—regardless of mice, cats or careless gardeners. Throughout the summer this one stalk grew to over six feet, formed more than six flowers and provided several hundred seeds for harvest.

I share these seeds as I share my story of loss and finally the greatest gift of all—the gift of hope and resilience and the knowledge that all living things are miraculous in their existence and perseverance.

We should all be as hopeful as this Cornell sunflower.

~Sheri Gammon Dewling

18

My Daughter, Rose

Perhaps they are not the stars, but rather openings in Heaven
where the love of our lost ones pours through and shines down upon us
to let us know they are happy.
~Author Unknown

I sat by my dear daughter, Rose, as she lay reclining next to me, eyes closed and a peaceful expression on her face. I held her hand and stroked her hair softly and told her how much I loved her. After a while, there was a slight commotion in the room and voices speaking in Russian, a language I was in the process of learning but which I didn't understand well as yet. Then someone spoke in English, "It's time to go. They need to cremate the bodies now."

I recoiled in horror. How could anyone even suggest taking my darling daughter and burning her in a fire! The very thought was utterly appalling to me! But then another voice cut into my thoughts: "They are not here." It was the voice of Rose's father-in-law and I immediately knew that he was referring to heaven and reminding us of our belief that our dear ones — Rose, her husband Piper, and their son Sean — were no longer occupying the three bodies that were laid out there side by side in their coffins, but had left this world for a better place.

"Are you in a place where you can sit down?" my mother-in-law had gently asked my husband, Ken, over the phone hardly even a week ago. She had then proceeded to tell us the terrible news — that our 26-year-old daughter was dead, along with her 26-year-old husband and their three-year-old son. They had been driving on an icy highway outside a remote city in Siberia on their way home from snowboarding in the mountains, when their car had skidded out of control on the ice and collided with a bus.

The news had been so unbelievable and unexpected that it had been hard for our minds to take in — like someone telling us that the sky is green or that grass is purple. We had simply sat collapsed on a bench outside the bookshop where we had been shopping when the phone call came, and we struggled to regain some kind of equilibrium in a world that was spinning out of focus. Ken and I were actually on a short vacation at the time, which is why the news of our loved ones' deaths was first told to my husband's parents, they being the only people that the American Embassy in Russia were able to contact at that time.

It had been a very difficult year for us, and everyone had advised us to get away for a few days to rest. We had driven from our home in Boston to a small town in rural Pennsylvania to spend a few days enjoying the quiet countryside. Four months earlier, one of our other daughters, Lillie, had been involved in a car crash in Boston when a drunk driver had come speeding out of a side street in the early hours of the morning and hit the car she was driving, resulting in the tragic death of one of the passengers, and injuring the four others, including Lillie. She was the most seriously hurt but miraculously survived a delicate brain surgery and was finally on the road to recovery after a very difficult convalescence.

Now here we were again, facing another tragedy. Those words — "They are not here" — pierced my consciousness and at that moment, I wasn't even sure if I believed in heaven anymore. In that instant, it was as though everything I had ever believed in was swept away like a computer that suddenly crashes, or like a movie that abruptly stops in the middle of the action, and you are left with only static and swirling dots.

I had always believed in God, except for a few years during my youth when I had rejected my childhood beliefs and had declared myself an atheist. But then my life had taken some surprising turns and I had grown to love God with all my heart and had spent many years living in Latin America and later in Siberia as a missionary with my husband and our six children. I couldn't imagine not believing in heaven after having lived in dangerous situations and depending on God for everything, and seeing so many miracles through the years. But here I was, deeply concerned about Rose and her family and knowing that their future and their happiness and wellbeing depended on there being an afterlife. Suddenly everything I had been so sure of seemed to have been swept away.

As I stood there at that moment, it occurred to me that my faith in God had always been connected to the Bible, so I tried to think of a Bible verse about heaven. I thought of the verse in John 3:16 which says, "For God so loved the world that He gave His only begotten Son that whosoever believeth in Him should not perish but have everlasting life." I pondered this verse for a moment and asked myself, "Do I really believe this, or are these just nice words?" Then another thought came to me, "You have a choice. You can choose to believe this or you can choose not to believe it. It's your choice." So in that moment, I responded, "I choose to believe," and immediately, I felt a gentle peace surrounding and supporting me, something that, to this day, has always stayed with me.

After we left that place, we all went outside and walked around and around the block. Everything was so cold and drab. We were all in a daze. Actually, we were waiting for the bodies to be cremated, and trying to keep ourselves moving about and warm while we waited. It was impossible for us to bring the bodies all the way back to the States to be buried, so we had opted to have our loved ones cremated in Russia so we could bring their ashes in urns back with us to be buried.

Finally, we were taken in a few vehicles to where the accident had taken place. The road was so lonely and empty. Hardly any vehicles passed by while we were there. It was hard to believe that there could have even been a bus coming at the very moment when they had spun out of control. We saw all the debris at the side of the road scattered in the snow. Up on a little hillside in the background, someone had placed a wreath of flowers in memory of our children.

I tried to imagine how it had been for Rose and her family to crash out there in the middle of nowhere and leave this world in such a remote corner of the earth. Suddenly as I was looking at the wreath of flowers, I saw the sun setting behind it and the sun's rays shone down directly on it and formed a crisscross of rays around the wreath. I grabbed my camera to catch this beautiful sight. Piper's brother noticed it the same moment as I did, and he too snatched up his camera to capture this picture. It came to me like a beautiful promise — that even there in the middle of nowhere, God's love and light had been surrounding them and had carried them safely through the tragedy and on to a better place.

That night we traveled on a train from Novokuznetsk to Novosibirsk where Rose and Piper and little Sean had lived as missionaries and humanitarian aid workers. I stood in the corridor of the train, gazing out the window at the birch trees and snow in the darkness, and poured out my thoughts to God. I felt as though He responded by assuring me not to worry about Rose and Piper and Sean because they were happy and had gone on to a new life, but that I needed rather to focus my attention on caring for our other children and helping them through the days ahead.

In Novosibirsk, we had a memorial service and it was so touching to see so many dear Russian people who expressed their love and appreciation for Rose and Piper and Sean, who had lived among them for the past several years, and had loved and helped so many. I couldn't help but think that despite their short lives, Rose and Piper had lived life to the fullest. Even though they had only lived 26 years on this earth, who was I to decide how long a lifetime should be?

I am so thankful for Rose and Piper and Sean and the wonderful times we shared when they were here with us. Often I feel the presence of Rose, close to me. And heaven is no longer an abstract place to me. It seems much more real now and I look forward to going there someday when my time on this earth comes to an end. In the meantime, I love life and I want to live each day, loving the people around me, my children and grandchildren, and God.

~Laraine Paquette

19

A Sign from God

*If instead of a gem, or even a flower, we should cast the gift of a loving
thought into the heart of a friend, that would be giving as the angels give.*
~George MacDonald

I t was 1985, and I was 18 and away from home all summer. I had
landed what I considered to be my first real job—a maid at the
biggest hotel in Glacier National Park. I intended to use every
day off hiking and otherwise exploring the park. One of the first
people I met was a young man of 19 with orange hair and a passion
for hiking that almost equaled his passion for the Lord. We hit it off
immediately. Rain or shine, we explored trails in Many Glacier Valley
whenever we had time off together. In addition to his incredible sense
of adventure, I also admired a spiritual maturity that I had never
before encountered in someone of that age.

June 10th—third day off (and therefore third hiking day). The
plan was "Iceberg Lake for sure," and then Ptarmigan Lake and Tunnel
if we had time—16 miles in all if we made it. Along the first three-
mile stretch of trail, one of the things we spoke of was how amazing
it would be to stand on a ledge below an overhanging waterfall and
watch the water cascade in front of you. And then, there it was, just
around the bend, 200-foot Ptarmigan Falls with just such a perfect
ledge about two-thirds of the way down.

We agreed that he would "check it out" while I waited on top for
the report. Twenty minutes and several snacks later, I began to wonder what was keeping him. I traced back and forth over a quarter-

mile section of trail that made a U-turn around the brim of the falls, but it was heavily wooded and I had a difficult time seeing much of anything in the canyon below. I even climbed down 50 feet or so from the trail in the place I had last seen him disappear, but it was wet and slippery from the fall's mist and I dared go no farther. About the third time retracing my steps along the trail I finally spotted what I had begun to dread seeing—a pair of boots sticking out on a rock and connected to a half-submerged body, a full head of orange hair flowing with the current.

I knew immediately that he was dead. After a few moments of tears and shock, I gathered up packs and belongings and began the hike back to the ranger station to report the incident. How do you begin a story like that? Rangers apparently determined I was level-headed enough to be of use on location, so I made the trek back up to the falls with five rangers in rescue gear and a chopper on standby. It wasn't until about three hours later when I finally returned to the hotel, the news having preceded me, that I broke down and collapsed into the waiting arms of my two very tearful roommates.

Already the next morning I received calls from several people in my home church saying that they were praying for me (amazingly, the news was broadcast over the radio before I even had a chance to call home). And over the course of the next few weeks I encountered some of the greatest acts of kindness from fellow employees (back rubs, special dinners, the offer of extra time off, etc.).

But the story doesn't end there. Something was still missing. I missed him terribly, but I also knew there was no doubt that he had been ready to meet his Maker. I finally decided that I needed to share this with his parents. I obtained their address, included some pictures I'd taken of the falls and the "rescue," and wrote a lengthy letter describing their son as the incredibly spiritual person who I knew.

Several weeks passed, and I received a return letter that just floored me. His mom wrote that she had wrestled and wrestled with God over the death of her dear son and just couldn't come to terms with the possibility of this really, truly being His will. She finally "laid out a fleece" and asked God for ten signs. The first occurred the very next day as they were visiting the gravesite; the shadow of a cross appeared on the hood of their car. She went on to list eight more things that came about during the next few weeks. Number ten was my letter, and it served to answer her most crucial question. Their family had since been overwhelmed with a feeling of acceptance and peace.

It is still amazes me when I think about it. We ask the Lord for signs, or we interpret various events as God speaking to us in signs, but I had never before considered the possibility that God could use ME as a sign to someone else.

~Ann Schotanus Brown

20

From Pain to Purpose

Don't waste your pain; use it to help others.
~Rick Warren

W hy were the police at my door? What did they want, especially at 7:00 a.m.? I pulled my mind out of my morning quiet time and opened the door.

"Are you Sandra Maddox?" the officer asked.

Why did he want to know? What could this be about? I hadn't broken any laws. My husband hadn't done anything wrong. And my daughter, Tiffany, was attending school a thousand miles away. What could possibly be wrong?

"Yes, I'm Sandra Maddox." Thankfully, my husband, Ron, had by now joined me.

"Ma'am, I'm sorry to tell you that your daughter, Tiffany, was killed in a car accident last night."

"NOOOO!" I screamed as I fell into my husband's outstretched arms. In an instant, my peaceful little world had shattered. God, this can't be true! Not my Tiffany. Why?

Time lost all meaning as I moved through the motions of each day, doing only what had to be done. Even breathing became a chore. It wasn't possible that I'd never see Tiffany's beautiful, smiling face ever again. God, why?

Every morning, there it was again—a fresh wave of grief slamming into me, like a powerful riptide pulling me under. I couldn't imagine ever smiling or laughing again. My very soul—my little girl—had been taken from me. How do you bury your only child? I raged at God. Parents aren't supposed to outlive their children! I knew God was good, but I could not see any good in this. Nothing made sense anymore.

She was still so young with so much to live for. She hadn't even had time to start her own family yet. No God of love would let this happen. Would he?

Every moment seemed to overflow with despair.

In the midst of it all, I found myself thinking of our last visits and of all the things she would say, all her funny little expressions. One of the latest was, "Mom, I think when you want answers, sometimes you have to get in people's faces until they give them to you. Y'know?" It made me laugh to hear her say that. Remembering it now both stabbed and salved my broken heart.

I had been beating myself up thinking about all the things I'd done wrong as a mother, my mind filled with "what ifs" and "if onlys." But what good was it doing? Nothing could bring my precious daughter back to me.

Just months earlier, our church had finished a series called 40 Days of Purpose, a campaign based on Rick Warren's book, *The Purpose Driven Life*. I found phrases we'd memorized then coming back to me now, right when I needed them:

God is more interested in your character than in your comfort.

We are made to last forever.

You are not an accident.

Was it possible God could have a purpose in my daughter's death?

I was stunned by the words the pastor spoke at her graveside service, "Look at the special gifts God gave Sandra in Tiffany's last days."

How could losing my daughter possibly be a gift? I pondered those words as my tears freely fell. I pondered and prayed and "got in God's face," as Tiffany might have said.

Could it be possible that God had been preparing me for this very moment my entire life? Certainly, it wasn't God's perfect will to take my daughter, but He had allowed it. Did He have a purpose for my grief and loss?

I thought about how my own mother had left me when I was a young child. I reflected on the abusive marriage I'd walked away from when Tiffany was 14. Hadn't God taken care of me then? Somehow, each trial we'd experienced made the bond between Tiffany and me stronger—even during her rebellious years.

And God reminded me of the prayer I'd prayed back then. "God, please bring Tiffany home—not home to me but home to you."

I thought of the last time I'd seen her, blowing me a kiss in the airport just a few weeks earlier. The beautiful red scarf wrapped around her neck had been my last gift to her. How could I have known this would be the last earthly glimpse I'd have of my daughter?

Was it possible God had not taken Tiffany away from me, but simply taken her home to himself? Did he need her more than I did? Was she dancing in his presence even now?

I'll never stop aching to hold my daughter. Tears still flow and holidays—those times that used to be so joyful—are terribly difficult to get through.

But slowly, I found myself asking God to show me his purpose in it all.

And slowly, doors began to open.

I was invited to speak at Tiffany's high school, where I let the tears flow as I told the story of the wrong choice she made when she got in a car with a boyfriend who'd been drinking.

God inspired me to write a book for children in Tiffany's memory—a book in which she, as a little girl, is the main character.

And then one day our women's ministry director at church asked if I would lead a new program: an outreach to young mothers of toddlers and preschoolers. I felt my breath leave my body.

Could I do it? Could I handle being in a room with all those "daughters"? How would it go? Would it bring back all the old pain and regret?

But by now, I knew this was about more than a choice—it was a holy assignment.

Slowly, the darkness was fading and the sun was rising in my life again. God was showing me purpose—a way to go on without Tiffany and leave a legacy for her in this world she'd known so little of.

Today I share my story wherever I can—before church groups, community groups, school groups—anywhere I am asked to go. It's amazing how often I meet people who've also lost children, people who need to know God cares. I tell them grieving is necessary, but that if they trust in God's good purposes, that riptide of sorrow may try to sweep them away, but it cannot hold them under.

Sometimes, before we can find the sunrise, we must find courage to walk into the darkness.

~Sandra E. Maddox

Grieving and Recovery

Helping Hands

21

A Compassionate Guide

A word spoken in due season, how good is it!
~Proverbs 15:23

I met Gene when our son was three; we'd always known he would die young due to his complex medical condition associated with Noonan syndrome. That day four years ago, as I watched Gene, a funeral director, shed tears in response to Evan's story, I knew he would be a source of comfort—for Evan, predictably, had crept into his heart.

I met Gene again last week on the second floor of a beautiful painted brick building with bright wood trim. The carport at the entrance was grand, with ornate pillars holding up the roof. My wife Penni and I sat down with him around a mahogany conference table. We had set up a meeting to plan the homecoming for seven-year-old Evan.

Evan died on a Friday morning. Later that day, Gene's crew came to our house and watched as 11-year-old Noah and I carried Evan to the funeral vehicle. "Hey Dad," Noah whispered. "It doesn't look safe."

Paddy, a funeral director himself, looked in from the other side of the car and told Noah, "You can follow us if you like. You know... to make sure Evan arrives safely." Paddy was just awesome as he scrunched his large linebacker frame into the back.

Talking through the details of your child's funeral is a crushing experience. But as we talked with Gene, he lightened our burden a little. He shared his memories about the day he'd first met Evan. And Penni asked about his children, especially his daughter who has Down syndrome. I don't know if what Gene did next was typical for his profession, but he showed us some pictures and short videos of his daughter. Penni just insisted, and Gene smiled with us as we saw his daughter in a cheerleading competition. In that moment, I knew that Gene smiled for Evan too.

Thursday, six days after Evan died, was the viewing for close friends and immediate family. Somehow, I survived the intense sense of loss. I occasionally saw Gene glance in the door. I started to walk over to him and before I could say anything, he said, "I got your back." I went back to my friends.

Friday was a totally different event as hundreds of people showed up. I was exhausted after the first hour and a half and asked Gene if it would get busier. He looked at me and said, "Scott, it's going to get very busy—especially between five and seven." It was only half past three.

Saturday, the day of the funeral, we pulled up to the church. The Royal Oak firefighters were going to be pallbearers and the big red engine was already in place for the processional to the cemetery. One of Gene's crew waved to us and gently held out his hand to indicate where the car should stop.

We made our way through the large church foyer and there was Evan in front of three large Christmas trees with towering windows behind him. The crisp December morning was bright, the sky was blue, and the sun shone brilliantly. There were picture boards of Evan's life and flowers of all colors. White balloons floated high in the air and the strings gently moved as people passed by to see Evan.

"May I have your attention," a strong voice commanded. I turned and saw Gene. He stood tall at that moment in his long black jacket. "It's time to enter the auditorium and make your way to your seats."

Gene then asked the family to come together around Evan and pay their last respects. The pastor asked us all to hold hands and we prayed. Gene gently asked everyone to leave except for Penni, Noah, sister Chelsea, and me. He then asked Penni and me to put our hands on the lid and close it. Man, that is a heavy thing to do. Gene locked the casket and we filed into the sanctuary. Gene led the way, followed by an immaculately dressed firefighter, and then us.

After a perfect celebration of Evan's life, Gene asked us again to stand up and follow Evan out. The firefighters did a formal salute as they loaded the coffin, which was draped with a University of Michigan flag, a fitting tribute to the medical team that served Evan so well for seven years.

With lights flashing and the fire engine leading the way, we couldn't help but notice all the cars that had pulled to the side of the road out of respect for our son. The hearse, just ahead of us, had a white balloon tied to the back door, signaling that a child had died.

Noah kept looking back and said, "Mom, look at all those people following us."

As we entered the cemetery we could see a large green tent off in the distance. We knew it was for us. Winding through the maze of burial spots and evergreen floral arrangements, we finally saw Gene. He never wavered. He marked the exact spot for our car to stop with his large flat hand. I couldn't believe the precision of it all.

He told us to stay in the car as his large crew waved in vehicle after vehicle, showing them where to park. When it was time, Gene opened Penni's door and led her to a seat by Evan. We watched as the firefighters placed Evan above his final resting place and they stood directly across from us, behind Evan, as though they were going to protect him until the end.

Gene asked everyone to get as close as possible around us inside the tent. The last service was peaceful and at the end we all sang hymns, starting with "Amazing Grace."

With the last note still in the air, Gene motioned us to the side and the grave attendants came in to lower the casket. I don't know if you have ever seen that but it is a very powerful sight as those long straps eerily sway and unwind oh so slowly.

Penni said we should sing, so someone started singing "Jesus Loves the Little Children." We all joined in, even Gene and his staff.

Gene handed each of us—Penni, Noah, Chelsea, and myself—a white rose. We dropped them on top of the coffin.

It was now time to place the first bit of dirt on Evan. I grasped the wooden handle of the shovel and I plunged it into the large mountain of clay.

As I threw the first dirt on the casket engraved "Evan Harrison Newport," words I had never planned broke from my lips: "This is for my son."

Penni was next. Then Chelsea. Then Noah. Others followed. Gene was last.

Gene guided us again, asking us to look up into the fresh winter sky. He passed out the white balloons that had surrounded Evan over the last three days. He gave Noah the one that had been on the back of the hearse. "Noah," he said, "this is a special one just for you."

We let the balloons go.

As they floated off to a faraway place, family and friends started to interpret what they saw in the sky. Gene said, "It looks like a giant flashlight." That was Evan's favorite toy.

~Scott Newport

22

A Little Child Shall Lead Them

Heavy hearts, like heavy clouds in the sky,
are best relieved by the letting of a little water.
~Antoine Rivarol

My friend Eileen's husband died suddenly after a short illness that took everyone by surprise. Dan was only 56, in good health—or so everyone thought—so how could he be gone?

After the funeral, family and friends gathered to share memories and offer comfort to the newly bereaved widow. Eileen was doing her best to be strong and stoic. She had always been the rock of her family, the kind of woman who could handle any situation and cope with whatever life handed her with grace and aplomb. She moved through the crowd of mourners graciously, accepting condolences, thanking people for coming, pausing to smile at the stories people told her about something sweet or funny or thoughtful Dan had done.

She hid it well but I—and everyone else—could see how shaky and emotionally fragile she was, and we were all tip-toeing around her as if she were a time bomb, being very careful not to say or do anything that might shatter her hard-won control.

Suddenly, in the middle of a funny story one of the mourners was telling about Dan, the one thing everyone was afraid would happen, happened. Eileen stopped smiling and her eyes filled with tears.

She looked down into her lap, her hands fisted tightly on her thighs, her chin trembling visibly as she struggled not to break down in front of everyone. But it was no use. Tears coursed silently down her cheeks as she lost the struggle with her terrible, overwhelming grief. Her shoulders started to shake.

Everyone froze. What was the proper thing to do? Should we go on talking, pretend we didn't notice, and give her a chance to compose herself? Should we say something? Should we hug her? Get her a tissue? Offer her something to drink? Should we leave her alone to grieve privately?

While the adults were hesitating, afraid of doing the wrong thing and making things worse, Eileen's eight-year-old granddaughter Lauren sat down beside her and took one of her grandmother's hands in both of hers. "It's okay, Grandma," she said. "You can cry. I'll just sit here and hold your hand while you do."

It was such a simple thing and, yet, so exactly the right thing. While the supposedly wiser adults hesitated, embarrassed and unsure in the face of such raw emotion, eight-year-old Lauren simply and honestly acknowledged Eileen's pain and grief, and offered her the comfort she needed at the moment.

Her innocent, unselfconscious action offered potent proof that simple acceptance and understanding is so often the best response to another's pain.

~Candace Schuler

23

Mother's Bracelet

When I was young, I admired clever people.
Now that I am old, I admire kind people.
~Abraham Joshua Heschel

My mother's silver charm bracelet began as a "grandma bracelet," with charms engraved with the names and birthdates of her six grandchildren. Some are profiles of a little girl or boy; others are plain silver discs. Then Mother added a charm for me and one for my brother, Art. After decades of marriage, she got a new diamond wedding ring, and added her original slim silver ring to the bracelet.

A tiny silver pig dangles from the bracelet—a tribute to my father's many years with the Hormel Company. There is also a charm from Portugal; I have no idea what its significance is other than knowing my parents had once taken a trip to Portugal. Eventually, one at a time, charms were added for her 11 great-grandchildren. Mother wore this bracelet often and she always wore it on Mother's Day.

After my mother died, Art and I made plans to meet at her home to distribute all of her belongings. Mother had lived in Burlingame, California. Art and his wife, Joan, flew in from Minnesota. My husband, Carl, and I planned to drive our pickup from Washington so that I could bring home Mother's Spode Buttercup dishes, which I had always loved, and a small chest of drawers—the only item my mother had which had belonged to HER mother.

As I walked out of the house to make that sad journey, I fell and broke my ankle. Hours later, after getting a cast, I left the hospital in a wheelchair with instructions to keep the ankle elevated for several days. Because of post-polio syndrome, I was unable to get in and out of the wheelchair without Carl's assistance. Travel was impossible.

Mother's condo had been sold, and we needed to empty it for the buyers, so Art and Joan sorted through Mother's things without us. I wanted so badly to be there.

Art arranged to ship the chest of drawers and Mother's china to me. I tried to think what else I might want to keep but I was grieving for my mother and in pain from the ankle. My mind wasn't functioning in high gear, and I couldn't think of anything specific. Mother and I had different styles; she was an elegant, stylish woman. I'm a "country girl," and our homes reflected our personalities. I didn't need any furniture; her clothes didn't fit me. Art called several times to ask about small items that he thought I might want but, in the end, we gave most of the household to the Salvation Army.

On Mother's Day the following year, I remembered the silver bracelet. Why hadn't I thought to ask for that? When Art had called to describe Mother's jewelry, in case I wanted any of it, he hadn't mentioned the bracelet. I hoped Joan had taken it, but when I asked, Art said no, he didn't remember seeing it. I was heartsick to think Mother's treasured bracelet had somehow been overlooked and ended up in a Salvation Army thrift store.

That summer, more than a year after Mother's death, I received a package from a jewelry store in Burlingame. The package was insured; I had to sign for it. I couldn't imagine what it might contain. When I opened the box, my eyes filled with tears. Mother's charm bracelet was nestled in the same container, lined with gray velvet, that she had always kept it in!

A note from the jeweler explained that Mother had brought the bracelet in to have a new charm added for her latest great-grandchild, but she had never returned to get it. When he had tried to call her, the phone had been disconnected.

"She was a lovely lady," he wrote, "and I knew this bracelet was a family heirloom." He had searched through his records until he found another customer who lived in the same condominium building as my mother. He called her, explained about the bracelet, and asked if she knew how to contact anyone in my mother's family. She didn't, but she talked to the building manager, and got my name and address. She then went to the jewelry store, paid for the new charm, and gave the jeweler my information. He shipped Mother's bracelet to me.

Each year on Mother's Day, as I fasten the silver bracelet around my wrist, I not only remember my dear mother, but I thank two generous people who made the effort to return a cherished family treasure to someone they had never met.

~Peg Kehret

I Am a Nurse

We cannot direct the wind but we can adjust the sails.
~Author Unknown

I had been working in ICU for just over two years when I met her. Hope came to us suffering from respiratory distress in the late stages of breast cancer. She was 39 years old and had been fighting her battle on and off for years. It seemed that everyone knew that she was not going to win the war, that is, except for her. She had a teenage daughter at home and an eight-year-old as well. She had been a single mother for years. She was also one of the lucky ones in that she had one of the best familial support networks I had seen in my time in the ICU. Her parents had long ago taken her and her children into their home to assist in raising them and caring for their daughter through all of the surgeries and treatments.

Hope was not an easy patient to care for initially. She was on Bi-Pap, which is a miserable experience for the heartiest of individuals, and was in considerable pain around the clock. She would have periods of very low oxygenation, which would result in confusion and combativeness. It made it difficult for some people to get along with her. She also had a few complicated dynamics involving the father of her younger daughter, which placed the nursing staff right smack in the middle. It was a very sticky situation that strained both her family and the staff, and we sheltered her as best we could. We also balanced the assignments so the same nurses were not taking care of her all the time.

She was with us for weeks, sometimes improving enough to move to the Medical-Surgical floor for a few days. Inevitably, she always returned to us. While she was not prepared to give up her fight, she let us know regularly that if she were going to die, she certainly would not be doing it in the hospital. The nurses and physicians caring for her were realistic about her chances, as were her parents. Nevertheless, as long as Hope wanted to fight, we were there to help her do that.

I cared for her often and in her moments of lucidity she expressed her regret and, surprisingly, the guilt she felt at having spent so much of her younger daughter's life battling cancer instead of being her mother. As we talked, I realized that Hope was actually much closer to letting go than she had let any of us believe. As trust developed between us, she let me in on the secret of her unbreakable motivation. She was holding on every day, trying desperately to last until her daughter's ninth birthday, which was just a week away. She didn't have her younger child come into the ICU often; she hated to let her baby see her there, hooked up to IVs and machines, unable to even get out of bed to care for herself. However, she was excited to have her coming for her birthday. She abruptly stopped talking about it then, and looked away from me, teary-eyed. I handed her a box of tissues and waited for her to continue. She would not say anymore, just kept shaking her head, until she finally whispered, "I can't go to her birthday party."

Watching this woman, this mother who was living the last of her days in the hospital, away from her family and friends, finally letting a few cracks show in her strong façade, was more than I could bear. I could not take away her cancer and I could not make her well enough to go home. I could, however, be her voice, her advocate, and act as her connection to the outside.

I was scheduled to work on her daughter's birthday. I sat down with her first thing that morning and asked her if she would like to throw a little party for her daughter, here in her room. She didn't say anything for a moment and her eyes filled up. I'm sure mine did too. Then she nodded her head and quietly said, "Okay." My husband brought in cupcakes. We got some colorful balloons and tied them to chairs. I went to the gift shop and picked out a stuffed dog (her daughter's favorite animal) for Hope to give to her. I brought everything to her room, including a birthday card for her so she could write a private message to her daughter. We wrapped her dog together.

When her daughter came in later that day, her face lit up as she realized she was having a surprise party. We all sang "Happy Birthday" and then stepped out to give the family some private time. I can't say now who was affected more: Hope and her family, or myself and the other nurses who realized we were watching the last birthday celebration between mother and daughter. My heart broke for them as I thought of my own baby, tucked in at home with his father. There were many tears that day, of both happiness and grief.

Hope died a few weeks later, peacefully, on our Med-Surg Unit. Her family was with her at the end and I ran into them in the hallway right after she passed away. I exchanged hugs with everyone, including her little girl, and expressed my sympathy. They seemed at peace, knowing that their loved one was finally resting. As I watched them walk away, I found myself hoping that when they later thought about Hope's final days, they didn't just remember her fight and the sadness. I hoped they also remembered those few moments of real happiness when she got to put aside her illness and love her family, cuddle her daughter, and celebrate the life she was leaving behind.

I love being a nurse. Many people search for years for their purpose and mine has been clear for as long as I can remember. This situation affected me tremendously and to this day, I am so glad to have been a part of Hope's life. I have since left the ICU to work in Labor and Delivery, which brings me full circle. Instead of assisting those in their final moments, I welcome new life into our world. I put a lot of heart into what I do, as I am sure my coworkers can tell you. Every patient I care for leaves with a tiny piece of me, and that is okay. There is enough of me to go around. I am all nurse.

~Melissa Frye

Mr. Fitz

Could we change our attitude, we should not only see life differently,
but life itself would come to be different.
~Katherine Mansfield

Giant. That was the first thing that came to mind. Mr. Fitsumanu was at least 6'8", maybe taller, and as wide as a mountain. His hands were like sledgehammers with fingers. When he talked it was as if thunder spoke English with a Samoan accent. "Call me Meester Feets," he would say, and at the age of 13, who was I to argue?

My father had just passed away and with him went my direction in life, or so I thought. Mr. Fitz would say, "Doan fink too mush how bad you feel, jus know you feel and keep koing." My father spoke very little English and would only speak to me in Samoan. Mr. Fitz, as thick as his accent was, had an extensive vocabulary. He seemed to always speak philosophically, which I liked. It would always make me think. Looking back, I guess I was looking for someone to fill the void left by my father's death, and Mr. Fitz, in many ways, was like my father and so I clung to him.

Mr. Fitz had just moved to Missouri, and he volunteered to teach Sunday school at my church. Mr. Fitz came into our classroom, and boy did that room get quiet. I noticed that he only had two fingers on his massive right hand. That didn't keep him from writing with it. Thumb and pinky, that was it. He noticed me looking at his hand and said, "Eet doan hurt me, doan let eet hurt you." My face must have been filled with horror or fear for as I turned to the rest of the class, they burst out laughing. I turned to Mr. Fitz and he smiled. I felt ashamed for staring, but his smile warmed me and I began laughing as well.

In his twenties he had worked in Hawaii at a shipyard as a steel cutter. As his shift was coming to an end his mind wandered to this new game he and his friends were learning, golf. He was paying little attention to his saw, slipped and three fingers came off. He quickly wrapped his hand, picked up his fingers and raced to the hospital. The doctors were unable to reattach his fingers. There was too much bone and tissue damage. Mr. Fitz would tell this story with a grin and then hold his hand up and say, "Hang loose. At least I can steel play kolf." That would always amaze me: the story and the fact that he still played golf.

Mr. Fitz and his wife had been childhood friends of my mother and father in Samoa. When he saw my name on his roll he asked who my father was. I told him his name and that he had passed a month prior. He picked me up and started weeping. A rush of emotions that I had tried to hide from my family, friends, and even my mother suddenly exploded from me in the form of uncontrollable sobs. I'm the youngest boy in my family and my younger sister and I were the only children still living at home. My older brothers would say, "You have to be the man of the house now. You better stop your crying." I hadn't cried a tear since before the funeral.

Now I cried, "I don't want to be the man of the house. I just want my father back. I want to let him know I love him."

Setting me back down, he said, "A man can steel miss hees fodder's love. To weep for anudder chance to profess your love tells me you are da man of da house. Doan fink too mush how bad you feel, jus know you feel and keep koing."

In the weeks following, my family and I would frequent Mr. and Mrs. Fitz's home. This made my mother very happy. She got to catch up on gossip and I got to help Mr. Fitz fix things around his house, while listening to stories of my father's childhood. Mr. Fitz always had something to fix and I, somehow, always had to fix it. He knew where the ladder was and I could climb the ladder and clean the gutters. It seemed his wisdom and my youth were a powerful combination.

One Sunday, after church, he asked my mother if I could caddy for him in a golf tournament on the last day of school. I heard this and begged my mother to let me go. She conceded, and missing the last day of school seemed trivial. Now was my chance to see the big guy swing those clubs.

The day arrived and I was ready to see Mr. Fitz swing those shiny clubs that looked as if they would slip right through those big paws of his. We parked and he pulled his clubs out of the trunk and handed them to me, showing me how to hold the bag on my shoulder. It was heavier than I had expected.

As we checked in and walked to the first tee, I realized that men were staring at us. At first I thought it was because of the size of the man walking next to me, but then I saw someone pointing to Mr. Fitz's hand and making a gesture with his own hand. Mr. Fitz looked down at me and said, "Eet doan hurt me, doan let eet hurt you." I had forgotten about his hand. A tournament official standing with the man making the hand gestures walked over to us, "Sir, are you at the right tournament?" he asked.

Without hesitation Mr. Fitz answered, "Yes sir."

The official, startled at the thunderous voice, stepped back, asked his name and informed us that we were with the next group and were up.

As we watched the other players tee off, I noticed Mr. Fitz smiling. After each tee off, his smile seemed to widen. I began to worry. Was this his way of dealing with his nervousness? These men were hitting those balls into the next zip code. Then Mr. Fitz was up.

Men had already begun to gather behind us. Mr. Fitz took the biggest golf club from the bag and strolled out to the tee box. He teed up his ball, took the club with just his left hand, and in a flash there was a whip, then a tink, and that ball was gone. If those men were sending their balls to another zip code, then Mr. Fitz was sending his to Mars.

Applause came from everywhere. Mr. Fitz laughed and then asked the crowd, "Did anyone see my ball?"

I was astonished at the way Mr. Fitz played golf with one hand and made it look like that was really the way you played the game. He came in fourth, and by the reaction of the other golfers, he might as well have won. He did in my eyes.

On the ride home, I asked, "It must have been a real challenge losing your fingers. Were you ever scared that you wouldn't hit your ball as well as those other men?"

He thought about my question for a minute, and then with almost perfect English said, "To lose something that you would take for granted will always be there is not the challenge. Making the best of what may come is." At 13, these words would forever be etched in my mind.

Mr. Fitz passed away in August the following year. He drowned saving his niece from a riptide. I loved this man and the direction he gave my life. In the short time I knew him, I realized the impact that he made on my life and to this day I appreciate him for it. Every time I think of him I can still hear him say, "Doan fink too mush how bad you feel, jus know you feel and keep koing."

~Highland E. Mulu

26

Life Is a Series of Choices

Each difficult moment has the potential to open my eyes and open my heart.
~Myla Kabot-Zinn

It was the hardest telephone call I'd ever had to make. "He's gone," I said quietly. "It's over." I could hear my father's sharp intake of breath, followed by a choked sob. From my mother I heard nothing. Sitting on the narrow bed in our spartan hospital apartment with my husband by my side, I proceeded to convey the news to my parents that their six-month-old grandson had died.

The days and weeks that followed would pass in a blur, and the only thing I could recall from the funeral was the way my friend Grace grasped my hand so very tightly, and how grateful I was that she did so. I remember the friends who came to our home during the traditional week of mourning, and I remember wondering whether I'd ever be able to smile or laugh again. At the time, it seemed unimaginable.

I tried to settle back into my old routine, and just over a month after our son passed away, I returned to work. I had wonderfully supportive colleagues, but it was still torturous at best. Being alone with my thoughts was simply unbearable; silence unnerved me completely. I stopped driving my car to the office and began to travel by bus instead, as being stuck in traffic on my own was wreaking havoc on my sanity. My colleagues did their best to be understanding, but sometimes working in an office full of women led to situations that I just couldn't handle.

The day I heard that one of my colleagues was bringing her newborn son for a visit was not a good one. I tried to remain calm, but on the inside, I was growing increasingly frantic, knowing there was no way I would be able to join in everyone's excitement. When she arrived, one of my coworkers ran past me, pausing only to ask happily, "Did you see the baby?" I hadn't, of course. Nor did I want to. It was nothing personal—I just wasn't emotionally ready to do so. My wounds were still too fresh. Seeing other babies was too painful.

Fortunately for me, my friend Lesly happened to be standing nearby. She quickly realized what was happening and made a decision. "I forgot something at home," she said to me. "Come with me to pick it up." I didn't say a word, and mutely followed her as she grabbed her bag and car keys, flooded with an overwhelming sense of relief and grateful that she was taking me out of there.

The loss of our child was not a secret, and after he died, I desperately needed to feel that his death was not completely in vain. I promised myself that if I could somehow use my experiences to help others with similar tragedies, I would. When I heard that the wife of a close friend of my brother's was struggling to come to terms with a baby who was stillborn, I sent a carefully worded e-mail to the friend, asking if his wife might want to talk. "Yes," he quickly responded. "Stacey wants to hear from you. She wants to talk to someone who understands what she's going through."

The connection was made, and Stacey and I began to share our stories and our sadness. We spoke of our frustrations—the people who couldn't comprehend what we were going through, the people who believed they were helping us when they told us that we had to "get past the loss and move on," that "there would be other children," and perhaps most perplexing of all, that "it was better for it to have happened now, rather than later on." Through our exchanges, we both grew stronger, each of us drawing on the comfort we felt in knowing that someone else understood. As we healed, our exchanges became less frequent, picking up again years later when we found ourselves pregnant at the same time and needed to connect with someone who instinctively knew what the other would be feeling.

I had never been much of an extrovert when it came to sharing my feelings face-to-face, and this was especially true when it came to the death of our son. Showing my vulnerabilities in person was not something I'd ever been good at. As such, being an expatriate writer with friends strewn across the globe had its advantages. While I was not capable of allowing the protective walls I'd built around myself to be breached in my day-to-day physical encounters, I found it much easier to let down my defenses in writing, online. It meant that I could avoid physical reactions when telling my story — people couldn't see mine, nor would I be forced to deal with theirs.

Writing became my primary form of therapy as I chatted and corresponded with friends in California and Norway, friends whose support became my lifeline whenever things looked bleak. "Remember," said my friend in California during one such exchange. "Life is a series of choices. You're going to get hit with a lot, but it's up to you to choose how you're going to deal with it." And I knew he was right. I couldn't change the fact that my son had died, but I could choose how to live with what had happened. It was up to me to decide whether I wanted to remain stuck in that deep, dark hole or whether I wanted to pull myself out and move forward. When it came down to it, I knew I needed to get out of that place, that I was not prepared to let the pain from my tragedy define who I was forever. I knew that it would hurt more to stay there than to find a way to heal somehow. Through my friends and through my writing, I found myself again, and time became my ally in dulling what my loved ones and writing could not.

This is not to say, of course, that there is no longer any pain. In the weeks leading up to both his birthday and the anniversary of his death, I am often agitated and anxious, not always realizing why until I look at a calendar. The passing years have given me tools that help me to navigate my way through the difficult times, though. I have written and I have shared, and I've been profoundly overwhelmed by the support I received as a result. Remarked my friend Isabel one day, "By being so honest and real you enable other people to admit to having feelings too. Imagine!"

And I think that Isabel just might be onto something.

~Liza Rosenberg

27

How to Help

Even hundredfold grief is divisible by love.
~Terri Guillemets

Please be gentle with this new person
That I was forced to become.
I need understanding and patience,
So please administer some.

I often feel myself floundering
In my daily activities now,
And some of the things that I used to do
Are harder to do somehow.

There are certain songs I can't bear to hear
And places where I cannot dwell,
And just folding laundry can make me cry;
(Shopping for groceries, as well.)

If the smell of a grilled cheese sandwich
Has me suddenly weeping tears;
Please understand that he loved those for lunch
And I made them for him for years.

And don't be afraid to mention his name.
I need that more than you know.

You are not the reason I'm hurting so much —
The loss of my son made that so.

Just offer your shoulder if I need to cry
And listen if I need to talk.
This road that I'm on is SO difficult —
The hardest I ever will walk.

Maybe someday I'll show you his pictures
And not fall apart at the seams.
Just tell me you know that I'm hurting so —
I can't tell you how much that means.

I know that the pain will get softer
So be patient with me till it does;
I never will be the same person again,
For, I'm not the ME that I Was.

~Beverly F. Walker

28

A Quilt of Memories

The best way to cheer yourself up is to try to cheer somebody else up.
~Mark Twain

I called her Mom Mom. She was my grandmother. We were very close, and the more time I spent with her the more I began to notice little things about her. She loved my cousins and me very much and enjoyed spending time with us. She was always ready to help others or to give to those in need. When times grew hard and she would question why things happened, her faith in God never wavered. But the one thing I remember most of all — she was the glue that held the entire family together.

I was five the summer my family found out she had cancer. How was I supposed to know why Mom Mom was getting sicker and sicker and then, all of a sudden, why she was gone? I struggled to understand. She had died just weeks before my birthday. Had I done something wrong? How could I understand it was the cancer that had so quickly taken my grandmother from me, and not something I had done?

I watched the people around me grieve. Some stayed busy. Some cried but then smiled through their tears as a good memory came to mind. My cousin, Caleb, was plagued by nightmares of Mom Mom's death. And me — I chose to grieve in silence.

After the funeral one day, I remember looking at the family pictures in the hall when I noticed something out of the corner of my eye. The door to Mom Mom's bedroom was open. Someone was inside.

I crept closer and peered through the doorway. My mom was busy pulling Mom Mom's clothes from the closet. At first, I feared she was going to throw them away. They held so many memories for me—like the blue dress with polka dots that she had always worn to church or the shirt with the flower print that she wore while gardening. Then I noticed my mom pause. She looked over the clothes, her expression thoughtful.

I took a few steps into the room. "What are you doing?"

"I… I was toying with the idea of making some quilts out of Mom Mom's clothes. I think there's enough material for five quilts—two for your aunts, one for Sarah, and one for you and one for me." She looked up then. "Would you like that?"

Tears threatened to fall. I couldn't find the words to speak, so I simply nodded. I could almost see it now, a patchwork quilt lying on my bed. A security blanket I could pull over my head at night and something I could look at in the daytime that would remind me of Mom Mom.

Memories. That was all I really had of her now. And it was those few memories that I clung to in the years that followed.

First, came my aunts' quilts, then my cousin Sarah's. Mine was next—or so I thought.

"It's been several years since Mom Mom's death," my mom said one day, "but Caleb is still having nightmares."

A lump welled up in my throat. I wasn't sure I liked where this conversation was going, but I didn't say anything. I waited, knowing there had to be more.

"I was thinking," my mom said. "Do you think Caleb would like a quilt—one made from Mom Mom's clothes?"

I glanced up startled. "I thought you said there was only enough material for five quilts."

"Well," my mom let out a deep breath. "I was thinking that I could give up the material for my quilt."

I stared at the ground. I knew what that quilt meant to my mom. I held my breath. I don't know whether it was God or not, but I heard a voice, a gentle whisper, that pulled at my heart. I looked up. "Could you make two smaller quilts?"

"You mean something like a lap quilt?"

I could see my mom was thinking about it, so I waited for her to answer.

"You know that might work."

"Then split my material," I said. "Give half of it to Caleb."

I saw the look of shock and confusion on my mom's face. "I meant to split my material, not yours. I would never do that to you."

"Split my material," I repeated firmly. "Please, I want to do this."

It was late August by the time the quilt was finished. I remember the long hours of sewing and stitching my mom had put into it. As I stared at the finished quilt, I couldn't help but smile. On every other square there was a memory colorfully stitched into the fabric.

There was a feather stitched on the green square symbolizing the Indian relics Mom Mom had kept in the attic for us to play with. On a pink square there were candies, just like the ones she had kept in the glove compartment of the old gray car. Down in the corner there was a shell stitched on a sky blue square. It reminded me of the scavenger hunts we had on the beach.

As we walked the quilt over to Caleb, a thought crossed my mind. Will it help him with the nightmares? Or will it only make them worse?

I bit my lip as we spread the quilt out for Caleb to see. I wasn't sure what he thought of it at first. But then as he slowly reached out and touched the material, he smiled fondly. What was he remembering? Perhaps it was the Halloween costumes Mom Mom had made for us. Perhaps he once again saw her bending over her flowers, her hands covered in dirt. Or perhaps memories had taken him back to the aquarium, where he once again touched the horseshoe crab and, with an impish grin, glanced back at Mom Mom.

After a moment, he looked at me. "Are you sure you want me to have this?"

A smile spread across my face. "Yes. It's yours."

My aunt told us later the quilt had worked. Caleb's nightmares were gone.

It was that summer I realized something. It might have been a difficult decision to share my material, but as I listened to my mom and Caleb talk about Mom Mom, something changed inside me. My heart was beginning to heal. I felt joy when I saw Caleb's excitement. More importantly, I felt peace.

~Meaghan Elizabeth Ward, age 17

The Woman Who Could Not Stop Crying

Have you ever been hurt and the place tries to heal a bit, and you just pull the scar off of it over and over again.

~Rosa Parks

Early on a Saturday morning, I was on my way to run some errands. Up ahead on the street in our quiet neighborhood I could see red lights flashing and a crowd of people standing on one side of the street. I slowed down, like most of us do, to check out the scene.

To my horror I saw a yellow tarp covering what had to be a body on the sidewalk. Around the body were eight or nine scattered, broken bicycles. Having been an avid cyclist most of my life, I simply had to pull around the corner, park my car and walk back to join the crowd of people who were quietly standing and staring.

"What happened?" I asked a woman. She filled me in.

"There was this group of bicyclists," she said. "Somebody had a flat tire and they were all up on the sidewalk while one guy fixed the tire."

She stopped talking for a moment, then pointed at the covered body on the sidewalk. "A guy in a big truck came around the corner too fast, lost control and plowed into all the bicyclists. Most of them have been taken away in ambulances, but that poor young man is dead."

I sat down on the curb. It seemed eerily quiet. The police were still marking the area with yellow tape and talking to the young driver of the truck. The truck itself had ended up on someone's lawn.

I never ran my errands. I must have sat on that curb for over an hour. Eventually I just went home, my heart aching for that young man and whoever loved him. Three months later I would realize why I "happened" on that scene and why I could not tear myself away.

My granddaughter, Autumn, was working at a job while in high school. One day Autumn called me saying she had a huge favor to ask.

"You have to help," she pleaded. "I work with this woman whose son died a few months ago in a bike accident. She works for a while, then goes to the back and cries her heart out. You know how to help people and you have to do this."

Click went my brain. The bike accident. The young man under that yellow tarp. The son of this woman where Autumn worked.

I told Autumn I really had to think this through. Could I help without being intrusive? This woman did not know me and I didn't know her or her son.

I went into what I call my "Quiet Zone," and came up with a plan, having no idea if it would work. I told Autumn to gently tell this woman that her grandma (me) did a lot of hospice stuff… and to explain hospice because this woman was from another culture and maybe didn't know all that hospice does. Autumn was to give Saheema my phone number because maybe I could help with her grief.

I was honestly surprised when Saheema called, and yes, she was crying on the phone. My intuition told me to see her on neutral ground… not my house and not her home.

I asked Saheema if she would meet me in a park. I described the park and a quiet place where we could sit at a picnic table and talk. The only time she could meet me was 7 a.m. Fine with me. I suggested Saheema bring family photo albums.

I got to the park first, with a big thermos of tea and two cups. I waited ten minutes, thinking she wasn't going to show up. Then I saw her walking slowly and tentatively toward me, carrying several photo albums.

Yes, she was crying. I got up and helped her put all the albums on the table. Before we sat down, I opened my arms and she came to me for a hug. Neither one of us said a word for at least five minutes. I just held her, this tiny woman, with a heavy accent, from a faraway country, who could not stop crying. I'd brought plenty of tissues, but noticed Saheema used colorful real handkerchiefs.

We spent an hour together, drinking hot tea, and looking at pictures. As she slowly turned each page, naming the faces of her large and extended family, we lingered a long time on every picture of her son. Pictures of him as an infant, then as he grew up, school sports, college graduation. Her son was clearly the shining star in her family and particularly in her life. He was tall, dark and movie-star handsome.

By the time we closed the page of the last album, Saheema was no longer crying. She actually smiled a few times and just dabbed at her eyes. We never spoke of my hospice life, or even an "afterlife." We were just two women who knew what grief feels like, two women from different cultures whose paths just happened to cross.

I'd like to believe that Saheema began to heal that day. A lovely letter arrived from her about a week later, saying "Thank you for helping me and being interested in my family and my dear son."

The best part was when Autumn told me Saheema was no longer going to the back room to cry.

~Bobbie Jensen Lippman

30

A Slice of Heaven

Earth has no sorrow that Heaven cannot heal.
~Author Unknown

As a mother whose son passed away six years ago, each special occasion is a struggle. I miss the wholeness of my family, finding myself wishing that all my children were together and we could share in the celebration of special days. One year, a week before Mother's Day, I started to feel anxious over how I would handle another Mother's Day celebration without my son. I did not want to waste another year of not fully enjoying a day honoring my mother and my mother-in-law, as well as "being in the moment" with our families. An idea popped into my head, which was a very non-traditional way of coping.

I made an unusual request of my husband. As Paul is very logical, I feared he would think I had gone over the edge, that I had finally lost my mind, but I have learned through my journey of grief to communicate my needs to others, no matter what the subject. Do not make the mistake of assuming what others are thinking or feeling. The openness of being able to relay your feelings to your loved ones is a key to finding your way out of the darkness of despair to the light of hope and joy. Not entirely confident of his response, I decided to e-mail my request to him for Mother's Day. I asked if when he was buying a Mother's Day card for me, he would also purchase a card from Andy. I told him to just listen to his heart and Andy would guide him to the right card. He did not reply, so I was not sure that my request would be fulfilled.

Mother's Day I awoke and thought of the fun-filled day ahead of us. A trip to my sister's to be with my family, which included my mother and father, my daughter and son-in-law and two wonderful grandchildren, my sister and her family, and my brother and his family — 18 family members together to enjoy the first part of the day.

To complete the second part of our day, we would then travel to Paul's parents' house and spend special time with them. To have our two mothers living is a special present. The thought of Andy not being with us flashed through my mind and my heart then saddened with that reality. The phone rang, and my daughter in Dallas, who could not be with us, phoned and wished me a happy Mother's Day. Her call helped me focus on the present instead of the past.

I turned from the phone, and on our kitchen island was a beautiful vase of flowers with two cards and two presents. My husband gave me his card and present. I am very lucky that after 21 years of marriage my husband still realizes how wonderful it is to hear that he loves and appreciates me as wife, friend, and mother to our children. I then turned to the other card sitting by the flowers and slowly opened the envelope. It was a lovely card and my husband had signed it with the exact same handwriting as Andy. Tears filled my eyes, but they were happy tears, not the tears of sadness. Paul then told me to open the gift. It was a kitchen knife, with the following note:

Mom,

I wanted to get you something that would make you think of me. So I bought you a slice of heaven. Every time you are cooking and using the knife, I will be with you cooking some delicious concoction and slicing a piece of heaven. Hopefully you will think of me and know how much I enjoy cooking and that *this gift will bring you as many years of joy as you have brought into my life.*

Love,
Andy

Andy loved to cook and we often spent time laughing and talking with family and friends gathered in the kitchen. What a perfect gift! For that day, we were all together. With my husband's compassion and willingness to indulge my "odd request," I was able to enjoy Mother's Day without a heavy heart.

~Jan Grover

Grieving and Recovery

Attitude Adjustments

31

Secret Shopper

Action is the antidote to despair.
~Joan Baez

Paul's funeral was on Friday. By Saturday afternoon, everyone was gone and the house seemed so empty, so quiet. On Monday, I struggled to get myself back to work, not sure how to get through the day. I took some inspiration from Paul, who had so desperately wanted to work as much and as long as he could.

People at the office didn't know what to say to me, nor I to them. There were more than a few awkward moments. Somehow, I made it through the day, and the week, even though I often excused myself to go sit in the bathroom and cry.

As soon as I drove out of the parking lot, I burst into tears and wailed all the way home. To keep the neighbors from calling the paramedics, I forced myself to be quiet as I walked into the house.

Inside, the paralysis set in. I could do little more than sit at the computer and play solitaire, trying to numb the pain. I repeatedly replayed the last weeks with Paul. Some small part of me still expected him to walk into the room, for us to somehow return to our former life, to wake up from the nightmare. I rehearsed conversations I planned to have with him, until I once again realized that there would be no more conversations. And I cried until my stomach ached.

I couldn't find the energy to prepare anything that resembled dinner. Some nights I ate hardly anything besides the candy in the dish on the desk. I had never been much for candy before, but now I couldn't seem to get my fill. Or maybe it was just because it was within reach. Chocolate chip cookie dough ice cream was the other staple of my new diet.

One reason I didn't eat better was that I hadn't gone to the grocery store since before Paul's death. That was one of several places I just couldn't face without him. Trips to the store with Paul were an adventure, which is one reason we nearly always went together. We started at the deli counter, where he ordered a "proper" selection of meats and cheeses for "nice" sandwiches. "Nice" was Paul's highest praise for a sandwich. From there we went on to the breads and condiments.

In the produce section, he maintained that bins were left open precisely so that customers could take samples. As he explained these things to me, he smiled and winked impishly.

Coffee cakes, sweet rolls, and donuts often "appeared" in our shopping cart when I wasn't looking. After feigning surprise, Paul explained that "that little gray-haired lady over there" must have gotten confused and accidentally put the items in our cart. Then he explained that it would be rude to return the items to the shelf, so we should do the honorable thing and keep them.

I demonstrated to him how I had played "racy car driver" with the shopping cart when my children were young, pretending to speed and rev the cart's "engine." He caught on to that game quickly, and soon incorporated the "race cart" into our shopping routine. What fun we had just going food shopping!

A further complication to returning to the store was that we had gotten to know the store manager, who would surely ask about Paul if I went in without him. I just couldn't handle that yet.

The day I got the call that Paul's ashes were ready to be picked up, I knew I wanted my friend Judy to go with me. I was nervous—this was another trip I didn't want to face alone. I hoped that Judy's company would make me braver—and it did. Having her by my side made it easier to reach out and accept the cube-shaped carton containing Paul's ashes. There had been no need to buy an urn because

Paul wanted his ashes scattered right away — on the lake where he spent his summers as a child.

I signed a few forms and we went to the car. I sat the box on my lap and took a deep breath, not sure what I was feeling. After a silent moment, Judy said, "What do you want to do now, Bet?"

I thought for a moment and said, "I need you to go with me to the grocery store. I haven't had the courage to go since Paul died. But I need food."

"Sure, we can do that. But you don't need to go without Paul. We'll just take him with us."

I looked at her blankly for a moment before it sank in. Of course, we would take Paul with us. As I was beginning to comprehend, Judy reminded me, "Paul would want you to have fun again. He'd see the humor in this." She was right, of course. "We'll let him ride in the cart with us. That way, we can talk to him while we shop, and you won't be going without him."

"Okay, I'm ready." One look at Judy and I started to laugh. At first, it felt strange. I'd nearly forgotten what it was like. But it felt good, too, and I knew Paul wouldn't want me to cry for the rest of my life. He'd be the first one making jokes. I realized that's why I now needed Judy with me — to help me find humor in the situation.

We drove to the store, took the box in with us, and sat it in the child seat. We told him we were back in the store and asked him what we should buy.

I pretended to answer him. "All right, I'll start at the deli."

We then proceeded to produce, where I explained to Judy about the samples.

I even bought a coffee cake for him. We played "race cart" down deserted aisles, and giggled as we made car sounds.

"Watch me take this corner, Paul. What's that? No, I can't go any faster."

Judy asked, "Paul, do you need coffee?"

I asked. "Which brand of paper towels did we decide we like best?"

As we were checking out, now with a lighter heart, I kept the tears away when the store manager came over and asked how Paul was doing. That marked the first time I managed to tell someone that Paul had passed away without breaking down completely. I didn't tell the manager that I had Paul right there, that he was in the box I was taking out of the cart while we were speaking. After Judy and I were outside, we burst into laughter at the absurdity of the scene.

With Judy's humor and Paul's ashes, I got through that first trip back to the store. It was several months before going to the grocery alone wasn't so poignant—and before I stopped reaching for Paul's favorite items. But each time was made easier when I remembered the day I took Paul with me—carton and all.

~Bettie Wailes

The Eight-Iron Victory

Turn your face to the sun and the shadows fall behind you.
~Maori Proverb

It's really difficult to hit an eight-iron when tears keep falling onto your hands. The first time it happened I knew in my mind what the problem was, but couldn't bring my heart to face the truth.

The second time was on the seventh hole, a short par four. After a decent drive I reached into my bag and pulled the eight-iron out for the relatively easy shot to the green. As I looked down at the ball, seeing the club resting comfortably on the ground, the tears flowed again.

I knew it was necessary to face the grief and anger that flooded my soul. Even as a 62-year-old man, I desperately wanted to sob like a little child. You see, the eight-iron was my father's favorite club, the one he so often used in winning our close-fought and exciting golf matches.

Playing the macho card, I had stifled the anger and hurt residing in my heart during the six months after his death. Now it was catching up to me, triggering spontaneous tears every time I reached for that club.

Often I wished he had died from a heart attack, even an automobile accident. That way only his presence would be gone, not the memories of the father I loved.

The awfulness of Alzheimer's disease had robbed me of not only my father, but also the memories of the man he was. My mind was a dynamic kaleidoscope of remembering only the withering body and a mind that had escaped reality. Memories of the man I had loved and respected focused on eyes that had lost their sparkle and a mind giving up the search for names.

I remembered the fear that flooded me when he was still mobile, but needed help finding the bathroom every single time. Grief and confusion did battle when I heard ugly, vulgar words coming from a man who never expressed anything more violent than an occasional "damn."

Sometimes when I pulled the eight-iron out I literally heard the last-day rattling breath of my father on the phone as he was dying on the East Coast while I was helplessly listening on the West.

That club, Dad's favorite club, became a symbol of something ugly, reminding me only of those awful last months. Golf had been my friend because of the numerous times I played with my father. Now it had become a torturous endeavor.

Maybe it was serendipity or perhaps a God-induced thought, but on the way to play another perfunctory round, I knew what had to happen. I wasn't looking forward to the game yet again.

After parking my car, I opened the trunk to get my clubs, dreading what I knew I had to do. I lifted the bag up just enough to extract only my putter and the eight-iron. Taking two balls and only those two clubs, I headed for the first tee. I had to face this demon.

The original thought was to overcome the psychological terror and deep anger by sheer willpower. I reasoned that by forcing myself to play this nine-hole course with just the eight-iron I would eventually erase or stifle the emotions I felt each time I pulled that club from the bag.

The first hole was a blur. My body was stiff, the swing harder than normal as I felt inner anger making me want to smash those Alzheimer memories into oblivion. My mind wasn't on golf, but on fighting to keep tears from flooding out.

I walked faster than normal, stomping on the grass, trying by physical action to rid my soul of these feelings.

Hole number two wasn't any different. I was being "the man," chasing victory by brute force, yet feeling anger rising and confusion winning.

On the third hole it happened. My tee shot produced the resounding "click" of a well-struck ball, and as I watched it climb into the sky, reproducing the type of shot Dad so often hit, the tears started. First just a moistening, but then pouring out as my whole body sobbed in a great release of pent-up emotion.

Walking to the ball I noticed the blazingly blue sky for the first time. The grass felt friendly. I could feel my heart beating in my chest.

When I reached my ball, the unimaginable happened.

I didn't even attempt to stifle those tears. Dropping my putter behind me, I took the eight-iron, saw its blurry outline near the ball, and swung towards the hole only about 20 yards away.

Once more I hit it just right. I watched it hit the green, take one full bounce, and then roll the last few feet directly into the hole.

I'd seen this shot so many times from my father as he chipped in to tie or win a hole. As the ball rolled firmly into the hole, my mind saw Dad's face with his quiet smile and glistening eyes as once more he pulled off the semi-miraculous shot.

The golf for the rest of the round was a blur, but the memories that filled my mind were as sharp as HDTV. Each shot I hit produced a memorable moment.

As real as it was during the original times, I heard his, "Great round. You hit some excellent shots." Whether he won or lost, Dad's respect for his opponents was genuine and encouraging.

I remembered his gleaming face as he said, "I knew you could do it!" the first time I ever beat him in a match. Even though it took me to the age of 32, his pride was genuine. My memory of that day also included how thankful I was that he never "let me win," but allowed it to be an honest achievement.

On the eighth hole I hit a really poor shot, and my memory rewound to how proud I was of Dad when we played with someone just learning the game. His patience and quiet teaching gave growing confidence to the person, and resulted in increased skill. Dad never took credit for the improvement, but gave full credit to the learner.

Finally the ninth hole came. Walking toward the last green my tears had stopped, my walk was lighter and my heart rejoiced.

Yes, the sad memories of my father's failing body and missing mind were still there. They were there, but the comfort of happy nostalgia had returned. My mind was free to remember the beauty of enjoyable love.

After putting out on the last hole, I raised the eight-iron toward the sky and said aloud, "Thanks, Dad, for showing me life and how to live it."

~John H. Hitchcock

33

The Willingness to Let Him Go

When we are no longer able to change a situation, we are challenged to change ourselves.
~Victor Frankl

He loved Myers's Rum, dark chocolate and the Three Stooges. From the moment I met him, I knew he was something extraordinary. For me, he was the first person I had ever known who had my back. What a difference that made. There was a new freedom born in that truth, and at the age of 21 I finally learned to have fun and play like a child. In Bill I had found a playmate, a cohort and a soul mate.

When they arrived at my door on that early January morning, I knew immediately what they were going to tell me. It was a drunk driver on a dark, wintry country road. They said he died instantly. At the age of 30, he had become a statistic.

The shock carried me through countless months, threaded with denial as I thought I caught glimpses of him crossing a street or passing by in a truck. On occasion, the sadness would overflow and the blessed relief of tears would carry away some of the pain. Most often there was anger and fear. I had lost my faith. I wanted absolutely nothing to do with any god who could have allowed this to happen.

For four years I continued our work with adults with disabilities. I did this in his name and as my reason to get out of bed each morning. The spark in my eyes was gone, and my smile was hollow. I simply did not know how to live without faith, and was unable to live my faith in the reality of Bill being killed. My life seemed to have lost all meaning and I simply did not care. I was dying from the inside out.

Finally, as the fourth autumn approached, I felt my spirits dropping lower with each falling leaf, and I knew I was in trouble. With what felt like my last breath, I reached out for help. Miraculously, my hand was grasped by someone who had the spiritual strength to hold on tight and point the way. On a cloudy Saturday afternoon, I curled up under an afghan in the corner of my sofa and began to sob as I shared my story of Bill. She sat quietly receiving my sobs, words and pain, without judgment or comment.

It was after I was completely emptied that she took my hands and looked clearly into my eyes and spoke. Quietly she said: "If you want to recover, you are going to have to let go of Bill." My eyes opened wide and my body immediately stiffened. She was asking me to do the one thing I honestly could not do. We talked for a long while and I attempted to find any other option. I was simply not willing to do this thing, yet I could not open my heart to God if I continued to cling to Bill and blame God for his death. I felt even more stuck than I had earlier that day. I had no idea where to turn.

Patiently she offered another suggestion: "Pray for the willingness," she said. "Just pray for the willingness twice a day. Keep it very simple. Do it whether you mean it or not. The willingness will come." I did not want to follow her suggestion, but could think of no alternative. Therefore, I reluctantly agreed to give it a try.

And so I began, a sour, mumbled: "Dear God, please help me to be willing to let go of Bill," every morning and every evening for the next ten days. One afternoon in the middle of work, I suddenly felt the willingness come. It was but a nudge, yet it was very clear. I rushed out of the room and sat quietly with God for a moment and cried "No, not yet. I am not ready." Nevertheless, I continued my daily prayer, a little less sour and with a bit more vigor.

A few days later the nudge came again; it was gentle, but very strong and very clear. I knew it was time, and I was willing! I did not have time to ponder the wonder of that: instead I received the grace to simply proceed. I sat down quietly in a chair and talked to Bill, and he was there! I poured out the words I had longed to say: my depth of gratitude for him, the intensity of my grief, the profundity of my love. I talked and talked until there was only one thing left to say. I sat quietly in his presence for a few moments, and then began to explain my need and desire to let him go, my awareness that we both could be free.

And then, with complete willingness and abandon, I told him goodbye. Before those words had even left my lips, I felt the power of God rush over and into me, lifting me up into love and peace I had never imagined possible. The light was turned back on, and I was fully connected. I sat quietly in the lap of love for the longest time; I had never imagined the power of God to be so loving and pure.

I hardly knew where to go from there, but simply decided to go on with my day and do the next right thing. When I went to a meeting that evening, I found people looking at me with wonder. Several people commented that I looked so very different and asked me what happened. I explained the best I could, words were so inadequate. The transformation of that moment has been alive in me ever since that autumn afternoon.

When times of darkness visit, I try to remember the power of the light and the love of that moment. I have learned to love more freely, give more openly, and live more joyously. Now, when I see Myers's Rum, dark chocolate or the Three Stooges, I feel deep gratitude for both the love of Bill and for the willingness to let him go.

~Cate Adelman

34

Learning About Loss Before It's Too Late

Life is what we make it, always has been, always will be.
~Grandma Moses

One day last week I woke up in a lousy mood. Why? We were out of coffee. I was late paying a MasterCard bill. My favorite clock had just stopped working.

I didn't even think of saying "good morning" to my husband Bob. After all, we've been waking up together for 32 years. As usual, we both got out of bed and headed right to our desks.

I checked e-mail and replied to people who were complaining about rainy days as if we were all living through a catastrophic disaster.

One more e-mail remained. It was from a fellow named John. And it turned out to be a breath-stopping shock.

The first time John wrote to me was about a year ago. He was responding to a column I had written about relationship troubles that Bob and I had overcome:

"Hello Saralee. My wife Donna pointed out an article by you she found moving. It brought her to tears. I'm a grown man who can be very emotional. I was pleasantly surprised that there was a happy ending and everything was fine. Few couples these days enjoy the closeness that you have with your spouse. I am proud to say that I have been with my beloved for 26 years and she's still the one."

When I saw his name on this current e-mail, I was hoping to read more about his loving marriage. He wrote:

"Two days ago my wife fell down a flight of stairs. I lost the only girl I will ever love. She was only 54 and in perfect health."

I stared at his words as my life was overhauled in less than one minute.

I could hear Bob in his study. He was in a bad mood because he kept getting cut off during a phone call to our veterinarian. I asked him to come in and read John's e-mail.

As he was reading, his demeanor changed. In slow motion, he went from appearing uptight and annoyed to sadly calm. With a deep sigh he said, "Thank you for having me read this."

I cried as I re-read the rest of John's note: "She was an organ donor and I am told that because of her good health she can help as many as 50 people. It has been nice talking to you about the love with our spouses."

I responded, "Your e-mail made me think about so many stupid things I get upset about. You gave me a huge wake-up call as to what matters in life and what doesn't." When I asked for his permission to write about this lesson, he kindly agreed and said, "I'm sure Donna would be honored."

I am the one honored to be writing about Donna's many legacies. She selflessly changed the lives of 50 people by giving precious gifts from her body. Through the words of her adoring husband, she leaves behind and continues to teach the profound yet often overlooked lesson: love is what is most important. I am also hoping she will help many realize, the way I did, that most everything is small potatoes compared to love, life and death.

And so this morning, it didn't faze me that I was out of computer paper when a deadline was imminent or that we, along with many others, are so hurting for money that we're on food stamps.

In silence, I said, "Thank you, John, for being so open with me about your tender love affair. Thank you for showing me that living in the moment is the path to joy, because all future moments are truly unpredictable. Thank you, Donna, for showing me that giving, in its most gracious and noble form, is done without expecting anything in return. Eternally, you will always be 'the one'—for John—for 50 peoples' lives you will now be an extraordinary part of... and for me."

And then I said "good morning" to Bob.

~Saralee Perel

My Son

If you suppress grief too much, it can well redouble.
~Molière

I didn't like Tommy. Love him? It seemed unlikely that I ever could. I knew our differences had to be resolved soon or I would have to stop trying to be his stepmother. Tommy's natural mother had died a year before and he and his brother had gone through a series of housekeepers and sitters, and now us.

When Tommy's father and I married it seemed like an ideal arrangement. His sons would have a mother and my daughters would have a father. Death and divorce leave many refugees and here were six we could combine to establish a real family.

Tommy was chubby and constantly stood in front of the open refrigerator door gulping gallons of milk. It wasn't necessary to correct him about anything, because with just a look in his direction tears flooded his eyes. I was certain that if his lower lip trembled one more time I would scream. I knew I treated the boy kindly, yet I was drowning in feelings of guilt about him. It was easier with Tommy's younger brother, though I never understood why.

When Tommy wasn't crying, or gulping milk, he was pulling on his T-shirt and stretching it. Sometimes he locked me out of my bedroom when his father was home so he could visit with him and I couldn't. Tommy would block the television screen so my daughters couldn't watch. In my eyes Tommy was rapidly developing into a thoroughly obnoxious child. He was only seven.

We'd been married several months and tension was building at a phenomenal rate. Each night I dreaded the ritual of tucking Tommy into bed and kissing his fat little cheek as he glared at me.

I prayed for guidance.

Tommy's father had told me about their loss. Nancy had been ill a long time and when he called the boys into the house to tell them she had died, Tommy's only response was to ask if he could go back out to play. My husband, caught up in his own sorrow, interpreted this as childhood innocence and avoided acknowledging and resolving Tommy's grief. The boys did not attend the funeral and the subject was closed. The prevailing attitude was that life was for the living, but part of Tommy had also died.

I was pretty certain the difficulty with Tommy was related to his loss. With no training in psychology, and no personal experience with death, I knew that by addressing the issue I might be opening a Pandora's box that I was ill equipped to handle. I had to take the chance, and with God's help I was provided insight and courage.

That night, as I tucked Tommy into bed, I sat down close to him. "Do you miss your mother?" I asked.

There was no trembling chin, no shining tears or hateful glances in response to this question. This time a volcanic eruption of grief burst from the little boy. As he cried and sobbed, I held him in my arms and for the first time we really touched. My hugs and kisses were given by choice, not duty, and his reception was honest and real. After the tear storm subsided, we talked.

"I understand her eyes were blue like yours," I said, still holding him. He nodded. I refused to allow him to withhold the rest so I probed deeper.

"What do you miss most about your mother?" I asked.

"I miss her pizza. She made really good pizza," he said. The sobs had quieted and now he was ready to talk.

"I met your mother once when she came to pick up your father after work. I worked there, too. She was a pretty lady." Tommy couldn't remember the incident but agreed that she was a pretty lady.

Though I knew he hadn't, I asked if he had gone to her funeral.

We talked about where she was buried. He had never seen her grave. We talked about her relationship with God, which I already knew was good.

I stretched my memory for any details I knew about his mother so that we could talk more about her. I knew so little. After a while our conversation drifted on to current, less emotional matters.

When I kissed the chubby cheek and hugged the little boy that night there was love in the kisses we shared. At last we had begun to communicate, and I was able to sincerely give of myself to him and he to me.

The next morning, when Tommy came into the kitchen for breakfast he casually called me "Mom." I hadn't asked him to. He just did.

I knew I would never take his natural mother's place. I didn't want to. She would always be special in Tommy's heart but Tommy also needed a real live mother every day. He chose me and I love him and his brother completely.

~Lorna Stafford

Last Laugh

Mirth is God's medicine. Everybody ought to bathe in it.
~Henry Ward Beecher

My father's funeral could have been a sitcom. There wasn't much to laugh about in the last few years of Dad's life. On Christmas Eve 1996, my mother had a stroke. It left her partially paralyzed and unable to talk clearly. Dad spent the next four years caring for her, in spite of his own battle with prostate cancer.

In November 1999, they moved to a nursing home, where Dad died in mid-February 2000. The final few weeks were especially difficult. He had grown up in an orphanage and the last place he wanted to be was an institution — or, more precisely, an institution was absolutely not the last place he wanted to be. He was an independent man, but he was no longer able to get around on his own, even to use the bathroom. And he was in so much pain that his moans often brought tears to the nurses' eyes.

He died during a snowstorm on a Sunday night. The memorial service was Thursday, the only bright day in a week of stormy weather.

He had left no instructions for a memorial service and he hadn't been to church for years. But he had been raised a Catholic and at one time considered entering the priesthood. So we asked the local parish priest to conduct the service, even though he knew Dad solely through our brief descriptions. We had no way of knowing that he would accidentally provide us with one of our most cherished memories.

My sister Sandra, who travels widely, has a knack for relaxing anywhere and a certain lack of inhibition. At one point, before anyone had arrived at the funeral home but the two of us and my son-in-law, who had driven us, she decided she was exhausted. So she lay down on the floor. Bill, one of the funeral directors walked into the room—and almost fainted when he saw what looked like a body lying at the front of the room.

That gave us a small chuckle, but there was more in store. The organist was the mother of the funeral home owner, a nice woman whom I'd met before. We'd picked a couple of songs for the service, and asked her to finish with "On the Street Where You Live." Both our parents loved show tunes. During our teens, if Dad came home with a few drinks in him, he often asked Mum or me to play his favorites on the piano, including "On the Street Where You Live." That, we decided, should be the very last song.

We dug out Mum's sheet music so Mrs. Anderson could practice before the service. Then, at the last minute, she asked us to pick a few more songs, explaining that sometimes services went on just a little longer than anticipated and that she didn't want to run out of music. So we made our choices, again emphasizing that "On the Street Where You Live" should be the last one.

People were starting to arrive. Dan, my husband, wheeled Mum in. She looked very nice, dressed in a red woolen jacket, hair freshly done, wearing a touch of make-up. This was the biggest social event she'd been at in years, and although she sometimes wept silently, she spent a lot of time looking around to see who was there, occasionally waving with her good hand.

One of the last to arrive was Dan's Uncle Andy. He and my parents had been friends as teenagers. He was a bit eccentric, to put it politely. He had lived alone most of his life and frequently wandered around unshaven, wearing appallingly stained or worn clothes. But he had gone all out for the funeral. His hair was neatly cut and combed, he was clean-shaven, and he was wearing an orangey-red denim leisure suit straight out of the 1970s.

Sandra and I rolled our eyes at each other, but said nothing. Mum gave him a big grin and held his hand for a few moments.

The music began. We were still greeting people when "On the Street Where You Live" started. Just as we realized what was playing, the funeral director came over to explain. "My mother is in the early stages of Alzheimer's. She can't drive any more, can't live alone, but she's a talented musician and I hate to take this away from her."

"Oh," one of us said. Sandra and I exchanged quick looks, silently communicating, "I'm okay with this if you're okay." We both knew that if it had been Dad, he would have been falling over himself to be nice to Mrs. Anderson. So we soothed Richard, telling him everything would be just fine.

As we took our places at the front of the chapel, we both noticed that Mrs. Anderson had taken off her shoes and was pounding the pedals in her stocking feet. The priest slipped behind the lectern. Conversation ebbed. Mrs. Anderson kept playing.

And playing.

Father Paul looked at us. I looked away. Sandra raised her eyebrow. Father Paul looked at Mrs. Anderson. Everyone looked at Mrs. Anderson. Finally, the priest went over, put his hand on her shoulder, whispered something in her ear. She nodded, but kept on playing until the song was over.

We had met Father Paul two days earlier and knew that he was a former mailman who had come to the priesthood somewhat later in life. A small man with protruding front teeth and short hair that stood on end, he looked a bit like Alvin the chipmunk trying to be a punk star.

The vestments, of course, didn't belong to a punk star image — the chasuble was creamy colored, flecked with darker threads, as though it had been spun from wheat. But he was wearing dark running shoes, possibly to make a quick getaway after the funeral.

And then he called our father Harold.

Dad's name was Frank. He had a great laugh and a great sense of humor. Puns, slapstick, political satire, all might provoke a chuckle or a roar. He was also deeply amused by children, animals, and the ridiculousness of everyday life.

When the priest called him Harold, Sandra and I studiously avoided looking at each other. Somewhere in a back row, one of my friends poked another and whispered, "Cheryl's going to have a fit." She was right, but not for the reasons she thought. Sandra and I were trying not to burst into a fit of laughter.

When we were teenagers, Bill Cosby was one of the family's favourite comedians. Sandra had started calling Dad "old weird Harold" after one of the characters in Bill Cosby's comedy routines. When the priest mistakenly used the name, we both thought of that. And smiled, knowing that somewhere out in the universe, Dad was smiling with us.

~Cheryl MacDonald

When Fathers Weep
at Graves

When someone you love becomes a memory, the memory becomes a treasure.
~Author Unknown

The mockingbird sits on the wire now, singing. How can it sing? It was only a few days ago that I saw the baby mockingbird in our driveway as we pulled in with our car. I was afraid we were going to run it over. But I looked back after I got out of the car, and it was fine, hopping across the lawn. It would take a hop, throw out its half-grown wings, take another hop and throw them out again. I watched it go all the way across the road like that, hopping and sticking out its wings in a comical way! I assumed it was the mother bird flying around it, protecting, guiding, and perhaps telling it which way to go. But she could not control it. Later I wondered when she had relinquished her guard and given in to the inevitable.

The baby bird had fallen out of the nest too soon. It was not going to take off flying because it was not ready. Cats roamed the neighborhood. I had often seen them darting between houses. In my mind's eye, the baby bird met its horrible fate. Either a cat or a car, since it seemed to take forever for it to get across the road and caused me to give up watching and go inside. I did not want to witness its demise.

Yesterday I saw the "parent" mockingbird flying around the tree in our yard. Was it searching for its child? I watched it fly from our tree to the tree across the street where I think it had its nest. Back and forth it flew. I couldn't help wondering if it was the mother bird or the father bird.

Today I saw the bird up on the wire, singing. How could it sing? How could this bird act like it never happened, its baby now gone?

My son ceased to be. He is no more. Fate stepped in and Donnie is gone. And it's nearly eight years. But I keep putting one foot in front of the other today as I did the day after I got the news. I take a day at a time. And it was a really long time before I felt like singing, that's for sure.

My husband lost a son, too. His grief was different from mine. He wanted to go to the cemetery often, and I could not stand to be there.

Our son was an accomplished classical guitarist, and Don never ceased to be amazed at Donnie's talent. I think I may have taken it for granted just a bit, since I could play the piano by ear ever since I was a child. I loved to hear our son play guitar, don't get me wrong! I knew he was extremely talented, but I just wasn't in awe of it the way my husband seemed to be. Don was the one who would not miss a recital. Even if I could not be there, my husband would miss work to go if it was at all possible. Once he drove three hours to Memphis for a recital when Donnie was going to school there.

After his death, Don would play Donnie's recorded music all the time. That was difficult for me. I'd even hear him humming or whistling along at times. To me, I guess it was like singing, and it was much too soon for that. I would invariably close the door to the room where the music wafted out so that I would not start weeping.

I would think to myself, "This is pretty easy for him. He visits the grave and listens to Donnie play guitar as if he were still here, and that will get him through this? It must be different for fathers."

I wanted to scream and break things most of the time. I felt as if my heart was torn from my body when I lost my son. I told myself it was worse for me because I had carried him, and I had known him nine months longer than my husband had. I didn't think my tears would ever quit or that singing would ever be a possibility for me again.

Then I found this poem. My husband had copied it and laid it on his nightstand.

When Fathers Weep at Graves
By Alice J. Wisler

I see them weep
the fathers at the stones

taking off the brave armour
forced to wear in the workplace

clearing away the debris
with gentle fingers

inhaling the sorrow
diminished by anguish

their hearts desiring what they cannot have —
to walk hand in hand

with children no longer held —
to all the fathers who leave a part

of their hearts at the stones
may breezes underneath trees of time

ease their pain as they receive healing tears
...the gift the children give.

It made me realize that my husband's grief was just as intense as mine. I recognized the fact that he did his crying at the cemetery where he could feel closest to his son. And while I could not stand to go there, it was his place of release. I realized a father's love is just as profound as a mother's, and the father-son bond just as sacred.

Love never dies! Not a father's love, not a mother's love, and not even a mockingbird's love.

In time, we learned to honor our son's passing in ways that worked for us individually. We came together and discovered ways to honor his life, to honor ourselves, and carry him inside that beauty. And somewhere along the journey we have both learned to sing again.

~Beverly F. Walker

38

A Call to Action

Action is eloquence.
~William Shakespeare

Two framed birthday cards hang on the wall in my office. I often glance up at them and smile because they guided me back to a path I'd wandered from and helped me heal.

I'm a writer. I have been since the late 1980s when my dad was alive. He was the guy who always cheered me on. Even when an editor didn't think my work was worthy, Dad always did.

So what happens when a loved one dies and he or she is the person who's so closely connected with another one of the loves of your life?

If you're me, you quit writing. You think it's a bad case of writer's block and that within a couple of months, you'll be back at the keyboards.

However, a year goes by and then two, then those years turn into five. You get to the point where you say, "I was a writer... once." It was fun but it's in my past, now it's time to move on.

Loved ones have beautiful ways of sending you a message even after they're gone. It's their subtle way of nudging you back to what you love and what you need to be doing with your life.

Mine came in the form of two old birthday cards I stumbled upon, both of them sent to me from Dad. One said "Happy Writing," the other, "Write a good book."

I sat down holding them in my hands. Did he know I was

struggling? Was he watching me every time I sat down to write and cried when the words would no longer flow? Did he sense that I'd given up on my dream when he died? Were these cards a way for him to be by my side each time I wrote?

Deep in my heart, I knew the cards were my way back and I needed to preserve them. I had them framed. I put the frame on the wall and sat looking at it. Each time I put my hands on the keyboard, I'd glance up at those cards and read Dad's words out loud. He was still cheering me on.

It worked because since I found those two cards, I've had four novels published.

We all grieve. We all have our own unique timetable for healing.

While our loved ones don't want us to ever forget them, they don't want us to grieve forever. Also, they never want us to give up our dreams.

If you look hard enough, they'll send you a subtle sign letting you know it's time to stop your grieving and do something that will make them smile. Achieve something you know would have made them proud.

I was obviously meant to keep those cards even before my dad died, so I could rediscover them at a time I needed to find the path back to my dreams.

Each day I write I can see him smiling. For me, there's no better way to honor a dead person's memory than fulfilling a dream you both shared.

Thank you Dad. I'm a writer again.

~Susan Palmquist

39

Chicago Peace

The weak can never forgive. Forgiveness is the attribute of the strong.
~Mahatma Gandhi

As I drove to my office, a feeling of complete forgiveness towards my ex-husband, Ron, came over me. I recall the moment as if it were yesterday. I was heading north on I-95 and as I crested over the Baymeadows overpass, I had such joy and forgiveness in my heart towards him. For the first time in over a decade, I was able to say, "I forgive you."

Ron and I had been married almost eleven years before we divorced. Our three small children and I felt abandoned and heartbroken. We stayed in Illinois for a while after the divorce but then the children and I moved back to Florida to be with my family. Ron stayed in Chicago.

It was wonderful to be in Florida, surrounded by my parents and siblings along with their families. They encouraged us and provided support. Ron visited us once. It was not a happy visit. He was on a layover to a Las Vegas gambling trip and visited us for a few days. At that time in our lives, Ron was several thousand dollars behind in child support. I was bitter he was spending money on a trip to Las Vegas. My children and I had sacrificed and struggled for many years. It just didn't seem fair to me that their father was taking a trip when we did without child support.

To finally be at peace with Ron was a miracle. At times I wanted to giggle out loud. I felt such a burden lifted from my shoulders to know I could finally forgive and move on with my life. Although I didn't share this with anyone, I'm sure others sensed I had a change of heart towards Ron.

Two weeks later, as I entered my office, the switchboard operator stopped me and said there had been an urgent call from someone named Al in Chicago. I was to call him immediately.

Al was married to Ron's sister and he had always been a wonderful friend to me, even as Ron and I were divorcing. We had lost contact over the years so I knew Al was not calling me to chitchat. I dialed Al's number and heard him say in a grave tone of voice, "Ronnie was found dead early this morning. I felt you and the kids needed to know." My heart stopped. I can still close my eyes and be back in that stuffy little conference room hearing words I did not want to hear. My first thought was for my children. They had just lost their father—a man they would never have the opportunity to know. They would never have the chance to know and love him like I once did. I left the conference room with leaden feet and made my way back to my office to locate my manager. I needed to leave immediately and tell my children the sad news.

We left early the next morning for Chicago. It was a somber group. My dad and sister were with us for the journey. My oldest was living in Missouri and would fly to Chicago for the funeral. The following days were a blur. Ron's funeral was held the day after Father's Day. It was the first Father's Day my children had spent with their father in many years. It was bittersweet.

Jason, our oldest, was stoic. During the funeral service, he played "Stairway to Heaven" on his guitar. Tears stung my eyes as the beautiful melody drifted from the church balcony. Jennifer, our only daughter, shed many tears when we left Chicago. In spite of the circumstances, she was happy to finally meet some of her dad's family. Joey, our youngest, asked if I thought his dad was in heaven. I said, "Of course your dad is in heaven. He's there with grandma and they are watching over us." However, I wasn't convinced. I was sure God opened the gates of heaven only for good dads!

We got home very late and the weary travelers went to bed. I awoke early the next morning and while my brood slept, I poured myself a cup of coffee and headed out to the backyard. My dad had purchased three rose bushes two weeks earlier and we spent a Sunday afternoon planting them. I wanted to ensure they had survived a severe storm that occurred during our absence.

I made soft footprints in the early morning dew. The day was just beginning. I was sad about Ron's early death but also relieved he would not suffer anymore. I wasn't convinced he had made it to heaven though! I am from Missouri—the show-me state.

The rose bushes stood intact. Not one of the three had been damaged during the storm. I leaned over to smell the sweet scent of roses and as I did a leftover white tag on one of the rose bushes caught my eye. I went inside for a pair of scissors, returned to the yard and snipped off the tag. When I glanced at it, time stood still. The name of the rose bush was Chicago Peace.

Then I knew. God had been preparing me for Ron's death two weeks earlier by putting forgiveness in my heart towards him for all the years of pain. I believe that my forgiveness released Ron and he made it through the heavenly gates.

~Teresa Curley Barczak

40

The Christmas Card

Forgiveness does not change the past, but it does enlarge the future.
~Paul Boese

When I was nine years old, my uncle Frank was killed in an automobile accident. He was driving late at night on a backcountry road when a big ten-point buck ran out in front of him. Uncle Frank had no time to apply the brakes. His death was instantaneous, and to make things worse, Uncle Frank was killed early Christmas morning.

Uncle Frank was my mother's only brother and she was totally inconsolable when the sheriff brought us the news. Mom and Uncle Frank were as close as any siblings could ever be — that is, until their big argument. I was too young to really know what the argument was about, but I knew they had a big disagreement and very angry words had been exchanged. Uncle Frank had stomped out of our house and we had not seen him since; he was killed two weeks later, before the two of them had the chance to reconcile.

There was too much pain in our family that year to celebrate Christmas very much. I hurt for myself, for the first loss I had experienced, but I also hurt for my mother because she seemed so tortured, so guilt-ridden. "Frank knew you loved him with all of your heart, honey," my father consoled my mother.

"I will never be able to tell him again how very much I love him and how sorry I am for all of the terrible things I said to him," my mother sobbed.

My uncle's death changed our family forever. My mother cried for a long time after my uncle's death, but she finally dried her tears and announced as we finished dinner one early March evening, "No one in this family will ever leave each other angry again. We will never go to bed while angry at each other. We will make things right immediately. Do I make myself clear?" We all nodded our heads in agreement and I think we were relieved that a part of Mom's tough spirit was back.

Still, the ensuing Christmases were very difficult for us. The fact that Uncle Frank died on Christmas Day hung over our family like a fog that refused to dissipate, and we all knew Christmas was especially difficult for Mom. She tried to make Christmas enjoyable for us but she could not seem to get rid of her own personal guilt.

Then came that fateful Christmas Eve; I froze as I pulled the mail from the mailbox. Among several other Christmas cards was one from my Uncle Frank. How could this be? Uncle Frank had been dead for five years. The envelope was dull and faded, and did not display any postmarks, but sported a postage stamp that had been outdated for three years.

I thought my knees would buckle as I walked the Christmas card inside the house to my father. The look on my dad's face confirmed my disbelief. "What's this?" Dad said in a whisper. "Is this some kind of joke?"

"Where has it been all this time?" I asked. "And how did it make its way to our mailbox without being postmarked?" The look of disbelief in Dad's eyes told me that we would never get the answers to our questions.

When my mother saw the Christmas card from Uncle Frank, she almost fainted, but Dad caught her and was able to help her onto the sofa. Mom just held the card and cried for a long time before she got herself together, and with shaking hands, gently opened it. Tears welled up once again in Mom's eyes as she silently read the last note Uncle Frank had ever written. Mom was unable to speak so my father took the card from her hand and read it to the rest of us:

"I'm so sorry, Maggie, for all the awful things I said to you. You were right and I was wrong. I was just too stubborn to admit it. I am coming to celebrate Christmas with you all. Phone lines are still down from the storm so I have not been able to reach you. I love you Maggie. Let's make this the best Christmas ever. Love to you all, Frank."

Uncle Frank was on his way to our home to celebrate Christmas with us and to renew his love and relationship with my mother. Knowing what had been in Uncle Frank's heart healed my mother and our family. I saw an almost instant relaxation in my mother's features; her face was once again soft and calm, her gait and stature displayed a life and energy that I had not seen in a very long time. My mother was finally at peace.

We never figured out exactly where that Christmas card had been for five years or how it finally made its way to our mailbox. In my heart I believe God had a hand in directing that long lost card to us so that my mother could finally have peace. If there was ever a Christmas miracle in our family, that Christmas card was it.

~LaVerne Otis

Grieving and Recovery

At the End

Not Alone

Sadness flies away on the wings of time.
~Jean de La Fontaine

September 4, 2000, my husband and I celebrated our 40th wedding anniversary. As he did each anniversary, he took me out to eat. Candlelight, flowers, steaks. A quiet evening alone. "This is great," I said, "but when we celebrate our 50th, I want us to renew our vows. Just a quiet celebration. Me, you and the kids."

"No way," he protested. "I had a hard enough time getting through the first one."

And he did. I never saw a man so scared in all my life. I walked down the aisle toward my husband-to-be, his face as white as my bridal veil. My Uncle Melvin said he thought he might have to come to the front of the church and hold him up. Or at least brace him so his knees would stop shaking. Perspiration rolled off his forehead all the way to his shirt collar. His voice sounded like a young teenager going through puberty when he repeated after the minister, "I, Glen, take you..."

At this point I nearly bolted—turned and ran out the door. Had I pushed him into something he didn't want to do? I consoled myself; it was he who asked me. I didn't run, and we stumbled through the ceremony without any major blunders except he put my ring on the wrong hand. I was so flustered by this time that I didn't notice.

I could understand why he didn't want to do it again. Although he'd rejected my suggestion, I just grinned at him. I knew how to get around my husband. Even though he was "the man of the house," I could coax him into seeing things my way without his even knowing it.

Five years later, we were nearing our 45th anniversary. Glen had been diagnosed with lung cancer. "Honey, you and I both know I'll never make it to our 50th. Let's do it on our 45th." His statement came out of nowhere.

"Do what?" I had no idea what he was talking about. Had the lung cancer hit his brain?

"Our vows. Get married again."

"I thought you didn't want to do that. We don't have to." I wouldn't think of coercing him into standing in front of a bunch of relatives again. Now was not a good time.

"No, I want to." He took my hand, his faded green eyes looking into mine, his head now bald from chemotherapy. But I saw the handsome young, dark-haired man with gold flecks in his eyes who'd proposed to me 45 years ago.

"Will you marry me again?" His voice quivered as it did the first time, when we sat in the car in Iroquois Park Overlook and he slipped a $200 ring on my finger—a beautiful, simple, white-gold band, a small diamond in the center with a circle of tiny chips surrounding it. Years later, he'd offered to buy me a more expensive set, but I refused. I wanted the rings that had sealed our vows.

"Yes," I said. "Yes, I'll marry you again." He kissed me as he did the first time I said yes.

"Then we better start planning." He beamed like a child getting his way—like it was his idea from the beginning.

"It won't take that much planning." I figured a small ceremony after church on Sunday afternoon would be appropriate.

"No. I want the works. We didn't have the money for a big affair the first time. This will be different."

"I don't need all of that. Just something simple," I protested.

"I do," he said. "I already asked Bub to be my best man, and I assume you want the girls to be your attendants. We'll have a big reception, wedding cake, the whole shebang."

"I don't think I can fit into my wedding gown. We don't need to go formal." "Yes, we do. Buy another one."

I was dumbfounded. He was excited and invited everyone he saw before we even thought about sending out invitations.

July 5, 2005, two months before our big event, he succumbed to cancer.

A week later, I received a call from the jeweler, asking for my husband. The lady said his order was ready. When I went in to see what it was, I opened a box with a gorgeous set of diamond wedding rings. The settings were identical to my old ones except the center diamond was much larger. I had to feel sorry for the poor saleslady after I gained control and stopped the crying and blubbering, explaining why I didn't need them anymore.

I returned the rings.

I grieved as I suppose all widows do. But recovery comes through time and God's helping hand. My husband has not truly left me. He had dreamed of taking an Alaskan cruise. I did that. He went with me in my heart. I wanted to go to Hawaii. I did that. He went along with me. I carried him in my soul. I laugh with him about each new adventure our grandchildren undertake. I cry with him when we lose a family member. We will be together until we unite in our new life in heaven.

This year I will face our 50th anniversary. But I don't need an expensive diamond to remind me of how much my husband loved me; I have 45 years of memories, three children and the last, most beautiful memory of all. He wanted to do it all over again.

~Jean Kinsey

42

A Final Savasana

If you surrender to the wind, you can ride it.
~Toni Morrison

I decided not to go to my 10:15 yoga class and instead went to the hospital to help my friend die. The ICU became my class. Yoga is all about unity, and we joined my friend around her hospital bed, dressed alike in our blue paper hospital gowns and matching masks. She'd been trying to heal for a month now — beeping machines and blinking lights keeping her alive — and for many weeks before, fighting off the ravaging beast we call cancer.

Today we faced the decision I'd only read about in the newspaper. When do you let someone pass on — freeing them from the tubes that can both save and strangle? She was alert enough to converse with us. Unable to actually speak because of her tracheotomy, her parched lips mouthed her wishes. Her son dabbed her mouth with a tiny pink sponge, rubbing ChapStick on pale lips, lightly purple after weeks of labored breathing.

"Just be sure," she said.

"Sure of what, Mom?" her son asked, leaning close and staring in to her eyes.

She didn't seem to have the strength to add more, but I think we knew. As with birth, when words are few, death also doesn't demand much talking. It is all in the eyes. My friend would only say goodbye if she knew she'd gone the distance and there was no more hope.

In her last days she continued to be my teacher. I always brought small gifts when I'd visit, trying to help even if I couldn't heal. Last week I brought her a small mirror I'd found among my daughter's make-up. It had been two months since my friend had looked into her own eyes. At first, I worried. What would she see in her face after weeks of such sickness? I helped her unclasp the mirror, her swollen and bruised fingers trying to hold tight. Her wide smile filled the moment. She saw the beauty of herself. Her own reflection brought her such peace. She held her gaze tight, nodding and thanking me for my gift. I hope she knew she had given me an even more precious gift, the reminder that self-acceptance is the greatest joy.

Today is the day that her children had decided that they were "sure." They didn't want her to struggle any longer. With dignity she could finally give in. As we gathered around her bed we tearfully embraced her as she found her final savasana.

I had always wanted to take my friend to a yoga class, but she'd always said, "I'm just not flexible enough. I wouldn't be good at it!" She would be proud to know she actually became a wonderful yoga teacher, bringing that peace of unity and self-acceptance to a small room in the ICU.

~Priscilla Dann-Courtney

Editor's Note: A savasana is a relaxing position often used to begin and end a yoga session.

43

When I Was a Coward

Courage doesn't always roar. Sometimes courage is the little voice
at the end of the day that says I'll try again tomorrow.
~Mary Anne Radmacher

I hadn't seen her for two weeks. The kids were on holidays and it was impossible to take the three of them into a nursing home. They were small and fidgety and there was nowhere to sit and they didn't understand. About dying.

I'd tried to take Blake, but he was only five and the oldest and he wouldn't be swayed.

"I hate walking through that room of old people," he said. "They might make me sick."

I explained they were old, not sick. Not sick in the way that could infect him, but it didn't make any difference. He hated the place and I couldn't blame him.

I'd come to hate it, too, had to brace myself every time I punched in the entry code and swallowed the stench of that nursing home air. I dreaded the bulging stares and the hollowed-out faces, the twisted, age-gnawed limbs, the sickly white heads and the wrinkles everywhere.

But I was an adult. I was her daughter-in-law. I'd walked beside her through every step of her cancer journey. I couldn't abandon her now, even though she was so close, yet so far away. Hanging on for no other reason than that she couldn't die. No matter how little she ate or how thin she became.

While my husband, Chris, minded the kids in the playground next door—he'd already had his turn—I went inside. I signed my name in that big blue book on the table in the foyer and washed my hands with that stinking antiseptic they keep in a bottle nearby.

I scooted through the common room with 20 pairs of eyes on me, staring at me, wishing they were me, or wishing I was here to help them or visit them or save them or I don't know what. And I pasted that fake smile on my face and pretended everything was all right and that I was happy and fearless and perfectly fine with all the stares. And I looked back into those eyes pretending not to be afraid, yet really so very afraid that one day I'd be there with them too. And I kept pretending until I made it to the corridor leading to her room and then I could breathe again, at least until I came to the bed where she lay and I had to face her.

Then I dawdled in and found her lying on her side facing the wall. She was fast asleep, as Chris said she would be. I saw the thinness of her cheeks and her eyes closed tight. I saw her thick, gray hair splayed out on the pillow above her, her mouth open and the oxygen tube in her nose. I saw the caramel coloured drip-drip stains of the liquid meal supplement spilt on her shoulder.

I put my hand on her arm and she was hot to touch, snuggled as she was like a baby under her blankets with her winter pajama shirt on top and a nappy on the bottom. She didn't move or wake, she was in such a deep sleep.

I shook her gently and I know I should have said something, should have said, "Rosemary, it's me. Rosemary, wake up."

I had wanted so badly to see her because I knew she didn't have much longer and I wanted her to know I'd come again, but even if she'd woken I don't think she'd have known me or what day it was.

I thought she'd been sick before, with her walking stick and the cancer growing in her lung and her strange, idiosyncratic ways. But she'd just been old then.

Now, this was really sick and she was dying slowly and painfully, without dignity. This is how we suffer as we watch them go and no one prints it in any of those "Coping with Cancer" booklets they hand out like painkillers at hospitals.

As I stood there, I knew I should have said something. Even if she was asleep, she might have heard me. But I couldn't break the silence that stuck to us in that room. I couldn't risk waking her and making her look at me with those clouded, confused eyes. I couldn't bear to hear her mumble or gasp or dodder. Fear stopped me and stood between me and the last words I should have spoken to her.

So I had to remember the last time—or was it the second to last time, there had been so many visits—that I saw her and had flipped through the pages of her "Grandma's Brag Book" photo album. Showing her the photos of my kids in all their beauteous youth. Photos of the babies I'd borne with her son to make her a grandmother.

Those photos reminded me of good times and I'd hoped they would remind her, too. Yet as I was thinking it was good for her to see the kids, even if it was only in photos, it was sad, too. And if I hadn't held it together, I would have wept and wept. For her. For the ache of losing her.

Then, while I watched her sleep, I let that fear creep between us and grow. I didn't push it away or bury it or slay it with my bravery sword. I wanted to wake her and say "I love you" so she would know, but I was a coward and didn't say anything. The words stuck in my throat like dry rice and caught there. And I hated myself for my weakness and for those rice words sticking in my throat.

Silent and cowardly, I slipped out of the nursing home, glad to be free of its stinking touch and glad for the autumn breeze despite its chill. And though I hated the mess of the dead, dry leaves papering the walkway, I was glad to see them too.

On the ride home, we hardly spoke, only, "The smell of that place is still on me. It won't go away."

"Me too," Chris said.

He opened the car windows and though the kids complained about the cold, we kept them open all the way home, hoping the stench would leave us.

And then, wouldn't you know it, the phone call came at 2:22 the next morning. We knew what that phone ringing meant, of course, thought maybe there would be a dash to the nursing home to hold her skeletal hand as we said one last goodbye, but there wasn't even that. She'd died in her sleep.

Peace at last and at the last, peace.

Her cancer made us die with her inch by inch, and though we're still alive because we're young and healthy and it's not yet our turn, we'll always remember the hell of her dying-but-living that consumed us.

Most of all, I'll never forget when I was a coward and let fear stand between me and three simple words. I let her down and for that, I'll always be sorry.

~Aleesah Darlison

44

Winning the War

Faith is the bird that sings when the dawn is still dark.
~Rabindranath Tagore

I remember it like it was yesterday. A sterile doctor's office and an extremely self-assured doctor. I can picture the room we were sitting in. The perfectly clean countertops and the well-organized instruments. The crinkle of the paper as my father sat on the small examining table and the quiet creak of the door as the doctor walked in.

"Cancer," he told us, a little too confidently. "He's got cancer."

"You must be mistaken," I said to him as I looked at my father, who had his head in his hands. "I mean look at him, he's in great shape. There must be some mistake."

My mother started to quietly sob as the doctor continued to inform us that my father had a brain tumor. It was on the right side of his brain and it was about the size of a golf ball. They could operate but could offer no guarantees.

"No guarantees!" I said to him. "No guarantees! How about a guarantee that he will see his grandchildren grow up or celebrate his 60th wedding anniversary! How about just guaranteeing us he'll see his son graduate from high school next year!" I was sobbing uncontrollably by then.

"I'm sorry," he said to us as he slowly turned to leave. "But we'll do the best we can."

As we each tried to compose ourselves to walk out of the room, my mother uttered the first word she had said since we received the news. "Why?"

So many whys were running through my head. Why us, why him, why now? Why, why, why? The list could have gone on forever.

As we walked into the parking lot my father mumbled something. I looked to my mother and without saying a word she shrugged.

"What was that?" I said to him.

He looked at us both, and a little more confidently this time, said, "It's okay. I can beat this. We can beat this."

It was that simple to him. As if the "this" he was referring to was just a common cold, instead of the rapidly growing tumor that was destroying his brain.

The next few months seemed to drag on. The operation went well and after he recovered from that and a round of chemo he seemed to be doing much better. Several tests later, doctors revealed to us that the tumor was gone. He was in remission. I cried for joy that day, as did my mother. I think the question was in the back of both our minds though: For how long?

We didn't have to wait long to find out. A few months later I was sitting at my parents' house flipping through the channels on the TV when I heard my father coming down the steps. He walked into the living room and became eerily still. I remember it so well because it almost seemed to be happening in slow motion. "Help me!" my father yelled. I guess he knew something was wrong because as I ran to his side he started seizing. I lowered him to the ground and ran to call 911.

At the hospital they did a number of tests. MRIs, CAT scans, blood work, you name it and they did it. Once again the doctor came in and sat down in front of us.

"I'm so sorry," he began, "but he's got another tumor."

Inside my head I was screaming, "What, another one? We beat the first one and now you're telling us there's another one!"

I slowly raised my head to look at the doctor and as a single tear ran down my cheek, I said to him, "Is it operable?"

As I waited for him to answer I could taste the salt from that single tear as it landed on my lips.

"I'm afraid not—not this time," he said. "We can try chemo and radiation. Maybe even clinical trials, but we definitely can't operate."

The reason for this, we learned, was due to the location of this new tumor. It was growing directly in the center of my father's brain, in and around all of his optical nerves. The operation was too risky. He could end up blind, or even worse, brain dead. The doctors told us that if the tumor continued to grow, my father would develop Alzheimer's symptoms. Chances were, they said, he would eventually forget who we were and even who he was. They said he would become incontinent and unable to care for himself. They said his death would be slow. So there it was, my father's fate laid out in front of us like some path through hell.

When I look back at that day, I try to convince myself that we didn't give up. I try to picture us fighting just as hard as we had during that first diagnosis. I try to remember telling ourselves we would do anything we had to do to cure my father. Looking back, I don't think my mother and I ever gave up hope, but what I know now is this: That was the day my father's outlook changed. That was the day he honestly knew that what we feared the most was happening. He was dying.

Over the next two months we traveled back and forth to Geisinger for chemo and radiation treatments. When they proved unsuccessful, they sent us to the National Institute of Health in Baltimore for clinical trials. Each visit it seemed they added more and more pills to his already large collection. We could have opened a pharmacy in our house. Nothing seemed to be working though. It seemed no matter how many pills we gave him, the tumor continued to grow.

After arriving home from what would be our final trip to the National Institute of Health, I decided to go for a walk. I asked my father if he would like to join me and he agreed. As we walked along the road that day I remember the searing August sun and how it seemed to touch every part of us. I could hear the tiny pebbles rolling across the road when they would catch the toes of our shoes and the occasional rabbit scurrying into the brush when we got too near. I could feel the wind rustling the treetops and ever so gently blowing through my hair. The memory that is most vivid though is the once rugged hand that slowly touched my shoulder and the uncomfortable words that followed.

"What's wrong?" I said as my father's weakened hand came to a rest on my shoulder.

And then it happened. My father spoke the words I dreaded hearing.

"I can't do this anymore," he said. "I can't be strong for everyone else. I am so emotionally and physically tired. I need my family's permission to let go." He cried. "Promise me you'll take care of your mother. Promise me you'll see she gets through this."

What do you say when someone you love asks for your permission to die? I said the only thing I could say.

"I promise," I said to him in a choked voice.

As I said those two small words I saw relief in his eyes.

"Thank you," he cried. "I love you so much."

"I love you too."

We walked the rest of our way that day in silent understanding.

That was the last heart-to-heart conversation I would have with my father. Two weeks later he was gone. He died three days after my older daughter's birthday. Her cake and ice cream were his last meal. We had eighteen months with him from that first diagnosis. In another situation that could seem like a lifetime, but to us it seemed no longer than the blink of an eye.

In the days and weeks that followed his death I often asked myself why. Why did God take him? Why not someone else? What I know now is that we aren't supposed to know the answer to that question, not in this lifetime anyway. To some it may seem that cancer defeated my father, but in truth it is the other way around. Throughout the whole ordeal his faith stayed strong and his smile never faded. Cancer may have defeated his human body, but it could never defeat his soul. He may have lost the battle, but in the end he won the war.

~Laura J. O'Connor

45

The Greatest Gift

We understand death for the first time
when he puts his hand upon one whom we love.
~Madame de Stael

My first thought was why burden me with this? As I sifted through my feelings, I realized it was a gift, the greatest gift my mother could ever have given to me. I felt honored she would select me.

We all knew Mom was terminal. The cancer had come back, and remission was no longer a possibility. The chemotherapy treatments that had taken so much out of her the first go-round were no longer an option. The right step was to roll a hospital bed into her family room and permit her to die with dignity. This way she would be surrounded by her family and cherished friends. A hospice nursing team was employed to monitor and help keep Mom as comfortable as possible.

Dad had recently retired and was home with Mom all the time. My three brothers and I, and our significant others including her grandchildren, would all gather at their home every night after work and school. We would slowly retreat to our own houses and repeat the routine the next day. Mom was in and out of it, sometimes lucid enough to hold a serious conversation, but the intravenous pain medication kept her sleeping or resting a good portion of the time.

She remained stable for almost a week. Then the hospice nurse pleaded with us to talk to her, to soothe her, to convince Mom we would be okay and she could let go. One of the promises she requested of me at this time was to help my dad adjust, keep him active and busy, assist him in moving on.

Mom had gone the better part of the next day without awakening. The whole family was present, socializing in another room, along with the nurse. Dad was sitting in a chair beyond the head of the bed, watching television. I was sitting bedside with my mom's hand in mine, stroking, tenderly rubbing her arm with my free hand. I observed her facial expression change ever so slightly, then the most amazing experience I have ever witnessed occurred.

I saw and felt her essence, her spirit, leave her body. Time slowed. Her skin turned an ashen gray, then quickly returned to normal color. I informed my dad, "She's gone. Mom just died." He asked me not to say anything to the others just yet. He approached the bed, broke down very briefly and said his final goodbye. I then went to the other room to inform everyone else. The nurse tried to take over; she would check and verify that Mom had indeed passed on. I answered, "Don't bother, I already know."

While everyone else crowded into the room, Dad suggested he and I take a walk. I got the impression, as we walked and talked, of relief. Relief that the suffering was now over and that lives that had been put on hold could move forward. He even asked my opinion on how long to grieve, as my mom had suggested a date partner for him. Even in death, Mom still controlled our universe.

No one ever questioned how I knew, without benefit of any medical expertise, the exact moment of Mom passing on. I guess it really didn't matter, except to me, the recipient of this miraculous moment. There was a movie made in 1993 called *My Life*, where Michael Keaton passes on in a very eerie scene. I get chills every time I watch it. This memory will be with me my entire life, etched in my mind. Thank you, Mom, for this, the greatest gift.

~Thomas P. Haynes

Happy Birthday to Me

Sometimes the biggest act of courage is a small one.
~Lauren Raffo

It was 7 a.m. The elderly man lay propped up in the hospital bed in his small apartment. His gold-silver hair lay softly against the pillow and his blue eyes looked enormous in his thin face. This man who was my father knew today would be his last birthday—his 88th.

I stood in the bathroom just off his bedroom combing my hair and preparing for the day. My mother lay in her twin bed a few feet from Daddy. Exhausted from caring for and worrying about him, she still slept.

Suddenly I heard Daddy singing. He had always enjoyed his birthday and had fun with it. His voice was weak and I strained to hear him. Tears sprang to my eyes as I made out the words: "happy birthday to me, happy birthday to me." With God's help I put a smile on my face, walked to his bedside, and listened to him finish the song. Surely, if he had the courage to sing, I could muster the courage to smile.

And he did enjoy his last birthday, surrounded by his family. A week later, on his and my mother's 52nd wedding anniversary, the angels took him home. My frail little mother, my teenaged daughter, and I stood at his bedside, held his hands, and sang old, familiar hymns as he closed his eyes in this world and opened them in the next. At the funeral the minister said we "sang him into heaven."

My father taught me many things, including how to throw a baseball like a boy, drive a tractor, and walk like a lady. He taught me to face obstacles head-on and to embrace each day and be thankful for it. But the greatest lesson I ever learned from him was summed up on that morning as he lay on his deathbed and sang "happy birthday to me" for the last time.

~Verna Wood

A Time for Tenderness

When you are sorrowful look again in your heart, and you shall see that in truth you are weeping for that which has been your delight.
~Kahlil Gibran

I met her for the first time under the worst of circumstances. It would have been easy to immediately dislike or ignore her. She was a stranger in a place where I hated to be, doing things I didn't want to see. Instead I immediately respected her for her sincere acts of compassion directed toward one of my dearest friends.

The young nurse spoke tenderly, telling Tammy everything she was about to do while she methodically checked tubes and wires and assessed monitors of red, green and yellow zig-zagging lines above the bed. She overheard me ask if Tammy could hear or understand us. She sweetly informed us that she always treated every patient as if they could.

"Hearing is one of the last things to go," she said, mindful of our sorrow. "That's why I never stop talking."

I caught a glimpse of her nametag: Bridget. I thought her name was as lovely as she. I blessed her for being so kind to my friend, then left the room to let the reality of Tammy's condition sink in while in the tearful company of her family and friends.

A long day learning the facts and details painted a grim picture. Brain damage from a horrible aneurism was permanent and irreversible. I realized this was my last chance to tell her goodbye.

I sat by her bed, remembering Bridget's example, speaking out loud to my silent friend. I recalled the wonderful years we shared growing up with one another. While life had taken us down different roads, no time or distance could ever rob us of those delightful memories. We spent summers together as kids, riding horses and having slumber parties. We healed each other's broken hearts, we laughed, we swam in muddy ponds, and we competed in horse shows and rodeos and cheered each other to victory. When each of us got married, the other was in the wedding party. She had girls, I had boys, and we kept in contact for all these years, never realizing it would end so suddenly or so early. Tammy was only 43.

Tammy never reacted when I squeezed her hand. She did not notice my soft strokes on her arm, but I touched and I talked to her anyway, because I had to tell her one more time how much I loved her and that I would never forget her.

As I was sitting by her bed and recounting the best of times, Bridget returned to go through her vigilant ritual. While she worked, she asked me about our relationship and I gladly shared my memories of Tammy with her—the beautiful woman, the loving wife, the wonderful mother and daughter, and my perfect friend.

Bridget pressed a pen hard against Tammy's fingers, hoping for any kind of response.

"Oh, Tammy," she said sadly to no one in particular when she got no reaction. "It breaks our hearts, too," she said, turning to me. "Some of the nurses can't even come in here because they identify with Tammy too much."

She continued, "How are the girls? What are they doing and how are they handling this?"

I gave her a report on Tammy's young daughters and her husband and parents. Then I thanked and blessed this little ponytailed brunette for asking and being so compassionate.

Alone again with my dear friend, I told her not to worry, that everything would be fine. I assured her that it was okay to die so young because we had lived a lifetime in a short amount of time. Then I kissed her and told her goodbye.

The gift of compassion comes in many forms. It is a nurse

speaking tenderly while she performs a difficult task. It is a dying woman who made arrangements for organ donation. It is a friend in the hallway who painfully retells again and again the heartrending news to each new person arriving. Compassion is a husband with the strength to quietly and confidently say, "We will get through this with the help of our church family." It is a parent who pleasantly receives friends and is gracious and hospitable under the worst of conditions. It is a friend who is willing to let go, lovingly, not bitterly.

I left the hospital thankful to have some closure, yet trembling from the intensity of the helplessness and sorrow. I also left with one final unspoken gift from my dear, dying friend. Tammy taught me, without ever knowing, to remember how important it is to take the time each day to be tender and compassionate, for we are not promised tomorrow.

~Brenda Black

Last Words

Death leaves a heartache no one can heal,
love leaves a memory no one can steal.
~From a headstone in Ireland

What I remember most vividly when stepping into Dad's hospital room was the assault on the senses. The bright green walls were meant to be soothing, but to me they screamed of the desperation of the inmates. Nobody used this color in their homes. The noise of the machines helping my father to breathe sounded like the hissing snake of death. And the insidious odor of decay persisted despite the competing smells of antiseptic and bleach.

I took a deep swallow to quell the nausea. "Hi Dad," I said quietly. He turned his face toward me, and what greeted me was a man who looked decades older than the last time I had seen him. While he had only been sick for a few months, I lived on the other side of the country, and the progress of cancer on his 59-year-old body was swift.

"Hi, honey," he wheezed.

The instant our eyes met, I knew that he had surrendered to what was coming. When I looked into my father's eyes, now clouded over with pain, I knew that he would never leave that bed again. And since I was boarding a plane in six hours, this would be the last time I would get to gaze at those eyes; I would never again feel the grip of his hand, never again hear the lilt of his voice.

He wasn't strong enough for small talk. I simply held his hand and let the quiet tears fall. I don't know if he saw them or not. Finally, when it was time to go, I summoned all my courage. I set aside my fears. I resolutely said, "I love you, Dad."

Those words had never been said in my family. My father never said them to me, and until then, I never said them to him. In fact, I'm sure I never heard them uttered in our strict, Irish-Catholic household. It just wasn't done. But my fear of rejection was outweighed by my knowledge that this was my last chance. And so I said it.

But he couldn't give it back. His once dancing eyes, now muddy and confused, looked away. "I'm tired," is all he said. "Maybe you better go."

As we walked toward the elevator, my husband squeezed my hand and whispered, "You did the right thing." The elevator doors slowly slid open; we stepped inside. Jeff pulled me to him. "It's okay," he said as I sobbed into his shirt.

Three days later, I sat with my nine siblings planning my father's funeral. We alternated between tension and relief, laughter and tears. We had never been an expressive family, but there was a tangible sense of being tired of the restraint. His death was hardest on my youngest sister, just a sophomore in high school. She seemed confused by how this could have happened. As we shared "Dad stories" back and forth, she was unusually quiet, but finally said, in an almost embarrassed way, "I saw Dad right before he died. He took my hand, looked at me, and said 'I love you, Caroline.'"

Her words hit me like a blunt force instrument. He loved her. Why hadn't he said it to me? Finding out that just a day after I left him he told my sister, his youngest daughter, that he loved her, was a blow. How could he be so cruel? Did he really not love me?

It was easy to hide the reason for my tears—after all, we'd just lost our father—who would begrudge a child her grief? But no one knew the true source of my sorrow.

I'll always wish that I had that moment with my father over again. I wish I had said, "It's okay, Dad—you can say it." But I don't have it. What I do have is the moment with my sister. I know now that the risk I took helped him to find the courage to say what he wanted to say—but she was his audience, not me. Dad found the courage and strength, on his deathbed, to say "I love you." I believe at least some of that courage and strength came from me. And I am grateful that at the time when he was most vulnerable, I gave him something of substance. Something that would help him to let go, and help my 15-year-old sister to let go as well.

So Dad, I wish you could have said it to me. But thanks for saying it to Caroline. And, by the way—I do love you. And I know you love me, too.

~Bridget McNamara-Fenesy

49

Little Bird

Some days there won't be a song in your heart. Sing anyway.
~Emory Austin

On our first Christmas without Mom, I was shopping with my daughter at a craft show and we found the perfect tree ornament: a little red glass bird. Mom used to sit in her wheelchair at the back window so she could watch the birds play in the yard. The previous Christmas she had delighted in the antics of a pretty red cardinal that would flit in and out of the sweeping branches of the old spruce tree.

Months earlier, when she came home from the hospital, she fretted, "What will they think of an old lady with only one leg?" Her little face was knitted with despair.

"They will love you, Mom. You're still the same person you always were, with the same huge heart." She trusted that I would be right and that she wouldn't get hurt. She had become my child.

My younger brother and I had been living with her, caring for her, in order to fulfill her fervent wish to return to her own home for as long as she could. It wasn't easy but it was worth every minute, and we would both do it again in a heartbeat.

She could be obstinate, and enjoyed thinking she was giving us a challenge. We would say to her, "Who's a monkey?"

She would flash her toothless grin (she didn't like her new dentures) and gleefully chirp, "Mee-eee!"

She wouldn't always do the things that were in her own best

interest, things that would have helped her. It took a lot of persuading to convince her to take her pain medication, for example. She had great faith in television tabloid news shows, and had seen a story on mothers who sold their children for street drugs. Based on that dubious information, she stubbornly refused to avail herself of any pain relief. Finally we were able to convince her that it was not at all the same thing, and she took her pills as they were needed.

Her hair stuck out all over her head in wispy tufts, prompting my brother to bestow upon her the nickname of "Yoda." To her it was a compliment; she knew Yoda was wise.

One morning as I was brushing her hair, gray with age and thinning from illness, she said, "A couple of summers ago I called the Humane Society about a bird."

"You did?" I asked.

"Yes. It was the last summer Dad was with us. I went out on the front porch to water the flowers. Remember how hot it was that summer? Well, I saw a bird lying on the table beside the impatiens. It was still alive but not really moving. I thought it might be sick, so I looked up the Humane Society in the phone book and called them."

"Oh, Mom," I said, still trying to tame her unruly hair. "Good for you. What did they say?"

She turned and looked up at me. "They said the poor thing was probably dehydrated because it was so hot out, and to try giving it a drink of water. They didn't think it was sick."

"What happened then?" I asked.

"Well, I took out a small dish of water. The poor little thing had a drink, and a while later it flew off."

"What a wonderful story, Mom. You saved the little bird's life!"

"I hope so. It was really cute."

"And now, you're really cute," I said as I laid down the brush.

It was her habit, after a bit of primping and preening, to crow happily to my brother, or my husband and daughter if they were over, "Here I come! Cinderella is ready for the ball!" Everyone did love her. We were in awe of her strength in the face of all she had been through.

She would watch television, with her lunchtime soup and sandwich in front of her. Hands bent outward with arthritis, resembling broken wings, she would clap and sing along to the theme song of *The Golden Girls* ("...thank you for being a friend..."). It cheered us to hear the innocent promises of our sweet songbird.

Sitting beside her, I would reach over and gently grasp her hand. She would ask, "What are you doing?"

I answered that I was just making sure she was nice and warm, but really it was because I couldn't get enough of her. A cautionary voice inside me said to touch her as much as I could while I still had the chance.

On her last Christmas Eve, I watched her decorate cookies with my daughter. It was an age-old tradition, the passing down of the shortbread recipe through the generations. We had rolled her wheelchair right up to the dining room table, where the baked cookies cooled and awaited the pastel frostings and coloured sprinkles my daughter had prepared. It filled me with pleasure to see them working together, Mom carefully spreading white icing on an angel cookie while her granddaughter lovingly looked on.

We are consoled now by knowing that she is as light as a feather, soaring high above us and enjoying every minute.

Birds and angels don't need both legs to fly.

~Diane Wilson

50

Mourning Ahead

Only in the agony of parting do we look into the depths of love.
~George Eliot

W hen did it start? Looking back, I'm really not sure. But now that we are going into our seventh year, it seems like it's been forever. You know how things start to happen but you don't really pay attention. Little things, not important events, but you only remember them when you look back. When was the first time she forgot where she was going? When was the first time she called two times in a row, forgetting that she had just called? To cover, she made it into a joke so I didn't pay too much attention. At first. Little things.

Can you grieve for someone who has not died? Someone who is still alive? Yes I think you can. I have done it. My mother has Alzheimer's disease. It is a hideous disease. The only positive thing about it is that the person who has it doesn't know what condition he or she is in. I tell people that my mother HAS Alzheimer's disease but my family and I SUFFER from Alzheimer's disease. It changes everything.

And I grieve. She is still here, but I grieve. She bears no resemblance to my mother. She is just a shell... but she is still here with me. I treat her with respect and dignity, the same way I treated her when she was aware. I can touch her. I can talk to her. But there is no response. I look into her eyes. Nothing. I hug her. I tell her I love her. I tell her she is the best mother in the whole world. Nothing.

Nothing at all. Where is she? What does she understand? What does she know?

And I grieve. I feel that I have been doing it for years and finally I have reached the end of the process. At first I tried to deny the signs that were right in front of me. Signs that she was slipping away. That took a while. Denial does. I had to take over and become the parent while she regressed and became the child. And she let me take over. She didn't fight me. Somewhere, somehow she understood that I would take care of her and that she was safe. The circle of life.

Then anger. Oh, so much anger and resentment. Not at my mother. Never at my mother. But at the disease that was taking her away from me one day at a time. A teacher, university professor, therapist, writer and lecturer by profession and now she can't remember what day it is. A mother, grandmother, great-grandmother, daughter, sister and aunt and now she can't remember any of the names of the people in her family. She used to know that we were familiar but that's gone now. There is no recognition now… nothing.

The bargaining and depression came together. I would think: if I do "this" then please let my mother be able to remember "that." Just for today. If only for one more time. And the depression turned to sadness. Every once in a while the depression will creep back into my life. Something will set it off. I don't seem to have any control over when, or where, that will happen. It remains with me to this day. To combat the depression and sadness, I remember that my mother doesn't have a clue as to her condition. She is well cared for, warm, comfortable and at peace. There is nothing more that I could or should be doing. That is a blessing.

And finally, acceptance. In order to get on with my life I needed to get to the point where I had to accept the reality of the disease and its progression. My life changed. The lives of my husband and my children changed. That is the reality of the progression of the disease. That first Thanksgiving she was unable to be with us, sitting at our table, was so difficult. Although she was still alive, she was unable to leave her house. I was the one who had to make that difficult decision. That was three years ago. And I grieved. And the first year she didn't call me to wish me Happy Birthday was bad. She always called at the exact time I was born to wish me Happy Birthday. She would then tell me about the day I was born. Every year. The same story. It was a joke between us. The first year she didn't call, didn't even remember it was my birthday, I grieved. There were many more "firsts" I had to deal with. But since we are going into our seventh year, there really aren't too many more "firsts" left. The loss has gotten easier to deal with and I have accepted the reality. This is just the way it is.

So although my mother is alive, I have already grieved for her. I have gone through all of the stages of the grieving process that a person goes through who is mourning the loss of someone who has died.

And when she actually dies, when her heart stops beating and she stops breathing, when she is really no longer with me so that I can touch her, hug her, tell her I love her, what will I feel? Of course I know I'll feel shock and an overwhelming sadness. I'll miss her. I'll cry and wish I could touch her just one more time. Tell her I love her one more time. Thank her for being the best mother in the whole world and a wonderful role model. All those things. But I know I will also feel relief. Immense relief. Relief that she is no longer suffering and that she is finally at peace. Relief that this terrible ordeal is over… for her and for us. And how about the guilt? Will I feel guilt? No. I do know that the one thing I will not feel is guilt. There is no reason to feel guilty for feeling the relief at her passing. I have nothing to feel guilty for. I did the best I could for my mother while she was alive and I have already mourned for her. I went through the mourning process while she was still alive. And I am at peace with that.

~Barbara LoMonaco

Editor's Note: Barbara's mother died a few days after she wrote this piece. She reports that, although she is sad, she is very much at peace with her mother's release from her seven-year ordeal.

Grieving and *Recovery*

Moving Forward

51

Love, College, and Chemo

And if we ever leave a legacy it's that we loved each other well.
~Indigo Girls

I was one of those happy people. David and I started dating during the second semester of our freshman year of college. Our love was that flawless kind of young love where life never gets in the way. We had years ahead of us to hold hands between classes, kiss under the bell tower at our university, and lie around in bed for hours talking about our future. After three weeks I knew I would marry him.

We went through college having a relationship that I could barely believe could be true. We never fought; David was too calm and gentle. I would have done anything for him and he would have done anything for me, but neither of us ever took advantage of that. He was my best friend, my rock, and the source of endless hours of laughter and happiness.

After three years together, David started to feel sick at the beginning of the semester. He would be out of breath after running a short distance, and he was always tired. After going to the health center, they told him he had bronchitis and sent him home. After all, what 21-year-old college guy isn't tired and out of shape? I remember lying in bed with him and noticing faint bruises on his arms. His heartbeat seemed too fast, so during that week I slept with my hand over his heart just to make sure he was okay. He said he was fine, but I had a pit in my stomach and knew that something was wrong. Really wrong.

The next day he called me at work and said, "Honey, it's me, I don't want you to worry but I went back to the health center and they are sending me over to the hospital to get some tests done. Everything is going to be fine." I really thought it would be. After all, we loved each other way too much for it to end up any other way. The next day David was diagnosed with T-cell acute lymphoblastic leukemia. In true David fashion, always caring about me more than anything, he turned to me and said, "Sorry I got leukemia...."

He had eight rounds of chemo and a stem cell transplant. We spent our last semester of college in the hospital watching movies and cuddling in his hospital bed. The nurses used to come in and tell us to please stop laughing so loudly because we were disturbing the other patients. Life was bad, but our love was good. When he came home from his transplant he was in remission and we were so happy. We moved in together and started talking about getting married after I finished graduate school. Life was on its way to being as normal as it can be for two people in their early twenties who have just looked death in the face. After seven months of clean scans and good blood tests, his doctor noticed that his thymus (a gland in the chest that I'd never heard of) was enlarged and that they needed to take it out. He said this was from the chemo. I'm not sure why, but when David told me about this seemingly harmless news, I sobbed. As happy as we were during those in-between months, I think deep down I was terrified and waiting for the other shoe to drop. David went in for his surgery, and after seeing the mass in his chest, his doctor told us that his leukemia was back.

Five more months of chemo and another bone marrow transplant, this time from an unrelated donor. David made it through the transplant and came home to our apartment. We both lay on our bed and cried with joy that he had survived and our lives could begin (again). Nine days later, on Halloween, he was admitted to the hospital again because a virus in his bladder was making him really sick and he needed some IV nutrition to regain strength. After three days in the hospital he seemed to be getting worse. Three days later, on my twenty-fourth birthday, he woke himself up long enough to write me an e-mail about how much he loved me and how I was a strong woman who could do anything. I sat on the edge of his bed that day and held his hand as he struggled to open his eyes long enough to tell me happy birthday. On November 7th in the middle of the night, I held my David's hand as he took his last breath.

The days and months that followed are still blurry to me. The first time I went back to our apartment after he died I lay on his side of the bed and sobbed as I looked at his tennis shoes on the floor, one lying on its side where he had last taken them off. Five hundred people came to the life celebration that we had instead of a funeral. I looked around in amazement at all the lives he touched. I would lie in bed and wonder if it was possible to actually die of grief. I wouldn't have cared if I did.

It has been a year and a half since David passed away. I still have days where all I can do is cry about David and the life we could have had but I have been able to find joy in life again. I got a new job that I love, moved into my own apartment (did you know when you live alone you have to kill bugs yourself?!), and even started dating again. Recently for the first time, I looked up at the sky while I was driving to work and actually noticed how gorgeous the sunrise was. I know David would want me to have a beautiful and happy life so I am trying my best to live in a way that honors the kind of person he was. I wanted my love for him to be enough to save him, but really, his love for me is what saves me every day.

~Lisa Tehan

The Blueprints

And in today already walks tomorrow.
~Samuel Taylor Coleridge

"I don't know if I can do this!" I sobbed and dropped to my knees.

"Yes you can. Together we can do it," my cousin said and knelt down beside me. She placed her hand on my shoulder and added, "C'mon, the sooner we get started, the sooner it will be over."

"That's the point. It will be final. The last of what's left of him will be gone." I covered my face with my hands and struggled to stop the river of emotion spilling over me. My father's death, it seemed, was only the beginning of the heartache and unbearable abandonment that I was feeling.

My cousin stood and faced the open closet containing the articles of my father's life: old shoes, six long-sleeved shirts, some jeans, some slacks, a couple of worn sweaters and a faded suede jacket. The scent of old suede, the sight of the right side pocket worn where he used to hook his thumb, a faint hint of the cologne he used to wear, assaulted my spirit. I stared at his belongings and wanted to wail.

My cousin wasn't going to allow that to happen though. She encouraged me to continue, to accept the grief and then go further and find closure.

Coat hangers slid across the metal rod. That's when I saw them—three sets of old blueprints rolled tightly and leaning against the back corner of the closet. My father had saved them for some reason, maybe as a reminder of the important man he had once been. I knew they must be at least ten years old. The yellowed paper, frayed edges and smudged fingerprints told me so.

In his short life my father had accomplished great feats in his construction business, only to throw everything away when drinking became more important. His business failed and he made drinking his first priority. I always found him slumped in a chair, chin on his chest and shoulders sagging in despair. A bottle of cheap wine sat on the floor beside him.

I didn't understand his illness and his abandonment of my sisters and me. Later on, I would come to realize this was not my fault. There was nothing I could have done to change him. God knows we tried, with AA meetings, several stays at recovery centers and a two-week stint at a county facility.

Now I couldn't resist the strange pull the blueprints were having on me. There were two large sets and one smaller. The smaller, I assumed, was for a single-family residence.

I reached inside the closet and wrapped my fingers around the small set of plans. His hands had gone over the paper and the details written inside many times. Carefully, I unrolled the thin paper. A beautiful two-story English Tudor emerged. A high-pitched roof, brick siding, and defined arches and gables were all there. I searched for a name on the prints and couldn't find one. Not an architect or a homeowner for that matter, and the specs were missing. This, simply put, was a rough draft of someone's vision. But whose?

"Look at this."

"Wow... it's beautiful!" exclaimed my cousin. "I wonder who the plans belonged to?"

"I haven't a clue. Look at the floor plan, it's so spacious and open."

She sat beside me and I spread the plans open across our laps. She shook her head like a revelation had just come to her.

"Looks like he left you something after all."

My eyes filled with unshed tears. "You might be right." I glanced back down at the floor plan. Carefully, I rolled the plans and placed the rubber band back on. We let a few heartfelt moments pass by in memory of who my father had been before the drinking consumed his life.

After a few minutes, we returned to packing his personal belongings. We filled two large garbage bags with his old clothes, his wallet and handkerchiefs and his shoes, except for one dressy pair. I held the left shoe in my hand. He'd walked in this shoe, traveled to meetings and then to bars. He'd worn it home and to my sister's wedding. I pressed the worn leather against my chest and then placed it in the box and whispered, "Goodbye."

Several months later, a friend needed to sell a parcel of land. It just so happened the acre was in one of my favorite areas—Wildwood Canyon, untouched and newly developed, with sprawling oaks and meadows growing wild with saffron grass. I jumped at the chance.

The top shelf in my closet had been home for the blueprints since finding them. Each day when I went to get my clothes out, I looked at them and smiled. They contained a dream and my duty became clear on a cloudy morning on the anniversary of his death. Instead of my clothes, I pulled the blueprints down and placed a call to a local architect. Within a month, those simple blueprints were developed into a full set of plans with specs, and six months later, the pad was graded and the foundation poured.

The first time I went to inspect the framing on the second story the sun was setting, the sky pastel and the wind gentle as it blew through the open walls. The plywood subfloor was covered with wood shavings and powdery dust, the scent intoxicating and familiar. I thought of my father and his dreams. In his lifetime, he had built apartment complexes and houses, and he had developed a mud and paint factory. He had accomplished much and then let it all slip through his fingers. Sadness filled me, but only for a moment. His life's path had taken a dark turn and he wasn't able to find his way back. In one fleeting moment, I realized he had left me a legacy.

I wanted to weep, but something held me back. Tears welled in my eyes and yet they didn't spill over. I felt my father's presence, near and yet so far away.

I have long since moved away from the Tudor that was once my father's vision. Proudly I sold the place two years after completion. Now when I think of the house, I think of him, and vice-versa. The original blueprints have a home in my attic now, and every once in a while, I pull them out and remember he was just a man, and he was also my father, one I still love to this day with all my heart.

~Cindy Golchuk

53

Six Words

The walls we build around us to keep sadness out also keep out the joy.
~Jim Rohn

We had six words in common, but somehow we built a friendship on them. I was a twenty-something struggling artist, barely making rent. David and his wife, Sonia, were in their seventies, immigrants who had been brought over by their children a decade before. In a heavily Russian subsection of West Hollywood, the three of us shared a sunburst-colored apartment building with a struggling actor, a surf-loving drummer, and a sad-eyed boy who had grown up in the Children of God cult and now worked at The Whisky on Sunset Boulevard.

David spent most of his time standing on the slightly elevated concrete slab that served as a courtyard, watching the neighborhood go by. He greeted me at the same spot nearly every morning, often pointing out various things around the block, accompanied by long explanations I had no hope of understanding. His wife, sick with diabetes, spent days in a hospital bed pushed against their living room window. Some nights I'd arrive home to find David reeking of vodka. He would smile sadly at me, mumble, "Sonia, no good." Neither one of us thought she had much time left, but she hung on for three more years.

When Sonia finally did pass, I was back east for the Christmas holidays. My roommate called late one night and said they'd tried to revive her on the living room floor while David watched quietly from the side. A few days later, a very young (and very close) friend of my family's was killed in a freak accident. As I walked numbly through the funeral procession, I found myself thinking of David and how strange it was our fates had suddenly taken such parallel paths.

I arrived back in Los Angeles several days after New Year's and found David in his usual place, dressed in black now, smoking a cigarette. He threw his arms around me as soon as I was close enough to reach. I cried and spoke soft platitudes that needed no translation. He nodded, but said nothing. I wanted so much to tell him of my friend, to let him know I understood that something was missing now, that Death had touched me too. I couldn't though; neither one of us had the words.

For several weeks, David remained in black, receiving visitors at his perch. The older women came to cook and clean, the older men to drink vodka and smoke. I watched it all from my balcony, feeling lost and alone, sad at my friend's passing, as David did the same from his. It wasn't getting easier, and I started to wonder if something had permanently broken, disabling me from continuing here.

Then one afternoon, six or seven months later, I was sweeping my balcony when I caught sight of David, shuffling across our street in a newly ironed suit with a small bouquet of flowers behind his back. He made his way up the stairs of the adjacent building, where one of the old Russian women who had been visiting him regularly lived with her son and two grandchildren. He rang the doorbell, and a minute later she emerged in a flowery dress, her hair neatly tied behind her ears. She accepted the flowers (with a giggle) and the two of them made their way down the street.

Broom still in mid-sweep, I stared blankly ahead, trying to process what I had just seen. This man, after watching his wife of 40 years linger with illness and expire before him, after being hobbled himself, unable to do much more than watch as the world went by, had somehow found life again. What had I done at 28, healthy, vibrant, the world at my feet?

A few weeks later, I followed up with a man who had asked me out several times over the previous year. I'd been annoyed at his upbeat persistence, preferring my own misery to company, but now I discovered a new faith in such acts of courage. It proved an auspicious move, and within six months I was moving out of my West Hollywood hovel and into a whole new life with him.

After the apartment had been cleared, I went back hoping to see David one last time. I found him, as always, leaning over the gate, peering down the sidewalk. He knew why I was there and he opened his arms, welcoming me. I stepped willingly into his embrace. I loved this man and knew I would not see him again. He was going to die here, as his wife had done, and I had so much yet to do. I pulled back, fighting emotion, and he patted me warmly on the shoulder, pointed and said, "Daughter," then touched his chest.

"Daughter." I nodded. One of six words between us, and it was, as it had always been, enough.

~Brigitte Hales

54

Broken Glass

Memory is a way of holding onto the things you love,
the things you are, the things you never want to lose.
~From the television show The Wonder Years

W hen my mother passed away, I was left in charge of her affairs. Grief-stricken, a few days after the funeral I drove to her house to assess the clean-up aspect of my job, as well as to take a peek into who my mother was.

My mother loved her things. Growing up in poverty, she vowed to never want again. As I looked around her home, filled with expensive collections and miscellaneous things, I realized that she had overly compensated for the needy little girl inside her.

Our relationship was never smooth. Emotional limitations affected her mothering, and I had a strong will that always rubbed my mother wrong. Things got worse when I became a teenager. Then my father died and my mother was left adrift in a sea of loneliness that eventually became an unreasonable bitterness. Our fragile relationship suffered even more.

Before my mother was diagnosed with her terminal illness, we had finally, blessedly, reached an accord. During the last days of her life I took care of her, and in the end there was nothing but love between us. We had accomplished a true level of karmic forgiveness—and I am eternally grateful for that.

So as I rummaged through her dresser drawers and closets, her things seemed to comfort me, even as it made me sad to think about how all her prized possessions would never be hers again.

For months I organized, sorted, boxed and arranged for the eventual estate sale. The man who was running the sale came to stick price tags on all the items. I chose not to be there that day, or during the day of the sale. I didn't feel I could handle someone bargaining for a lower price on my mother's "priceless" possessions.

A few days before the sale, I went to my mother's house to drop something off. I walked in and headed up the stairs, but I was not prepared for the scene that awaited me.

There were hundreds of neon orange and yellow tags everywhere. All my mother's things had been reduced to penciled-in dollars and cents. The white couches my mother loved and worried over each time the grandchildren visited, her cherished Lladro collection, the old sewing box that she had since she was 14, the dishes she ate from only months ago. Now mere items in a sale, they were no longer really hers. Soon to belong to nameless, faceless people who would never know her but would use her things and call them their own. I felt like a traitor, somehow having a hand in the evil deed of cheapening these memories with meaningless price tags.

Breathless and numb, I needed to find one space that didn't have a tag screaming out, horrifying me. There was nowhere to go; tags mocked me from every room. I stumbled into the bathroom that was blessedly empty. I glanced at my reflection in the mirror and saw dark rivulets of mascara-stained tears. I collapsed on the floor and looked out the door that led into my mother's room, and I saw the antique bench that used to be my grandpa's. A $20 tag hung from one of its etched handles. I remember my mother telling me years before that the bench had reminded her of her father because it had sat at the foot of his bed. It had reminded her of him, and now that bench reminded me of her.

My grief grew to include the loss of my father, the loss of my grandma and grandpa, and then finally back to the fresh loss of my mother. Every one of those dear people haunted me as I sat on the bathroom floor.

Blindly I reached for my cell phone and called a friend. I was sobbing so much that she could hardly understand me. After she consoled me for about 15 minutes, I was able to hang up, wash my face and leave my mother's home, never to see those items again. At my car, my hand trembled and I couldn't unlock the door. I needed my mother to reassure me, to comfort me. But I was alone in the driveway and my heart was aching desperately.

Without thinking, I raced back into the house, ran up the stairs and straight into my mother's bedroom. I grabbed my grandpa's bench, raced back out and stuffed it into my car.

I cried on the entire drive to the storage space that I had rented for all the items I was keeping. I was emotionally and physically exhausted when I got there and opened the door. Boxes and boxes of unsorted pictures, crystal and china, my mother's cherished tea cup collection, all welcomed me and gave me a bittersweet comfort.

I added my grandpa's bench and as it slid between two stacks of boxes, I heard a dull crunch, and then breaking glass. Horrified, I pulled out the frame that held my parents' wedding portrait from 1959. My beautiful, young, happy parents looked at me through a spider web of cracked glass. I ran my fingers across the broken glass and carefully brushed away the splintered patch in front of their faces. As I saw them smiling at me, I no longer felt alone in that cold storage space.

I realized then that my mother's things—tagged and ready to be sold—were like a pane of glass in a frame. Palpable, breakable, and replaceable. Something fine and pretty that only serves to cover the truer, more meaningful and beautiful picture underneath.

I smiled for the first time that day. Marveling at how simple it was, I felt my heart releasing her things and it felt good to finally let them go so that they could bring joy to someone new. The metaphorical glass that I had surrounded my mother in had broken into a million pieces and had fallen away. I no longer needed those tangible things to connect me to my mother. She was firmly—unbreakable and irreplaceable—in my heart forever.

~Amy Schoenfeld Hunt

55

The Chinese Chicken Incident

We acquire the strength we have overcome.
~Ralph Waldo Emerson

The most vivid memories from my childhood involve the road trips I'd take with my family to see my grandmother in Brooklyn. They weren't particularly long drives, but to me, as a kid, we might as well have been taking weeklong journeys across the country. Squeezed between my two older sisters in the back seat, my father was at the wheel, leading us in a non-stop cavalcade of car games and sing-a-longs, his voice booming above the honking horns and noisy traffic outside. My mother, while occasionally chiming in with an off pitch note of her own, sat in the passenger seat casually looking on but mostly engaged in her own world among the cacophony of noise inside and outside the moving vehicle.

Growing up, it was always my dad who was the driving force in our development towards adulthood. His were the admonishing yells when we did something wrong and the encouraging words when we did something right. Many nights I sat with my father in my parents' bedroom at the foot of his recliner while he explained the lessons I brought home from school, dictated my papers to me, taught me about Greek mythology or solved logic puzzles with me. All the while, my mother lay in bed falling asleep with yesterday's *New York Times* in hand.

He was the creative pulse that made our house tick. He encouraged me to write, my older sister to take photos and my other sister to save the world. He was a surgeon, but could be found as often in the kitchen as he could in the operating room. Whereas many fathers spent Sunday afternoons on the couch watching football, mine was in his chair watching cooking shows and taking notes. Meanwhile, my mother spent her Sundays in her little makeshift office in the kitchen pantry paying the family bills and scheduling our upcoming week.

I remember the smell of the kitchen when my father decided to make dinner. It had the aroma of a French bistro one night and a Chinese restaurant another. Pans and dishes and food were everywhere. I watched him in awe as he transformed that kitchen into a five-star restaurant and became the master chef he wished he could be. On the nights he was too exhausted from the day's surgeries, my mom took the cooking reins. Her kitchen was more like a diner serving the essentials — meat loaf, spaghetti, hamburgers. It was good. It was practical. It was boring.

When I was 15, my dad got sick. The car rides were less frequent and often to the doctor, my mom at the wheel and focused on the road ahead. The car songs were not as boisterous and the games not as fun. The lessons were now at the foot of his bed and they didn't last as long. My mom still pretended to read her *New York Times*, but I could see her wide awake glances from behind the paper. The cancer quickly drained him of most of his energy. So the gourmet restaurant was eventually shut down for good and the diner took its place as blue-plate specials were served every night.

When I was 16, the cancer finally got the best of him. He had kept a smile on his face until the end, probably for our sake, but most likely because that's how he wanted to be remembered. He was a fighter, but even he didn't have enough fight in him for that. And while he kept the brave face and the rest of us broke down in tears, it was my mother who told us everything would be okay.

While my sisters were off at college dealing with their loss with the support of their friends, I was left home alone with my mother.

The two of us only had each other. Being a teenager, I felt sorry for myself. I don't know how much support I provided. I was a boy who had lost his father. I never thought about my mother as a woman who had lost her husband. And she never gave me reason to.

My mom would pick me up after school every day. Family road trips had become the two of us on the short ride to our empty house. On the way she would do her best Barbara Streisand impression singing along to the sounds coming out of the radio. She didn't care how out of key and off pitch her warbling was. And neither did I.

She attempted to help me with my schoolwork. But I had reached the age where I could do it on my own. I didn't need anyone to write my reports for me anymore. The one time I let her help, I nearly failed. But I appreciated the effort.

My mother was trying to be a mother and a father to me. But as hard as she tried, she couldn't fill that void left by his loss.

On my 17th birthday, she decided to make me Chinese Chicken. This was my father's specialty and my favorite dish. He would marinate chicken in a mixture of hoisin and plum sauce, sauté it in a wok with red peppers, water chestnuts, bamboo shoots, broccoli and cashews until the mixture filled the kitchen with the most succulent aroma, making my mouth water with anticipation. As I sat in the den waiting for dinner to be ready, the odor from the kitchen began to make its way towards me. It hit me in the face like a punch from a heavyweight. At first sour, then stale, and finally burnt. The pungent odor was accompanied by the crashing of pots and pounding of countertops. I couldn't take it any longer and disobeyed my mother's earlier instructions to stay away at all costs.

When I entered the kitchen, I saw a woman I hardly recognized. She stood frozen above a smoking wok, vegetables and poultry strewn about the kitchen, bits of cashews in her hair and flour covering her face like a Kabuki performer. And there, I could see it, however faint it was—a vertical streak which extended from the corner of her eye down her cheek breaking up the purity of her white mask.

It was then that I finally realized I wasn't the only one trying to fill a huge void left in my life. I lost a parent, but she had lost so much more. I would never be alone as long as I had my mother. But she had to be everything to me and I couldn't be everything to her. How could I not have seen that she needed my support maybe even more than I needed hers?

Ever since my father died, that one tear was the most I ever saw my mom allow herself in front of me. She is the strongest woman I've ever known. She is the fighter. And she was the backbone of our family all along. And for that, I owe her everything.

And so I ran a towel under the sink and helped my mother wipe the flour off her face. "I was in the mood for spaghetti anyway, Mom."

~David Chalfin

Hand-Me-Down Funeral

We do not remember days; we remember moments.
~Cesare Pavese, The Burning Brand

My last argument with Daddy was the one about his funeral. He didn't want one. "What's the point of a funeral?" he wanted to know. "It's a big waste of money. When the time comes, here's what you do."

He pulled out a plain white sheet of paper with instructions. Neatly typed, of course: "Cremation, minimum container, no memorial service." He'd drawn it up himself.

Tanned, seemingly healthy, he looked like he should be out on the golf course, not at the breakfast table making funeral pronouncements to my mom and me. But he started out quiet that day, more subdued than usual. Facing heart surgery in a month and a detail man, he was going to leave nothing to chance.

"Life," he said, "is like a stock portfolio. It needs to be well-planned."

That was his style. Facing his possible end, he was obsessed with the details. Mama was used to his obsessions, but I was impatient.

I took one look at the paper and started right in. "First, you're not going to die. And even if you were, this is a terrible idea!" I said. "People need a way to say goodbye."

"Not to the tune of thousands of dollars," he said.

"But people need closure," I told him. "A funeral wouldn't be for you. It would be for the people you leave behind."

He was unconvinced. In fact, the debate seemed to enliven him.

"You know what else," he said, voice rising. "All those clothes in there, you ought to get rid of them when I go. Give them to charity or whoever wants them. Don't be saving stuff when I'm gone."

Unchallenged on the clothes, he rushed to have his customary last say.

"A funeral," he said, "should reflect the way you live your life. Remember that. I'm not about to pay top dollar for mine."

When the conversation resumed, a month later in the hospital on the eve of surgery, he pulled out the paper again. I was grateful this time there was no time to talk.

The hospital TV vendor arrived, and Daddy turned his attention to telling her how he wasn't interested in paying $6.00 a day. When she disappeared around the corner, he sneaked over to the TV hanging by the vacant bed beside him, to see if they'd forgotten to shut it off.

If the evening news had appeared, it would have been his last little bargain. But the only free ride turned out to be a dull in-house video on low sodium diets.

Sadly, his luck ran no better with the surgery. Complications set in the very first night, and the paper that had been such a lively topic for theoretical debate suddenly took center stage in a real-life drama. With Mama, I now read it over and over as we planned for his funeral, or non-funeral, and struggled to find ways to say goodbye. Without wasting too much money.

Calling hours — no service, no flowers — was the final compromise. There were no speeches, other than the private stories about a birdied hole or the fish that got away, and the flowers that came over the deceased's objections were quickly dispensed to my mother's list of "shut-in friends."

But the unexpected memorial unfolded over the next couple of weeks when Mama, trying to honor his wishes, started inviting some of his golfing buddies to come try on a few of Daddy's shirts.

"You know he would not want these to go to waste," she said. "Now you just come see what you'd like before I ship them all off to the church."

Mama was a quiet and sensitive woman. No sooner had she said it, than she was worried she might be leaving someone out. So she quickly began to figure who else would be interested in his closet cleaning, and issued invitations to the rest, in order of their family relation and their closeness to my dad. First, she approached my sons.

"They'll never go for this," I thought. "They'll think it's morbid to wear them." I was wrong.

One morning, I looked up from breakfast to catch the cuff of Daddy's PJs walking by. My eyes traveled up the full length of the six-foot frame.

"Morning!" said the older one. They fit perfectly. With his back turned, he looked just like Daddy the year he put Grecian Formula over his gray.

Then the younger one padded in wearing Daddy's huge white athletic shoes.

"I think they'll bring me luck," he said, in a surprising show of sentimentality.

The parade went on, with Mama calling cousins and friends to come up to the house and see what they could use. After I flew back home and called to check on her, I heard a nightly report on the diminishing inventory.

Golf shirts, jackets, dress shoes. There was something for everyone. With each bit of clothing that went out the door, there was a "thank you" and a story about Daddy. Golfing buddies told how ecstatic he'd been to shoot his last birdie, and how they'd always counted on him to bring the crackers in case anyone got hungry before the turn.

Invariably, they'd say, "I'll think of him whenever I wear this." One added, "When I put on his sweater, I can hear him laugh."

He was right about the laughter. It was real. It was Daddy's new way of getting in the last word.

~Pat Snyder

57

Chicken Soup for the Soul

The Gift of Compassion

In the midst of winter I finally learned there was in me an invincible summer.
~Albert Camus

My heart freezes as the ringing phone pierces my sleep. My husband jolts awake to answer and as I hear a guttural moan from his lips, I sit up on full alert. He thrusts the phone at me. "Kevin didn't come home from class," he groans, fear and disbelief in his eyes.

I spoke to Kevin this morning, as I have every day since he left his first suicide note more than a year ago. He was upbeat and excited about the community justice event he had organized for this weekend.

"What happened?" I ask into the receiver, dreading the answer.

"I talked to him this afternoon and he seemed fine," my daughter-in-law blurts out, panic in her voice. "He said his headache was livable today. He was on campus but didn't go to class. And the police won't do anything until he's been gone more than 24 hours."

I make plane reservations, frantic because I'm in Kansas City and he's disappeared in California. I fixate on how we're going to find him as I call family and friends to see if they have talked to him. I hope he's only been in a wreck or has helped the wrong street person and is lying hurt in an alley somewhere. And I'm stunned to hear myself praying that if he is dead, that it isn't by suicide.

I'm numb through the three-hour flight as I try not to think, try not to imagine the worst.

The next day I attend his community event. I know that if he is going to appear it will be at this program, a product of his all-consuming passion for social and environmental justice. I situate myself so I can see all three streets that lead into the park. I will myself a glimpse of his car and the shuddering sigh of relief I'll breathe when I see him. But he doesn't show up.

In my rush to Kinko's that afternoon to copy missing-person flyers I'm lucid and focused, yet feel jostled by the disturbing crowds of people who swoosh by with their lattes. I glimpse baby carriages and hear snippets of the screech of tires in the background of my urgency. I wallow in my Pollyanna world as I assure myself that everything will be fine.

I spend another restless night with a vivid dream of Kevin as he walks down a wood-paneled hallway. In my dream, he is gazing around in wonder and notices me watching him. He waves goodbye as he flashes me his engaging grin, and with a glimmer of joy in his eyes, he turns and continues down the corridor. I wake from a fitful sleep sobbing with hope that we'll find Kevin and that he will be as serene as he appeared in my dream, the wrinkles on his forehead softened now that his headaches are healed and he understands that it's no longer his responsibility to relieve the suffering in the world.

It's the third morning now and I call the hospitals again as others drive through town to search for him. My heart pleads "NO!" as the phone rings, but I snatch up the receiver with a prayer that someone has found him. And they have. My chest crumples as the park ranger begins to explain how he found his car, then his note, and then his body.

I begin my new life as if I'm enshrouded by lead veils that settle in for the long haul and restrict access to all senses—touch, taste, smell, hearing, sight. Only the sixth sense is active—heightened perception and spiritual connections. I'm bombarded by confusing "signs" that feel like vital links to another realm, wild coincidences that point me to an omniscient power whose presence I had only read about before Kevin's death.

I agonize that my sanity will implode as the lines of reality blur while I try to find a footing in this new definition of my life. But there is no footing. There is no place of comfort, no Pollyanna resolution, just a harsh stripping away of the life I'd always envisioned: that guided by my nurturing, my children would grow up to be thoughtful, compassionate souls who would live out their lives in peace.

As the years pass, the lead veils gradually lift and occasionally float away altogether. Sometimes, on those days when the veils are lighter, I wonder whether I truly want to shed them permanently. If I give up my devastation, then what's left in my soul? What kind of mother would I be if I no longer mourned the depth of Kevin's despair every minute of every day?

His ten-year battle with constant, debilitating headaches rendered him powerless to reach his humanitarian goals. I hovered over him to gauge his reactions to every medication change and every new treatment and therapist. With each setback I saw his confidence diminish and his enthusiasm for life wither under the burden of his sense of failure.

What would I say to him if we could relive his last year? What do I comprehend now that I didn't even fathom before he died?

I would say that his own healing had to come before he could heal others; that society and family responsibilities are utterly irrelevant when weighed against the glorious gift of his life. I'd encourage him to leave school and his professional life and embark on his own spiritual quest to find the peace that I have learned is possible. My immersion into yoga and meditation has given me a deep knowing that there is a place within each of us that is at peace even in the midst of our suffering. I would pry open his heart to those "signs," the preposterous coincidences that make me shriek with laughter and shake my head in awe as a glimpse of that connectedness overwhelms and comforts me.

It's been seven years now. People who hear about my loss entrust me with their deepest fears about their own children. Because I know their stories can be more devastating and horrifying than mine, I worry sometimes that my empathy for their anguish may draw my own veils back down.

But as their pain begins to envelop me I'm urged on, guided by that inner peace that helps me muster my courage, buoys my spirit, and offers me the gift of endless, abiding compassion.

~Sami Aaron

58

The Uninvited Guest

Enjoy when you can, and endure when you must.
~Johann Wolfgang von Goethe

I sit on the park bench eating cheesy popcorn and watching young children on the playground. I am enjoying the day, the sun on my face, and the smell of fresh grass.

Randomly I think, I wish Samantha could run and play with them.

And there it is, the cold hand in my cheesy popcorn, the presence taking up too much space on the park bench, blocking my sunshine. My Grief.

"Really?" I say. "I didn't invite you. Get your hand out of my cheesy corn." Instead, I end up having to scoot over, making more room for My Grief. Grief comes and goes when I least expect it. I'll be in my car, driving along listening to music and I'll catch it in the corner of my eye, kicking the back of my seat.

"Hey Heather."

"Aww crap, what are you doing here?"

"It's been a while. I thought I would stop in for a visit."

"Well, make sure you fasten your seatbelt and be quiet. My daughter's sleeping and I don't want you to wake her up."

"Can I change the station?"

"No."

"Can I play with the window?"

"No, you can just come along for the ride."

So we go on the ride together, fingernails thumping on the dashboard as a reminder of who decided to show up today. Yes, I am quite aware of your presence, you don't need to remind me.

Grief's appearance used to rattle me, send me into the bathroom crying hysterically. Render me useless for a day. Sometimes it still does, but as Grief has been established as a consistent visitor in our household, we have drawn up a contract. We have an agreement.

As the mom of two children, one who died at birth and one who has a progressive disease, I will grieve. I will grieve for many dreams that will not come to fruition. I will grieve for a life I thought would be different.

I will grieve at times. And I will not grieve at times. I will laugh at times. I will not laugh at times.

Grief can come into our house but is not allowed to stay. If allowed to stay, it would devour the corners of our house. It would suck up the oxygen in the room. It would consume me.

And that is not acceptable.

Grief tends to run within the Special Needs community I am a part of; I bump into him quite often, even visiting other families....

"How are you?"

"My daughter has pneumonia. She is in the hospital on a ventilator."

I look around and see Grief, sitting on the couch, smugly picking at dirty fingernails.

And I meet those who sadly keep very, very close company with this unwanted guest. Grief hangs over them like a shroud. It is hard to laugh. It is hard to love, because in copious amounts Grief tends to ooze; like a nasty septic wound... draining life from us.

But we still have to laugh, we still have to play, we still have to live... life carries on.

I cannot, at the end of my life say... well, it was long, hard and I was sad.

Surprisingly, our relationship is not based entirely on conflict. My interactions with Grief have allowed me to see myself raw, unprotected, and exposed. At times I feel that I have lost my skin... yes, here I am. Be careful, that's my beating heart you see there. Do not touch.

I am no longer afraid to approach others regarding their own tragedies. I bring up the tough conversations. How is your mother? I am sorry for your loss. I am so sorry your daughter is in the hospital. I hug, I cry, I listen. Not because I am an über-sensitive person but because I know Grief sometimes travels alone except when he travels with his favorites… Isolation and Loneliness.

Sometimes Grief shows up at a party… drinks my wine, eats my last bite of fudgy dessert. It's an annoyance really, but since Grief is not a constant life guest, I have learned to tolerate the time we spend together. Sometimes we even enjoy an introspective moment or two.

We have set the rules and sometimes they are followed. We cannot have a permanent impy, uninvited guest… we don't have the room… not in our lives, not in my heart… life is too short and despite the bad things that can happen… life is too sweet.

~Heather Schichtel

59

The Voice from Beyond

A memory is what is left when something happens
and does not completely unhappen.
~Edward de Bono

We have a dead man on our answering machine. I don't mean to say that I hear dead people. At least, not all dead people. Just one, and his message is pretty bland.

This past winter, an ailing friend of the family, Skip, abruptly went into a long-term care facility. He called to let us know what was going on, but got our answering machine. We heard Skip's message and visited him the next day. He died that night.

No one had erased Skip's message by the time he died and afterwards, my father-in-law didn't have the heart to. The message on our answering machine might have been the last recorded moment of Skip's life, my father-in-law reasoned. Erasing it would, in some way, be like erasing Skip from this planet.

So Skip has stayed on our machine for months. It's a bit weird checking the answering machine because I always have to press the skip button on the first message. In other words, I have to skip Skip.

Thanks to modern technology, we now can have recorded mementos of our loved ones long after they die. But it can be hard to draw a distinction between the sacred and the inane when dealing with the dead. It's sort of like a 21st century version of cleaning out a parent's house after a funeral. Unless you want to inherit a houseful of stuff you don't need, you have to make some choices.

The same should hold true with a recorded image or audio record. A touching birthday party or a poignant last few words can be irreplaceable.

But this message from Skip just isn't that special. All he says is that he's not doing well and to call him. If anything, it's a bit depressing. I wish instead that we had an earlier message from him, maybe saying he just won the lottery or that he felt great after taking a hike.

In the back of my mind, I also worry that we might be holding Skip back by holding onto him. I remember hearing a theory that the spirits of the deceased can't rest if we don't let them go. My town threw a wonderful memorial for Skip at the theater where he worked, one sure to have given him a sense of closure. Wouldn't it be awful if he were ready to ascend to the next plane of existence, only to be held up every time we checked our answering machine?

I figured fate would've taken care of the message by now — the first power outage would be God's way of releasing Skip from our machine. But though we did have a couple of power line-destroying storms this winter, each time the power came back Skip's message was still there.

So now we have to wait for the inevitable accident. Some day someone is going to slip up and press the erase button on the wrong message. Whoever does it will feel terrible, but it'll probably be for the best.

Of course I've thought about accidentally on-purpose erasing the message myself, but if I follow my father-in-law's reasoning that would essentially make me a murderer.

So my only hope lies in my eight-month-old daughter. She loves the telephone and already has shown a healthy inclination towards destroying the house. It only seems a matter of time before she gets her hands on the answering machine.

Until then, I'll just keep on skipping Skip and pray that he's resting in peace.

~Craig Idlebrook

A Hierarchy of Grief

We must embrace pain and burn it as fuel for our journey.
~Kenji Miyazawa

Mary was the first one to tell me that our children were in an accident. They had been dating less than a year when a drunk driver hit them from behind as Neil walked Trista home after a study date at our house. Trista suffered a massive head injury and was taken to Boston by helicopter. Her parents took her off life support the next day. Neil's brain damage was subtler, unapparent at first.

His eyes flew open when I reached his side in the ER.

"Hi Mom," he said, filling me with relief. He knew me!

Things quickly changed. He became agitated. He thought he was in a gym. He wanted the collar off his neck. He was in pain. His broken shinbone jutted off at an unnatural angle, his only injury we were told at first. Later we learned that his brain was also bleeding. He too needed to be transported into Boston for intensive care.

Even in those panic-stricken early hours, I felt the weight of the other mother in that room, the presence of Mary. I wanted to cover Neil's cold and shivering body with my own to warm him. I thought of Mary. Wouldn't she rather feel Trista cold and shivering than just plain cold? It was so unlike Neil to yell, to demand. It was hard to listen to. I wanted to take the collar off his neck, make him comfortable. I kept thinking of Mary and how she would give anything to hear Trista's voice again, even if she were complaining. My grief felt constricted next to Mary's. How dare I grieve at all? How fraudulent it felt, like I was hijacking the very word from someone who knew true loss.

But I have losses, too. Neil recovered. He left the hospital after two surgeries. He had physical therapy. He walked with a cane for months. But he has changed. He doesn't like crowds. He has short-term memory loss. He doesn't laugh as much as before. His friends from high school sensed it right away. They didn't know how to relate to him anymore. The ones from his theater group, who once gathered around his makeshift bed in our living room entertaining him with dances and song, started coming around less often. Eventually they stopped coming by at all.

Six years after the accident Neil still suffered. He took anti-depressants and saw a therapist. He smoked cigarettes. He still saw Mary from time to time. I wondered if when she looked at him, she saw the kid who went to the prom, the high school graduate, the college student, all the things that Trista would never be. And he has had successes. He graduated from Skidmore College with degrees in mathematics and the classics. He taught math at a private high school in Vermont. But he was asked to leave before the year was out. "Too depressed," the headmaster said. Now he works at his father's restaurant supply store and is applying to graduate school. He wants to teach again.

Because our children's accident involved a drunk driver, there was a trial; there were hearings for sentencing and hearings for parole. For each one, Mary and I were asked to write victim impact statements to read before the court. We stood before judge after judge over the years, telling our respective stories. Our parallel if uneven tragedies were held up for display over and over.

Sometimes Mary spoke ahead of me. Occasionally I went first. Sometimes she read from prepared statements, but often she just spoke from her heart. She told of memories: shopping trips and Girl Scout camps. School plays and holding hands. All the things that she would miss about her daughter.

"What yardstick do I use to measure that?" she asked.

But I need a yardstick, too. It may be different from Mary's. With tinier notches perhaps. Or at least spaced more widely apart. But I have things to measure, too. Neil's pain from fractured bones; hardware in and hardware out. His slow progress through physical therapy. His struggles with memory loss. His pain from the loss of his girlfriend and having his whole world turned upside down.

So I told my story to the judges, too. No embellishments. No drama. Just the facts and from the heart. I was aware that Mary was listening. I knew that her loss was greater than mine. But we were in this together and the judge needed to hear from both of us, bearing witness to our children's separate tragedies so that justice might take place, knowing that it never could.

I have come to believe that grief has many faces. There is no one right way to behave in the face of it. No correct approach. There is no one set of circumstances that warrants it as a reaction and no specific behavior that qualifies as an appropriate response. It just is. I have come to understand that the whole gamut of human emotion is legit when it comes to coping with loss. Even how we define our loss is personal and valid, different as it may be for each of us. I'm not sure where I stand in this hierarchy of grief. I may not be on the top rung, but I'm not on the bottom either. All I know is that I belong on the ladder.

~Carolyn Roy-Bornstein

Myfather@heaven.com

When love is lost, do not bow your head in sadness;
instead keep your head up high and gaze into heaven for that is where your
broken heart has been sent to heal.
~Author Unknown

Hand my father the telephone and he'd clam up. In all the years since I moved away from home, I can count the number of times he called me on the fingers of one hand. Each time he did, it was because my mother forced him to pick up the phone and dial. I know because he'd tell me, usually when she was standing right next to him.

It became a family joke.

When he bought a personal computer after he retired, I figured he'd just use it for spreadsheets to keep track of his finances. I hadn't counted on e-mail.

From the moment he got his first e-mail account, he became an e-mail junkie. His friends weren't into computers, so he started bombarding his stockbroker with questions and attached articles until his broker threatened to quit if my father sent him one more e-mail.

Whenever I came to visit, he badgered me to get an e-mail account so he'd have someone else to write to. After a year, I overcame my technophobia and gave in, much to his stockbroker's relief.

The minute I gave him my brand new e-mail address, he deluged me with jokes, financial information, news articles and whatever else he found interesting. I signed on daily just to see what he came up with. I was never disappointed.

In return, I sent him short notes, copies of articles I was writing, and URLs for websites he might find useful.

For the next couple of years, apart from visits, e-mail was our main form of contact.

Although my father and I had always had a good relationship, sharing common interests allowed us to grow closer. I was sorry I had waited so long to get online.

My father became such a fixture at the computer that my mother swore she'd wrap the cables around his neck if he didn't come up for air every couple of hours.

Even Puss Puss, the cat, learned that if she wanted my father's attention, she'd better head down to the computer. My father often went downstairs, ready to work, only to find the cat already curled up in his chair. Rather than disturb her, he brought in a second chair and they'd sit in companionable silence while he surfed the Web and e-mailed me his finds.

As my father's health began to deteriorate, surfing the Web became too tiring for him. Gradually, I took over the role of e-mail guru. I subscribed to health newsletters so I could send him articles with the latest information on his health problems. I checked the stock market news several times a day so I could track his investments and pass on tidbits of interest.

I also joined several joke groups so I'd have a steady source of material to e-mail him every week. He'd print them out and bring them to his dialysis sessions, where my mother read the jokes out loud to all the patients after they were hooked up to their machines—talk about a captive audience.

Eventually, the effort of signing on and printing e-mails became too much for him. The computer sat alone and unattended as my father struggled with the mundane tasks of living. Activities we take for granted—getting up, getting dressed and eating—took all of his strength. He kept his e-mail account, and I checked it on my increasingly frequent visits home, but now junk mail filled the inbox.

After my father's death, my mother gave his computer to my cousin. Without my father to share my "finds," surfing the Web lost its appeal. I unsubscribed from the joke groups, checked the market news less often and no longer scouted for new websites.

The other day I checked my e-mail address book for its semi-annual updating. Nestled in the C's, I found my father's old e-mail address. Although five years had passed since his death, I could never bring myself to remove his listing. Maybe now was the time.

As my hand hovered over the delete key, memories of all the information and love we exchanged in our e-mails resurfaced. I moved my hand and clicked on "edit" instead. Rather than delete him, I changed his e-mail address to samcooper@heaven.com.

I know the World Wide Web is still earthbound and e-mail hasn't reached those exalted heights yet. But who knows? Maybe one day it will. I'd like to be ready when it does.

I know my father will be waiting.

~Harriet Cooper

62

Grieve Bee

I don't know why they call it heartbreak.
It feels like every other part of my body is broken too.
~Missy Altijd

After a full week of teaching elementary school choir, Saturday couldn't have come any sooner. I had just nestled into my recliner after a delightful day in the sun, zipping about town on my mobility scooter. I am an energetic 46-year-old woman living with a form of Parkinson disease that stiffens my body, so bike riding is a thing of my past.

I had stopped at the market to pick up a carton of soy milk (I'm healthful that way) and a box of my favorite sweet cereal, Froot Loops (I like to keep my dentist in business). After donning my most comfortable sweatpants and Ragu-stained T-shirt, I was set for a lazy night in front of the tube.

So there I was, munching my artificially flavored rings and gripped by the National Geographic special on snakes. Right in the middle of watching a cobra swallow a rabbit whole, it hit me: memories of my dad, who had passed away only weeks before, consumed my thoughts.

The grieving process is a strange and miraculous thing and can overtake you at any time, even as you eat a bowl of colorful cereal and watch a snake gulp down a cute animal. The floodgates opened as wide as the cobra's mouth, and I started sobbing.

I found myself wishing and wishing for the heartache to just stop; that something else, anything, would preoccupy my mind. Then suddenly a giant bee hovered in front of my nose. The buzz was deafening, and I cursed myself for leaving my front door open to air out the house during the day.

Shrieking, I hurled my bowl of cereal overhead. As soy milk rained downward, I struggled out of my recliner. This is not an easy task when you have a mobility disease, but the buzz echoing in my ear was a great motivator.

Thud! I hit the floor. Crawling on hands and knees, I slithered toward the kitchen, as the mutant beast hovered only inches above. I grabbed a dishtowel, and where a person without a mobility issue could whip that towel with a mighty snap, striking the buzzing foe, I lifted my towel and it went... blorp. I could have sworn I heard the bee snicker.

I blorped left, then blorped right, I believe it napped whilst I blorped left once again. It lunged at me, chasing me all over my apartment, my arms flailing about as though my hair was on fire.

I made it to the bathroom and slammed the door shut. Arming myself with a can of white linen-scented Lysol, I was now ready to do battle with the fuzzy buzzer lurking just outside my door. My intention was not to actually kill the bee, but rather encourage it away from me, meanwhile, making it the only bee in existence that is 99% germ free.

After a deep breath, I courageously swung open the door, which promptly caught on the bath mat. That threw me off balance and I fell to the side, immersing my left forearm in the toilet.

The winged Kong flew in, buzzing, and I screamed and sprayed valiantly. All you could hear in the following seconds was buzzing and screaming and hissing, and mind you, my arm was still in the toilet.

I escaped and made it back to the living room and watched Kong fly about my home. My heart pumped, my mind raced, and my left arm was dripping. I frantically sought a remedy.

Just as I was going to grab a bottle of 409, it dawned on me. I dashed to the front door, opened it, and the bee flew out.

I plopped back down in my soy milk-soaked recliner and smiled, for my bee trouble suddenly reminded me of all the times my dad would laugh at me if a bee or spider wandered inside, and I'd start flailing. I then cried happy tears as the sound of Dad's laughter rang out in my memory.

I was content for those few moments, until I had to contend with the 12 mosquitoes and six moths that flew in when the bee flew out.

The message here is: let yourself grieve... and be mindful of what you wish for.

~Claire Mix

Grieving *and* *Recovery*

Across the Generations

63

The Funeral that Made a Family

It is never too late to give up our prejudices.
~Henry David Thoreau

He was the love of her life, but most of his family never knew she existed. They loved one another for more than 50 years, but they never married, never shared a home, never had a child together.

When they met, my grandmother was a pretty, lonely young widow with a toddler daughter (my mom) and he was a handsome, young bachelor who dated widely but had never found "the right one." From the beginning, they knew they had found something special. They knew they had discovered a lifetime love.

But there was a problem. A big one. She was from a strict Baptist home, and he was from a family of Jewish immigrants from the Old World. Their parents told them that if they married, they would not be their children anymore.

It was agonizing—they loved their families and they loved each other. They were told they had to choose. But how do you rip your heart in half? How do you tell your heart whom to love?

And so they lived more than five decades in a delicate balancing act—loving one another intensely yet never marrying and never living together. We, her family, knew him well. But most of his family never knew of her existence. They thought he was a lonely bachelor all his life. Those who did know never spoke of her.

They had great happiness. He was a gourmet cook who came over every Tuesday and Thursday to create an amazing meal. They were avid about fishing and spent one day every weekend in their boat on the lake. They took amazing trips every summer—they visited all the latest restaurants—they celebrated birthdays and "anniversaries" and holidays. For more than 50 years, they shared their lives and were happy.

But they also had the sadness of never being affirmed as a couple, of never sharing a home, of never sharing events with his family, of never having a child together. It hurt even after decades.

After 50 years of the same happiness and the same sadness, my grandmother passed away. Not long afterwards, her companion of a lifetime died as well.

Somehow, in the midst of his final days, his family learned about the great love of his life. Our two families came together at his funeral. They asked us to sit with them at the service and the burial. (The rabbi was confused but supportive.) Afterwards, we shared a meal. Around those tables, stories abounded. Having never known my grandmother, they had not really known him.

You didn't know that he loved to fish? Well, they went fishing together every week. Let me tell you about the time she caught the biggest fish. You didn't know he was a great cook? Well, let me tell you about his terrific spaghetti.

You never heard about their trips? Well, we have these great pictures of them down in Florida.

It was at the lunch that my young daughter Kate met his equally young grand-niece Abigail. They looked at each other curiously—two little girls in the midst of a room full of grown-ups.

They were shy at first. They were not sure how to get started being family with someone they'd never met before.

Then Abigail had an idea. "Would you like to see the doll I got for Hanukkah?" she asked. Kate nodded. The doll came out.

They began to play, quietly at first. Before long they were chasing one another through the room—shouting and laughing. Then they joined hands and started singing "Ring Around the Rosie." Round and round they twirled—smiling, giggling, and holding hands.

All of a sudden everything got quiet as every adult in the room noticed them. All the aunts and uncles and cousins and grandparents—those who had always known and those who had just found out. They all stopped and watched. Then they smiled. Then they laughed. After all those long years of being apart, two families had finally come together, all because of two little girls and a doll.

A decades-long love was finally complete.

Kate and Abigail are friends.

Kate and Abigail are family.

And now we all know.

~LeDayne McLeese Polaski

64

Phone Calls

The art of living lies less in eliminating our troubles
than in growing with them.
~Bernard M. Baruch

"Mom, Mom, wake up, Aunt Gloria is on the phone," said my daughter Jen as she shook me awake.

"Tell her I'll call her back. I don't want to talk now, it's late," I mumbled. I had fallen asleep during my favorite evening television show and didn't want any long conversation. I wanted to curl back up and retreat into my dreams.

"No," Jen insisted. "She said it was urgent." I reluctantly agreed to talk to her.

"Sallie, Mom is gone. I can't believe it. I just talked to her earlier this evening," my sister said.

"Gone where? What are you talking about?" I replied, yawning.

My brother-in-law, Ray, then got on the phone and said softly, "Sallie, your mom passed away about an hour ago and your dad is wandering around the hospital. We need to get there right away."

This couldn't be MY mother he was talking about. My mom was NEVER going to die. Who would comfort me, nurture me? Sure, I had my husband, but my mom was special. This was not supposed to happen until I was a very old person. I was only 44.

My husband came into the room and gently took the phone from my hand.

"We'll be there soon," he replied and hung up.

"Where are you going?" I asked, following him around like a lost puppy.

"To the hospital."

"But, you can't do that; I'll be here all by myself!"

"Then you can come with me, if you want," he said tenderly, putting on his jacket. In his wisdom, he knew better than to push me.

Reluctantly, I decided I would rather brave it at the hospital than stay home alone.

When we arrived I looked for my sister and her husband. Gloria rushed up to me and hugged me. I stood still, not yet comprehending how this nightmare had started.

"Like I said on the phone, I just talked to Mom about eight o'clock. I can't believe she's gone," Gloria said. "I need to see her. Come on, Sallie, let's go find her." And with that she took my arm and started leading me down the hallway.

"Wait! I don't want to see her," I said.

"Well, of course you do," my sister insisted. "You have to go say goodbye."

"No, I can't. I can't," I said, yanking my arm away from her.

"Well, I've never heard of someone not wanting to say goodbye to their mother," she fumed.

"Gloria, we all grieve in our own way," my brother-in-law counseled her. "Leave Sallie alone."

With that Gloria stomped off down the hall to find my mother. I leaned against a wall and started to sob. It hit me. My mom was dead.

"Sallie," my husband whispered, putting his arms around me, having witnessed the dialogue between my sis and me. "Your dad needs you. This is very hard on him too. Let's go see if we can find him."

I approached the nurse's station and announced who I was and asked where I could find my father.

"He's been wandering around here for at least an hour," the head nurse stated. "He seemed lost and couldn't remember any phone numbers. We found your sister's number in his wallet."

"Where is he?"

"In there," she said as she pointed down the corridor to heavy mahogany doors. "We thought the chapel was a good place for him to wait."

I dreaded seeing him. He was so emotional he choked up when he heard the National Anthem at baseball games. I didn't want to face him or his pain—our pain.

As I walked toward the chapel, I heard my mother's words coming back to me, "You're so your father's child. You have his brown eyes, dark hair and his strong determination. The day I found out I was pregnant with you, he was so happy he took me shopping and bought out the baby department."

As I neared the doors, I hesitated. In the last hour my world had turned upside down but I had to pull on my inner strength. I might not be able to see my mother lying still on a gurney but I could be there for my father.

I stopped as I turned the handle on the chapel door. I took a deep breath, as I whispered, "Come on, Mom. You're our guardian angel now. We'll take care of him together."

Easing my father's heartache became my goal over the next year. I knew he was hurting tremendously. He had cradled the love of his life in his arms as she suffered a massive coronary before the ambulance took her to the hospital.

We met often after the funeral and it was so awkward without Mom there. All my dad wanted to do was talk about the good old days. So I would sit and listen. I learned a lot about my parents and their life together. After our talks I would come home and draw a hot bath and sit in the bathtub sobbing. We were working through our pain together.

The first year was the worst: the first Christmas without Mom, my birthday without her homemade chocolate cake, and Mother's Day. No sharing the joy of my first grandchild or my son's wedding.

The old adage, "Time heals all wounds," wasn't working, at least it didn't seem that way. Then one day a few months later the phone rang.

"Hi honey. I um... um... wanted to run something by you," my dad said nervously.

"What's up, Dad?"

"Well, uh, I've met someone. Her name is Theresa and I'd like to take her out to dinner, nothing fancy mind you. But I didn't know how you'd feel about that. She would never take the place of your mom, you know that," he rambled on and on.

"Wow, Dad," I said, taken aback. I'd never even considered the possibility of this happening. I thought for a moment. "You know, Dad, no one should be lonely and I know she'll never replace Mom, so you go have a nice time."

"Thanks honey," he said, sounding relieved.

That's when I knew we had both started healing. I still think of my mom when I hear a special song she liked or something I wish I could tell her. She will always be in my heart, but we must continue living until the day we are together again.

~Sallie A. Rodman

65

Grandma on the Block

Anyone who says you can't see a thought simply doesn't know art.
~Wynetka Ann Reynolds

"Mrs. Woooolff!" I hear the cry as soon as I step outside. It comes from the three young sisters a few houses down. They pound up the street and stand in front of me, all smiles and news.

"I can ride my bike without falling!"

"I got a new backpack!"

"My favorite color is purple!"

I respond like any grandmother would: "How wonderful! Let me see! Purple is my favorite color, too!"

And it is appropriate that I do so. I have become an official Grandma on the Block for several kids. But for these girls I am more than that. I am like their substitute grandma. Their grandmother passed away last year after a long struggle with cancer and I was their Mom Mom's dear friend. She and I knew each other for 30 years. We wrote books, took classes, and meditated together. We celebrated family joys and sorrows with each other. I met the girls when they were newborn and followed their progress as my friend shared their baby steps taken, beginning words spoken, new skills acquired.

When my friend died, her oldest granddaughter started knocking on my door. She would hand me a picture she drew and then leave. The first picture was of two stick figures standing side by side. They were females, one a little larger than the other, looking forward.

There were no smiles, however, and other than a few sketchy wisps of hair and an inked line where a skirt might have been, no details.

My friend, this five-years-old's adored grandmother, was an artist and always said that her granddaughter had the gene passed on to her. The picture I saw was a simple one, the kind any young child would produce as she was learning to draw. It was black and white and, given the circumstances, sad. I thanked her and put it on my refrigerator door.

"You can come see it any time you want," I said.

She nodded, turned, and went back down the street.

The next week there was another knock and another drawing. Again there were the two figures, but this time they had hairstyles and a hint of a smile. I put it next to the first on the refrigerator. She seemed to like that.

Her sisters came with her the third time. They were too young to really understand the impact of their grandmother's passing; they just wanted to see if I still had the pictures. I did. And then I had another. This time the figures were in full dress and seemed to be holding hands. I could see the artistic potential now that my friend had noticed.

The intervals between drawings lengthened but the knocks became more frequent. The girls came to visit my pet cockatiel Eloise. Sometimes one or another would come by just to say hello—and to check out the refrigerator door.

Over the course of the year there were more drawings. If I was out, I would find one slipped under the welcome mat, a corner peeking beyond the grassy edge. By the end of the year I had a handful of drawings on the door. I could see the progress of grief being worked out, one picture at a time. We never discussed her grandmother but the drawings showed her emotions.

In the last picture she gave me, the two figures were clothed and smiling. There were flowers all around and the sun was beaming at the top of the picture, its rays spread out in all directions. I think those drawings allowed me to deal with the grief I was feeling, too. As I watched my friend's granddaughter grapple with her sadness I could empathize and work on my own. Being the grandma on the block helped both of us.

Today she came scooting up on her pink bike to tell me about her trip to Disneyland. It sounded like she had fun. I was glad.

~Ferida Wolff

Gracie's Angels

I brought children into this dark world
because it needed the light that only a child can bring.
~Liz Armbruster, on robertbrault.com

Three weeks after finding out his next great-grandchild was on the way, my grandfather stepped into heaven. I cried, naturally, but for some reason, the "big tears" just wouldn't come. Odd for me, because I was pregnant and extremely hormonal! I rationalized to myself that since I was a nurse, I had seen Papaw Billy's suffering; therefore, I knew he was in a much better place. I focused all my attention first of all on the funeral plans, and then after the funeral was over, I concentrated on making sure my grandmother was taken care of.

Almost five months after the funeral, my daughter and I were swimming in the pool when my husband called me inside. Our beloved Maltese, Gracie, had jumped off the couch and wouldn't walk. She wasn't crying or whimpering; she just refused to walk. I asked my husband to take her to the vet. I kissed her little nose, and told her, "Girl, you'd better be okay, because I don't think I could handle it if something happened to you." She looked at me with the saddest little brown eyes as if telling me that she was sorry.

I got the call from my husband, who was crying. He said that she had broken her back and needed to be put to sleep. I told him to go ahead because I couldn't bear the thought of her being in pain.

I hung up the phone and wondered how I would break the news

to my five-year-old, Shelby, who thought Gracie hung the moon. I took her into my bedroom and told her that Gracie had gone to heaven to play with Papaw Billy. Shelby took the news well; her little lips quivered and she cried a bit. Nothing like me, however. I was practically hysterical. Being six months pregnant by then, I knew that getting that upset couldn't be good for me, but I was inconsolable. When I could finally speak, I asked Shelby if she'd like to see little Gracie before her dad buried her. Surprisingly, she said she would.

My husband brought Gracie home wrapped up in a navy blue towel. We placed her on the floor and unwrapped her. She looked so peaceful, just like she was asleep. Shelby studied her for a minute, and then decided we would have a funeral for Gracie. My husband went outside to dig her grave. I just sat on the floor holding Gracie and crying.

When the time came, we trooped outside. My grandmother who lives next door came and joined our solemn processional. I handed Gracie to my husband and he laid her to rest beside Gus, our Yorkie who had died the year before. Shelby bowed her little head and said, "God, please ask Papaw Billy to take care of Gracie. She's the best dog in the world. Amen." I took Shelby's hand and started to walk away, but she hesitated, pulling me back. I didn't want to watch my husband put the dirt on my beautiful white dog, and I certainly didn't want Shelby to see it. I kept telling Shelby, "Let's go inside. Let Dad finish." Shelby looked up in the sky and said, "Here they come! The angels are coming to get Gracie!" At that very moment, a gentle breeze picked up. We stood silently watching Shelby. She continued to look at the sky, and then finally she said, "Okay, now we can go. Gracie is with the angels and she's going to play with Papaw Billy." My grandmother began to cry softly and nodded her head as if to agree with her.

Not long after that sad little funeral in our yard, I took Shelby to the library. She picked out a book called *Dog Heaven*. When we got home, we settled down to read it and on the first page, we saw a picture of a small white dog surrounded by angels. I immediately began to tear up, but Shelby just looked at me in the way that only a very smart five-year-old can and told me, "See Mom!! I told you the angels came to get Gracie!" As we continued to read the book, we saw a picture of an old man sitting on a cloud playing with the white dog. Shelby smiled knowingly and said, "And look Mom, there's Papaw Billy, playing with Gracie!"

Our family still grieves the loss of our beloved Papaw Billy and our little furry Gracie. We've since had several additions to our family, including a new baby girl and a new dog, that Shelby appropriately named Angel. We still visit the two tiny graves marked by two hand-carved crosses, and when we feel the gentle breeze ruffle our hair as we stand silently, I thank God for the faith of a small child and her words of comfort at a time when I needed them the most.

~Mandi Cooper Cumpton

Lillian's Daughter

The past is never dead, it is not even past.
~William Faulkner

Some months after my mother died, I was at the fish counter of her local supermarket, the place where she had always bought tiny amounts of fish for herself with the greatest concentration and intensity. The counterman had become something of a friend.

"So how's Mom doing? I haven't seen her in a while," he asked as he handed over my salmon and tilapia.

And there I stood, hand outstretched for my package, speechless. Despite how calm and collected I'd felt that afternoon, I dissolved into tears. "She died in December," I said, and bolted.

It was another of those post-loss ambushes that seemed to come in a steady, pummeling stream for those who are new at grieving. I could have—should have—expanded on my answer. Explained more gently. But that explaining was somehow just too daunting on an ordinary Tuesday afternoon when I had let down my guard.

I have had so many of those moments. And so, I'm sure, has anyone who's ever grieved for a loved one.

For me, the worst moments would come as dusk settled, the time when I would invariably be on the kitchen phone calling Mom on hers. Our conversations were so insignificant, so non-cosmic. They were about what each of us was making for dinner, about the weather, about the kids, the grandkids, and in her case the great-grandkids.

Nobody could have prepared me for the excruciating pain I felt in those early days when I reached for the phone... remembered... and stopped.

I would have given anything to hear my mother's voice, her laugh, even her grumbling about this or that. It was the "never again" part that was so overwhelming.

I spent days, weeks and probably months reviewing my sins of omission and commission in my relationship with Mom. I lamented the times I didn't visit her, take her grocery shopping, spend a Sunday afternoon keeping her company in her apartment when the weather, or her infirmities, made it impossible for a lady in her late nineties to go out.

The most overwhelming thing about loss is that there's no going back. No replaying the tape. It is what it is.

So when grief was still raw and new, there was that hollow feeling of guilt, especially in early morning or in the dark of night, and when I talked about it to my husband or my daughters, they assured me that I had been a good daughter, that I had done enough. How I wish I could have believed them.

But guilt is the handmaiden of death. Just ask anyone who's done that inevitable litany of "I should haves."

I adored my mother. But like most mothers and daughters, we had our differences and occasionally, our epic battles—many more when we were both younger and more volatile. We were very much alike, and that made our connection deeper—and more fragile.

The months—and now three years—have passed. I am no longer nearly as lost and sad as I was just after her graveside funeral, and through the Jewish custom of "sitting Shiva," receiving friends and family for that first week as we remembered and grieved together.

That earliest mourning left me dazed, drained and yes, relieved that Mom's struggle was over. Her last weeks were difficult, and in dark dreams, they return to me. My daughters tell me that they've had those dreams, too. Bedside vigils linger in the marrow, maybe forever.

One of the early hurdles was the final closing of Mom's apartment in a Philadelphia high-rise, the apartment that still carried her sweet smell in its walls. Going there for the inevitable cleanout was beyond painful. Just opening the door to that world, with the familiar furniture in place, the familiar pictures on the wall, the books, the amiable clutter, turned into a grotesque parody without my little blond mother there to greet us.

I still wince when somebody I haven't had contact with for these last years asks how Mom is doing.

I still sob when I hear certain music that reminds me of her, or when I come upon a note in her familiar handwriting. Those are the "gotcha" moments.

Grief, I am learning, is no neat process. And there are sometimes no words for the feelings.

But I count it as a blessing that I have absorbed this loss, and that the transition finally came when I realized that I am still Lillian's daughter, even though she is not here. I am still part of her, just as she is part of me—and always will be.

Sorrow is a wild and primitive place, and there are no neat schedules as to when it releases its grip.

It is a long and difficult journey, one that each of us must take alone.

But with it comes growth, wisdom, learning, healing and yes, that phase the experts call "acceptance."

Yes, I am still Lillian's daughter.

And so enormously proud to be.

~Sally Schwartz Friedman

68

New Englander at Heart

Tomorrow hopes we have learned something from yesterday.
~John Wayne

It was an evening in March 2002 when my dad called to report my 80-year-old grandfather was having problems. A few months earlier, Gramps, as we called him, had been in an auto accident. Luckily no one was injured. However, Gramps lost his license. My grandmother passed away many years ago, but Gramps still lived in that old farmhouse outside Merrimack, New Hampshire where he had been born in 1922. It was obvious that he couldn't continue to live alone way out in the boondocks, so my dad decided Gramps would sell his property and move somewhere where his lack of transportation wouldn't be an issue.

My parents had divorced in 1981 and my father had remarried and moved to Florida. My younger sister was a graduate student at Dartmouth. My older sister was married, living in Boston with her husband and twin toddlers.

It was decided, and not by unanimous vote, that Gramps should live with me—just for a short while.

I had been close with Gramps when I was younger. He let me stay at his farm for two weeks every summer when I was a kid. I remember rides on his tractor and picking apples in his orchard. Sometimes we went camping at Lake Winnipesaukee.

As I grew older, I got busy with college, then took a teaching position at a university in New York State and only talked to Gramps on the phone. I was living in Buffalo, New York, and whenever I called, Gramps would always ask how things were going "down south" even though I lived even farther north than he did, on the Canadian border!

To both our surprise, in July 2002, Gramps relocated to my two-bedroom townhouse apartment.

He was not happy.

He wanted to stay in Merrimack where he had lived all his life. Merrimack, he claimed, was an hour from Boston if he needed anything from the city, an hour from the White Mountains if he needed anything from nature, and an hour from the seacoast if he needed a ship to get out of the country.

Almost worse than his homesickness was his immediate boredom.

"I'm a New Englander," he would tell me. "I can't sit around all day watching TV and playing solitaire!"

So I got him a part-time job as a greeter at Walmart where he stood at the front of the store, smiled and said: "Hello! How about that weather? Do you need a shopping cart today?"

It was a job he was born to do.

Whether working or not, Gramps was still getting up at five o'clock every morning to cook bacon and eggs over easy; a real "New England breakfast" he called it, as if no one else in America ate bacon and eggs.

When I was a kid, it had been fun to get up with Gramps as the sun was rising. As an adult, I was used to sleeping late and rushing to make it to classes on time.

But with Gramps I was awake at five o'clock, even during semester breaks, and I never needed my alarm clock. I actually did get a lot more work done and was better prepared for class each day.

And then there were the cats. I had noticed a group of stray cats around the apartment complex. I'd see them climbing on the garbage dumpster or heard them fighting at night, but I never paid much attention.

Gramps adopted them.

The huge gray cat with the crooked ear is Zeus. Atlas is the black one who walks with a limp. And the calico is named Athena.

Zeus, Atlas and Athena. Did I mention Gramps was a fan of Greek mythology?

The cats wouldn't eat canned food. We tried a variety of flavors, like Ocean Whitefish and Turkey with Giblets, but they wouldn't touch it. Every morning Gramps shared his bacon and eggs; then for dinner they got chicken livers cut into tiny bite-size pieces. So besides taking him to work, Gramps needed rides to the butcher shop once a week to get fresh chicken livers.

Often, in the evenings, Gramps would watch John Wayne movies. Gramps professed that John Wayne was the best actor ever and he was sure the man was a New Englander. I didn't have the heart to tell him John Wayne was born in California.

Now the agreement was, while my father looked into some other long-term options, Gramps was going to stay with me for a short while. To me, a "short while" is ten days, five weeks, maybe six months. I'm sure six months is the maximum cut off for a "short while." But four years later, Gramps was still living with me.

On a rainy Sunday night in early September 2006, Gramps turned off the movie *Rio Lobo* and sat down across from me at the kitchen table where I was grading tests. He cleared his throat loudly.

"What do you need, Gramps?" I asked without looking up.

"I believe there's something I've never told you," he said. "And I need to say it."

I sat back and took off my glasses. "Okay."

"I am blessed," he replied, nodding his head. "Truly blessed. Do you know why?"

"Because you have the complete set of John Wayne movies on DVD?" I replied.

"No." Gramps chuckled. "I'm blessed because I have you. You're a good grandson. I don't recall I ever told you that."

I smiled. "Thanks. I'm blessed with a good grandfather."

"You know, I was worried when I first moved here that I'd miss

New Hampshire too much to be happy. But I discovered something important."

"What's that?" I asked.

"Being a New Englander isn't about where you live." Gramps pointed to his chest. "It's about what's inside. Even if I'm not in Merrimack, I'm still a New Englander at heart."

"That's good to know, Gramps."

"I thank God for blessing me with two things," he said. "I was born a New Englander and I have you. I'm a lucky man."

Then he got up and went to bed.

And that was it, almost as if Gramps had planned it.

The next morning I woke up just after six o'clock. I had to look at the clock twice before I could believe the time. I hadn't slept that late in four years.

I lay in bed and listened: no rattling pans, no sizzling bacon.

I shuffled into the kitchen. Three cats sat by the refrigerator waiting for breakfast. Zeus meowed loudly.

The church was packed for Gramps' funeral.

My dad and his wife showed up along with my sisters. The manager from Walmart, the cats' veterinarian and the butcher were there too.

I still felt lonely.

Now I live alone again.

Alone, with three cats. They continue to sleep on Gramps' bed, although if I sleep too late they wake me. Whenever I think the apartment is too quiet I put on a John Wayne movie for company.

At the funeral, my father pulled me aside and said, "I appreciate all you did for your grandfather. I hope he wasn't too unhappy, being away from Merrimack and all."

"Don't worry," I told him. "Spending the time together helped Gramps and me realize something important. We were actually blessed with each other."

~David Hull

69

Dancing into Heaven

Even if happiness forgets you a little bit, never completely forget about it.
~Jacques Prévert

M ost of us are not afraid of death; we are simply afraid of dying. Will it be an ordeal for ourselves and those who love us? Working with Hospice and sitting with family members during their last days has taught me that we die the way we live. Those who live courageous lives face death with the same positive energy. Sharing their dying can be a rare privilege.

Such an experience impacted my life profoundly when I had the honor of being with my 94-year-old uncle until he drew his last, peaceful breath. My uncle was an advocate of Dr. Norman Vincent Peale's philosophy and practiced it to the end of his long, successful life.

Uncle Ray outlived my Aunt Maude by ten years. After 55 years of marriage, the family was concerned about his living alone. It was unwarranted. He lived those next ten years fully and without self-pity or complaint. Although his adopted son died at two years of age, he had a close, loving family of nieces and nephews.

His quality of life was exceptional. Two months before his death, he was still playing golf — only nine holes and no longer counting strokes — but thoroughly enjoying the beautiful golf course and blue Florida sky overhead. His mind was sharp and clear, and he retained his curiosity about life. A year earlier he had called me and said, "I'm thinking about getting a computer. Now I want you to tell me the truth. Am I too old? And am I smart enough?" I assured him he was not too old and definitely smart enough. We e-mailed one another from then on.

His wonderful caregiver came every day from 5:00 to 7:00 to cook for him. On Thursdays, she spent all day with him, running errands and weather permitting, playing golf with him. She was a godsend in his life.

During the summer of 2004, he had a few minor health problems and spent time in the hospital. Needing to get his strength back, he entered a rehabilitation center. When he was ready to come home, I traveled to Florida to help him do so. Two days after my arrival, however, he became ill with an infection and had to go back into the hospital. To the family's dismay, a downward spiral began that ended in his death three weeks later. Those weeks will remain in my mind and heart for the rest of my life.

I think of it as a sad but extraordinary time. Sad because he was dying, and there were some difficult hours; special because of who he was and how he handled the last days of his life.

There were touching moments I will never forget. He would quietly sing to himself. He would give himself pep talks, saying, "C'mon boy, you can do it." One afternoon, while we both rested, I heard him say, "Things always seem to work out in the end."

There were difficult moments, a few hours of pain when he asked me to hold his hand, and we prayed together until the medication took effect. I told him I wouldn't leave his side and that he didn't have to be afraid. He smiled and said, "I'm not afraid." When it came to positive thinking, he walked his talk.

About a week before he died, while he was still perfectly alert and coherent, we were sitting together in the twilight of his hospital room, talking about this and that. Suddenly I heard the word, "Maude."

"What did you say?" I asked him.

"I saw Maude," he responded.

I asked, tentatively, "You mean in a dream?"

He hesitated and said, slowly, "Well, I guess you could call it a dream."

He paused. "No, it was real. I reached out and touched her. I could feel her. It was real."

I waited. Finally, he continued, "She wore a long, pink dress. She was tall and slim, and she was beautiful!" He added, "She wanted to dance."

I remembered how much he and Aunt Maude had loved to dance.

"Uncle Ray," I said, "when Aunt Maude comes again, I think you should dance with her."

I went home that night full of the joy and light of their love.

The last four days were spent at a hospice facility. The loving care of the staff comforted me as much as him. My chair by his bed opened up into a chaise lounge. A CD played soothing music. Family continued to call every day and tell him that they loved him. He slowly withdrew from us, however, his eyes staring toward the ceiling, appearing to be listening intently and talking to others invisible to us. When I spoke to him, he would smile politely and listen, but eventually his eyes would shift as though seeing someone behind me. I felt as though I had interrupted an important conversation.

The last day, he slept deeply. I read passages from my hospice book and the Bible, encouraging him to look for and relax into the light. He waited until his dear caregiver joined me that afternoon. Ten minutes later, as we stood on each side of his bed, he took one quick breath and never took another. It was so peaceful that neither of us could believe he was gone.

I shall always be grateful for the privilege of sharing those last weeks with my uncle. As I told a friend, Uncle Ray taught me how to live, then he taught me how to die, and then he danced with Aunt Maude into heaven!

~Libby Grandy

Nancy

A hug is a great gift — one size fits all, and it's easy to exchange.
~Author Unknown

When I was ten years old, my mother needed a babysitter for me. She was still at work for a few hours after I got home from school. The only person available in the neighborhood was an old lady named Nancy, and at the time I was terrified of her. She was grumpy and hated everyone. None of the neighborhood kids could get too close to her yard or she'd come out screaming. We couldn't even play ball anywhere near her house because if the ball happened to land in her yard, we knew it was gone forever. I tried to avoid this woman at all costs.

When my mother broke the news to me that Nancy would be my new babysitter, I cried. I thought I had done something wrong.

When that first day with Nancy came, I didn't want to leave school. The bus dropped me off at the end of the street and I walked as slowly as I could up to her door. Before I got to it, she was already standing in the doorway. She opened her screen door, let me in, and said, "Take off your shoes and leave them right there. Let me take your jacket, I'm going to hang it on the back of the sofa." And that was it. She went and sat down at her kitchen table, put her oxygen mask on and lit a cigarette.

Whenever I passed by Nancy's house, I always saw her sitting at that kitchen table with a cigarette in her hand and her oxygen tank next to her. The table was centered in front of her sliding glass doors so she could stare outside. Her living room TV was also positioned so that she could clearly see it from the kitchen. I figured this was her way of watching her afternoon soap operas while still being able to patrol her yard to make sure no sneaky little kids came around.

That first day at Nancy's house was scary. She made me sit at the kitchen table with her and do my homework right away. She set down the rules for me and demanded that I abide by them. My homework came first every day, I couldn't swear, couldn't interrupt her while her soaps were on, and couldn't complain about the smell of her cooking.

This same process went on every day. I came home from school to the smell of her dinner simmering on the stove, she took my coat while I took my shoes off, and I did my homework as soon as I sat down. I abided by every single rule and I was very polite when I spoke.

One day, I came home from school crying. This boy in my class was moving away and I was devastated because I thought I was madly in love with him. Nancy was at the door like usual, waiting to take my coat. When I came in, she took it and placed it on the couch. She asked me what was wrong and led me into the kitchen to our usual seats.

I was crying too much to talk so I didn't tell her why I was sad. She just gave me a hug and held onto me. She rubbed my back and assured me that all things happen for a good reason and that when my pain passed, I'd be a stronger person.

After that, Nancy and I began to talk more and more every day after I finished my homework. I told her everything and she told me things the way they really were. She spoke her mind as honestly as possible and sometimes she cussed like a sailor while doing so. But I respected that. Nancy taught me the meaning of honesty. She also started to let me taste that food she was always making.

I began to stay at Nancy's house even after my mother came home from work. I liked her. She was fun to talk to and her house always smelled good, so I stayed there instead of going home most days.

Then one day, I saw something on the kitchen table that was not normally there. There was her usual crossword book, a pen, and her ashtray, but there was also a small stack of papers. When I asked her what it was, she told me it was her "will." She explained to me that a will was basically a bunch of papers that said where her stuff would go when she died.

I got worried and asked her if she was dying. She laughed and said, "No, not yet, but I can't wait for the day. If it ever comes, don't try to save me." Then I decided to ask her about her oxygen tank. I knew what it was because it said "oxygen" right on it, but I didn't know what it was for. Nancy told me she had a disease called emphysema, a lung disease that makes it difficult to breathe.

Hearing this, I was baffled and upset. I asked her why she smoked. Nancy said, "Honey, when I die, I want to die happy. Cigarettes and soap operas make me happy. I'd like to die right here with everything I love. My chair, my soaps, and a cigarette burning in my hand."

That was one small conversation we had among many for months to come. Nancy became my best friend. She taught me to do what makes me happy and not take anyone's crap. She told me she trusted me with her life. She always told my mother, "I can put a thousand dollars in front of her and walk away. She won't touch a dime of it. I trust her with anything." She was right. I wouldn't have touched a dime of it, and I was finally glad someone appreciated that about me.

One day when I got out of school, I noticed one small change in Nancy's house. She came and greeted me as usual, took my coat, and helped me get my homework out. But I didn't smell anything. She had always eaten the strangest foods and it always excited me to wonder what I'd smell that day. But today, there was nothing cooking on the stove and no smell at all. I didn't ask her about it; I just figured that maybe she was ordering out for once.

When all my homework was out, we both sat down. Nancy lit a cigarette and turned to watch her soaps while I started to look over my homework.

When a commercial came on, Nancy put her cigarette in the

ashtray and put her head down on the table. Usually when she did this, she asked me for a quick shoulder massage, so I got ready and said, "Nance?" She didn't say anything, and when I said her name again, she fell to the floor beside my feet. Her face was pale and her eyes open.

I began to cry and scream as I jumped up. I ran next door and pounded on the neighbor's door. A girl I hung out with, Alysha, answered the door. I was in a panic and she couldn't understand me when I asked for the phone. I tried to say "Nancy" and when I did, she understood. We called an ambulance and then our parents.

The entire neighborhood was outside to see what was happening. When everyone noticed my hysterical crying and the ambulance crew entering Nancy's house, looks of horror struck their faces. My mother hadn't known exactly why I called her because I was difficult to understand, but she knew when she found me outside in Alysha's arms.

Nancy died that day. Sometimes I wish I had called the ambulance from her house, rather than Alysha's, so they could have instructed me on how to resuscitate her. But then I remembered what she said about not wanting to be saved from death and wanting to die with everything she loved. She was watching her soap operas and smoking a cigarette while sitting in that favorite chair of hers. But I was there too. And now I realize that I was a part of that group, the group of things she loved. Nancy loved her chair, her soaps, her cigarettes, and she loved me.

~Shaylene McPhee

71

A Gift of Time

The human spirit is stronger than anything that can happen to it.
~C.C. Scott

During the second week of January 2001, my mother became very ill and was rushed to the Red Deer Hospital, and was subsequently transferred to a hospital in Edmonton, Alberta. After a six-year battle with cancer, my mother's specialist held her hand, as he told her there was nothing else he could do to help prolong her life. This caring doctor told my mother she had the choice of being hooked up to a dialysis machine for the last few months of her life, or as an alternative, could simply go home. He advised my mother that without any medical assistance, she would possibly survive another month.

Before making her decision to leave the hospital, my mother asked my eldest sister Karen if it would be possible for someone to care for her, if she decided to return home. Karen consulted with all of us and my brothers, sisters and I made the decision to take this on as a team effort: we would all be caregivers during our mother's final days. My youngest sister Kim and I had already taken a break from work; my eldest sister—a nurse—arranged for a month's leave of absence and three of my brothers adjusted their work schedules so that we were all available to provide homecare for our mother.

Before my mother returned home, my brother Kevin arranged for delivery of a hospital bed; furniture was rearranged in her wee den, and within hours my mother's home was transformed into an environment that could accommodate her care. On the day the Edmonton hospital transported my mother back to Red Deer, two of my brothers and I stood at the front door of my mother's house as the ambulance arrived, waiting to welcome her home.

What do you say to someone who is dying? How do you greet them each morning and how do you say good night? What do you talk about during their lucid hours? I don't think any of us had thought about this until the ambulance arrived and the porters carried our mother into her home and placed her in the new hospital bed. I can still visualize my mother reclined in the bed, looking at her adult children sitting all around her. It was our mother who spoke first. She simply said, "Well, what do we do now?" Then she laughed. In our nervousness we all laughed too, and from that moment, we learned to cope with the situation one day at a time.

During her first week home from the hospital, our mother's local doctor assisted her with a living will, including a do not resuscitate order that we had to post on the wall. Mother decided to arrange her funeral and took careful consideration of where she was to be buried, ordered the urn and selected the hymns for her service. Our mother also asked us to arrange for all of her grandchildren to visit, before her health deteriorated to the point of making their visits too stressful. I can still envision Mother holding my nephew Bobby, as he lay sobbing on her chest, while she stroked his back and murmured how much she loved him.

My husband and our children, Michelle and Andrew, visited my mother one evening and it was painful to watch them both cry as they said goodbye. I clearly remember how Andrew's tiny body shook as he sobbed in my arms. Michelle returned on another day to spend an afternoon with her grandmother, and I stood outside the door to my mother's den watching them both deeply absorbed in conversation. There was no thought of what might happen in days to follow; they were simply enjoying each other's company. It was a very touching sight.

The weeks passed quickly and with help from Alberta Home Care, visits from our mother's local doctor, her minister, friends and neighbours, we managed to get through the good and the bad days. Each of my siblings took on a specific role during the last month of our mother's life. My eldest sister Karen was our mother's nurse; my older brother Keith cooked and brought us our evening meal on a daily basis; brothers Kevin and Kelly performed all the errands related to our mother's pending funeral and service; my youngest sister Kim took care of the laundry, and my role was "miscellaneous activities" that included massaging my mother's feet every afternoon.

While growing up, Mother had "trained" all of her children how to massage her feet. Although all my siblings attempted to avoid this task as much as possible throughout their youth, I had always found it to be the best way to have quality time with my mother. Consequently, this became one of my duties during the last month of our mother's life.

On a sunny afternoon several days before my mother died, I started massaging her feet and we began to talk about many things we hadn't discussed in years; we talked, and talked, and talked. At one point during our conversation, I remember caressing my mother's feet while thinking about how beautiful they were—such tiny, perfectly formed, unblemished feet. I massaged my mother's feet for hours, until she drifted off into an afternoon nap.

When she woke from her nap, Mother discussed how it was her desire that we prepare her body for the funeral home after she died. I stood in stunned silence while my mother explained that after we prepared her body for the journey to the funeral home, she had made arrangements for an immediate cremation once her body was placed in the hands of the mortuary staff. Unknown to us at the time, our mother had completed her final preparations. Three days later she deteriorated very quickly and on a Sunday afternoon, with all her children gathered around her, our mother drifted into a coma that lasted only a few hours. Our mother left this world just the way she planned to, with all her children gathered around her, while she quietly took her last breath of life.

My brother Kevin telephoned the doctor and minister and they quickly arrived at her house. After the doctor examined Mother's body and signed the death certificate, and the minister said a prayer, they left us alone with her.

My brothers then left the room, so that my sisters and I could prepare our mother's body for the funeral home, just the way she had asked us to. We washed her body, each of us taking turns gently cleaning her face, neck and chest. I remember washing her hands and thinking that my mother had melted away into a tiny woman, a mere shell of the woman she was just a month before. I massaged her beautiful feet one last time, before helping my sisters dress her in one of her favourite outfits. We then combed Mother's hair and asked our brothers to come back into the room for one last goodbye.

My eldest brother Keith had already arranged for the funeral home to transport Mother's body and the funeral home van arrived about a half hour after we had finished cleansing and dressing her. When the funeral home staff walked into the den, they were shocked to see an immaculately dressed elderly lady propped up in bed, appearing as if she had just closed her eyes for a moment. We quickly explained the situation and the funeral home staff made every attempt to be respectful and caring while they transferred our mother into the van.

Similar to the way my siblings and I greeted our mother the day she arrived home from the hospital, we stood in her front doorway watching her leave home for the very last time.

As traumatic as our mother's homecare was for all of us, I'm aware that like me, each of my siblings has personal and special memories of various events during the last month of our mother's life. I'm sure we will cherish these individual memories for the rest of our lives. On reflection, we had a full month to say goodbye to our mother, each in our own way. It was truly a gift of time.

~Kathy Dickie

72

The Miracle of the Easter Pies

You give but little when you give of your possessions.
It is when you give of yourself that you truly give.
~Kahlil Gibran

Twelve years ago, my mother-in-law, then age 78, went in for open-heart surgery. She suffered complications, and on a sweltering day in late June, she passed away.

My wife and I drove from the cemetery to her one-bedroom apartment in Brooklyn and started to go through her belongings. We scoured her drawers, cabinets and shelves, poring over her clothes, photos and mementoes, deciding what to keep, give away or throw out, and were almost finished. Antoinette—or Nettie, as everyone called her—had lived on little her whole life, so we expected no hidden fortunes. But how mistaken we were. We opened the freezer and looked in, and there were her pies.

It was quite a find. In early spring every year, Nettie would make an announcement. "I'm making the Easter pies," she would say. "Going to be busy, so nobody bother me."

The pie was an Italian specialty called pizza rustica. Her mother had once made the same pies from a recipe her family brought to America from Naples. Little Antoinette watched her mother prepare the pies for Holy Saturday, slicing the smoked ham and hot sausage into bits, filling the dish with fresh ricotta and Romano cheeses, brushing the beaten egg wash onto the crust to give it a glaze.

Nettie made 15 or 20 pies every April for more than 40 years. Her mother had handed down her recipe, but Nettie never looked at the sheet of paper, every spring making up the proportions in her head all over again. I can imagine her standing in the kitchen pressing the dough with a rolling pin, her cheeks smudged with flour, her fine hair in disarray.

The pies came out looking like two-inch-thick omelettes—stuffed with cheese and flecked with meat, all topped by a heavy, flaky, dimpled crust baked golden brown. Nettie wrapped the pies in foil and labeled each for its intended recipient (the size of the pie you got was a measure of her affection for you). Her doorbell would start ringing at noon as relatives came from all over New York City and Long Island to collect this family dividend.

Now we had discovered that Nettie saved a few wedges of the pie, including one for herself, labeled "Nettie" (as if even in her own home, she had needed to earmark her handiwork for herself). My wife and I looked at each other in surprise, saying nothing. Then we reached into the icy mist and took out the pies one by one, putting each in a plastic bag.

In moments, we left her apartment for the last time and walked out into the hot, still afternoon for the drive home, holding the pies as tenderly as we might an urn.

That Sunday night, as we gathered at the dining room table with our 15-year-old son and 10-year-old daughter in our home in Forest Hills, my wife served us one of the pies, steaming hot and giving off a savory aroma. She sliced a wedge for each of us, and we ate silently, scraping our plates for crumbs.

I'd eaten my mother-in-law's pies every spring for more than 20 years, and they always tasted good. But now the pie tasted better than it ever had, as if somehow flavored by the tears of our grief. With each bite I recalled with fresh clarity everything Nettie had meant to all of us over the years—how she had raised her daughter without a husband around, all while toiling as a seamstress in a factory, and especially how she had lavished love and attention on both her adoring grandchildren.

I'd never felt so grateful to anyone. Eating the pie that night felt almost sacramental, as if I could actually taste her kind and generous spirit.

Afterwards, my wife waved us all into the kitchen. She opened the door to our freezer and pointed toward the back. And there it was: one last slice of the pie, the one that was labeled "Nettie." "This one I'm saving," she said.

And so she has. And there Nettie's pie remains, untouched, unseen, but never forgotten. Other families leave behind insurance policies or furniture or jewelry, but Nettie left us her pie. That single slice will serve as heirloom enough, and feed our hearts year-round, giving us all the Easter we'll ever need.

~Bob Brody

Grieving and Recovery

New Beginnings

73

First Day

I may not be there yet, but I'm closer than I was yesterday.
~Author Unknown

My daughter Elisa recently e-mailed me pictures of her daughter Gillian smiling and ready for her first day of school. I'm certain my granddaughter hugged her mom goodbye with fear and excitement and walked away into a brand new world, just as Elisa hugged me about 25 years ago. But I wonder what Elisa did after Gillian disappeared into that swarm of first-day students? She probably choked back a tear and marveled at how quickly the time had gone: all those natural and sentimental feelings of parenthood.

The day I dropped Elisa off for her first day of school I returned to a quiet and empty house for the first time in my life. I'd been raised in the crowded, loud and rollicking house of Irish immigrants. A brother or cousins or neighbors or a priest or aunts and uncles were always eating and drinking at our kitchen table. I married young and had five children of my own, the best way, rapid fire, so you can deal with them when you're young and energetic and stupid. But then my wife died (of a rare, quick, and deadly cancer) and I was now widowed and young and sad and stupid. The eldest was ten when Luanne died and Elisa was three and I was busier than a one-legged man in a butt-kicking contest waiting tables and wiping noses and helping with homework and driving to soccer games and cooking and trying to finish my first novel.

Thank God for that hurricane of confusion. If I had time to deal with the dread and perplexity of facing a life, alone, with five children I probably would have given up. But if you have kids you can't give up.

I remember when Elisa was about Gillian's age she woke me up at two in the morning. She stood in front of me in the half-light of the bedroom. Her hair was mussed and her Flintstone pajamas were rumpled. She had been crying. In a voice that barely trembled she said, "I can't remember what Mommy looked like."

I didn't say a word. At that moment her grief was inconsolable. The world had snatched another thing from her: Luanne's face no longer existed as a ready and reliable memory. For Elisa the time to cry and say goodbye to her mother wasn't at the official funeral, but in her pajamas on a warm August night 25 months later. On this night, with Elisa, I did the only thing a father can possibly do in this situation.

I made hot chocolate.

Elisa was sitting on my lap, drinking her chocolate, when I asked her if she wanted to look at some pictures of her mother. She nodded a silent yes. As I rummaged in the closet for photo albums I wondered if I were doing the right thing. At times it had been comforting to look at old pictures and re-read poetry I had written for Luanne. At other times it was like picking a scab.

But Elisa and I sat down on the kitchen floor and soon—it would have been sooner, but I spilled my hot chocolate—pictures were scattered all around us. Elisa latched onto a picture of Luanne holding our older daughter Rachel. "That's me, huh Dad?"

I couldn't lie, "No, Ellie, it's not."

She asked, "Can I have this picture?"

I said yes and she walked to the refrigerator, grabbed a magnet and positioned the picture halfway up the door. She returned, kissed me and hiked off to bed. It didn't matter to Elisa that she wasn't the baby in her mother's arms. There was something in the image: Luanne's eyes, her hair, the way she held the child, that resurrected the spirit and memory of her dead mother. All the kids had their moments like this while dealing with their mother's death.

My moment was Elisa's first day of school.

I dropped her off and returned to a house strewn not only with five children's detritus but with the overwhelming fact that I was alone. Not suddenly, but finally, the grief had me to itself. Man, it hurt. It hurt beyond pain and tears; it ached to the point of surrender.

You can delay grief with activities or chemicals, but you cannot deny it forever unless you choose not to heal it. Elisa's first day of school was also the first day I faced, and precisely the time I began to mend, the actual and excruciating emotion surrounding the death of the woman I loved.

~Rob Loughran

74

In My Hands

I know not what the future holds, but I know who holds the future.
~Author Unknown

It's 5 a.m. here in Alberta and the household is asleep. I am not. I am visiting my sister and brother-in-law, and being with them is like being inside a wonderful, accepting, loving hug. They are very good to me and I feel so at home with them. Can it only have been two weeks since my beloved passed away? It feels like forever, and it feels like a heartbeat, and time seems irrelevant.

I find myself in a strange place in my life. After 31 years of marriage I am alone for the first time. I went from my parents' home to my first, brief, teenaged marriage. When that ended I still had my daughters to care for. Then I married my late husband. And now? It's just me. I have never been "just me." I was always a part of something bigger. I have never been "manless." I have no idea who I am or what I want in life. I cannot fathom being single, or worse, ever being in a position of trying to find a good man again. If that ever happens.

I feel like I am in a big ocean on a little raft, and the waves are getting choppy. I have no idea what to do with this. Does that sound strange? I don't know what I like, I don't know what I want, I don't even know what I want to do for a living. I don't know how I feel. I'm really in limbo. I guess this is a time that faith is called for. It's good that I am familiar with this thing called faith.

When my daughter flew in on the day my husband died, she brought me a lovely hand-bound journal. I have been writing in it every day. As wacky as this sounds, I write to my deceased husband every day. It is my way of settling things in my mind, of gently letting him go, of assuring myself that he is okay, he's happy and he doesn't hurt any more.

The morning after my husband died, I got up and brought my beads out to the dining room table. After I had my shower, I found both daughters and my granddaughter at the table, making necklaces. We proceeded to bead for an entire day and part of the next. We made lots of jewelry, and we reminisced about my precious husband, the only father they really knew.

We talked candidly about what had healed inside us and what has been ripped open. We laughed about funny things from the past, and we ached knowing the pain that he endured during his long illness. We put words to feelings that had remained unspoken for so many years. We did some big time healing, right there at the dining room table, with the power of women loving women, each contributing her strength and her love. We shared our fears, our vulnerabilities, and our sick familial sense of humor. We were women doing what women know instinctively how to do—keep the home, heal the family, mend the wounds, be strong as only women can. And I was happily the crone, the elder, the earth mother, the matriarch.

I am surprised in the face of my husband's death to learn how strong I am. I had no idea. I thought I would fall apart, perish even. I thought I would be inconsolable, incapable of reaching out to others. I thought I would be numb, frozen, as cold as my beloved was after his spirit left his body. How quickly the flesh turns cold, like stone. I thought I would be broken—all the king's horses and all the king's men, couldn't put me back together again—but I don't need the king's horses or his men. I just need to be open to my spirit, open to the love of those I trust, and to the prayers and quiet power of love alive and active in my life.

I need to grieve, not with a petulance that won't allow for healing, but with a fierceness that lets out the pain, and lets in the Light. I need to allow the animal in me to writhe in anguish, let out her guttural cries, allow her time, feed her Light. I need to accept that grief is not a tidy little package that you open for X number of days or weeks and then wrap up again and put on the shelf. It is an unpredictable, independent wildebeest. We ride it as we would ride the waves, only instead of water, we ride the waves of pain, up and down, back and forth, one moment submerged, gasping for breath, and the next, rising up from the depths.

A twisted, delightful part of me revels in my newfound freedom to be whatever I want. I can be unpredictable. I can do crazy things. I can think nutty thoughts. I can be a dichotomy in mind, body and spirit, and it's okay. I can do anything I want right now. I can feel my way into discovering who I am.

Who is this woman, this incredibly complex, unpredictable, and impractical woman? What do I do with her? She feels a bit untamed. Should she really be entrusted with her life? Hello! Have you seen inside her head? Would you leave anything as important as a life to that? And yet, here she has it—a whole new life to live—and not a single clue as to how to do it.

So, I go forward now, as I always have, putting one foot in front of the other, one step at a time, not looking out over the whole mountain because it is too scary, too vast. I look down instead to where my feet are. I look there, and maybe three feet in front of me, but no further. And I begin to take my steps, one two, three, four... deep breath... five, six.... Maybe one day it will be different, but for today, this is enough. This is sufficient.

~Ruth Knox

Lost and Found

If I had a single flower for every time I think about you,
I could walk forever in my garden.
~Claudia Ghandi

I wear black. Oh, all right, sometimes I wear black and white. My choice of color, or lack of color, was a source of conversation between Mom and my sisters. Once, they high-fived each other when I arrived in town to visit. They had bet I'd be wearing black, and I was.

"It's easy to pack," I bristled. "What could be easier than black and white?"

"What could be easier? How about a little happy color? You always look like you're going to a funeral." Mom did an imitation of a sad and weepy woman, dabbing at her eyes.

"No, I don't! I look professional."

"Oh, yes, I forgot. You are my serious Suzie. I really think the milkman left you on the doorstep." Mom rolled her always-merry blue eyes.

I rolled my eyes right back at her, along with a look of disdain.

"Ooh, that look! I know that look," she said, laughing. "You're mine. Your father gives me that look. When you were a teenager, I got that look from you all the time. Don't take life so seriously, SuzieQ!"

For my 50th birthday, my husband, Bill, threw me a birthday party. It was one of the last balmy summer nights in September, when plants are at their fullest. The garden was lush with flowers; tiny lights twinkled, along with flickering lantern candles scattered on tables. Under the moonlight, my family and friends gathered to toast the anniversary of my birth.

I had made a conscious decision to show Mom and my sisters a thing or two. For the party, I dressed in a turquoise pantsuit and a turquoise scarf with hot pink roses on it. I found silk turquoise sandals on the clearance rack.

"These sandals will fix them. They're the corker!" I mumbled, squeezing my pinkies into them.

Mom went crazy. "Look! She's wearing color."

At the end of the night, Mom hugged me. "How can my little Suzie be 50 years old? You don't look like an old lady when you wear color!"

She hugged my husband, too, and said what she always said to him, "You're a great guy, Bill."

It was the last birthday I'd ever celebrate with her.

She died suddenly. I never said goodbye.

Just after my mother's memorial, morning dawned with that sinking feeling about the reality of death. A friend invited me to go to an art festival. I was glad I said yes as I strolled along in the happy yellow sunshine, sipped on freshly squeezed lemonade and tried to forget grief.

The shops were having a sidewalk sale to coincide with the festival. I was drawn to a rack of jackets outside a boutique. One jacket caught my eye. It was denim, but patches of color were sewn like a quilt on it. The kaleidoscope of colors included lots of turquoise. It made me think of my birthday.

It fit perfectly. It was too much money. It wasn't black. I didn't need a jacket.

I bought it anyway.

The first time I wore it, I shook my head and wondered if a force I couldn't understand made me buy it. I chuckled thinking what Mom would say if she could see me.

Most every time I wore the jacket, someone commented on it in a favorable way. It got to where I played a game with myself to see if someone would say, "Oh, what a colorful jacket." Or "I love your coat!" I wondered if Mom was having a ball in heaven watching the game.

I purchased rhinestone turquoise earrings. Was Mom's spirit invading me? No one loved rhinestones and sparkly things more than Mom.

Then, it all came to an end.

On a trip to Washington, D.C., the Metro station platform was full of jostling commuters at rush hour. I was lugging a suitcase and my briefcase. It was hot. I took off my jacket of many colors, and laid it across the top of my suitcase. I clutched my purse and the handles of my luggage while I looked up at the platform map. When I turned to head to the correct train, my jacket was gone. I retraced my steps looking for my jacket. I searched everywhere. I went to the Metro offices hoping someone turned it in to the Lost and Found. I called a few times after I returned home. My jacket had a small angel pin on the collar so it would be easy to identify. No luck.

It made me sad. I actually moped about it and felt ashamed. I told myself it was just a jacket. I even tried telling myself maybe someone needed the jacket more than I did.

My husband shopped for another one, but couldn't find it. The store suggested he try looking on their website under clearance. No luck. I scolded him for trying, because the jacket was expensive when I first bought it. I didn't deserve another one when I was careless.

I tried to figure out why it bothered me so much. If someone stole it, I felt violated, of course, and dumb for not being alert. But, I also realized the jacket was connected to the loss of my mother in my mind. I felt wrapped in my mother's love when I wore that jacket even though she never even saw it. I had to let it go and let her go.

Unbeknownst to me, Bill didn't give up.

Funny thing was I had my passport photo taken wearing the jacket. There were also a few other photos of me wearing the jacket. He downloaded the photos and had an exact photo of my "coat of many colors." He put it in his search engine. Each day he would check to see if there was a match. One day just before Christmas, he received a notice that there was a jacket available on eBay. He bought it.

When he told me, I felt wrapped in love. It was like the sun broke through the darkness and color came back into my life.

It arrived in the mail just after the New Year. We laughed that it might actually be my jacket, but it wasn't. I checked the collar to see if there was an angel pin or pin pricks. No pin and no holes in the fabric. The jacket was brand new and he bought it at a bargain price. It was exactly like my old one. I tried it on and it fit perfectly. I felt happy.

It wasn't because of the jacket, although seeing it was like greeting an old friend. The joy I felt was the sense of knowing how magnificent it is to be loved. I grabbed my husband and gave him a fierce hug. Mom's spirit and love dwells within me. I could almost hear her whisper along with me, "You're a great guy, Bill."

~Suzanne F. Ruff

76

The Light of Morning

Find a need and fill it.
~Ruth Stafford Peale

Thirty-two years ago my infant daughter quietly tiptoed into my life and then left as quickly as she came, seeing the light of only one morning. She arrived on a warm August evening and departed before the morning dew had a chance to settle on the pink roses outside my hospital window. Angela was nine hours and one minute old—but in my heart, she had lived a lifetime.

"She's an angel," my mother said, trying to console me.

My best friend said, "Now she's with God."

"She's in a better place," they all said.

I know everyone tried their best to make me feel better, but none of those well-meaning words worked for me. The mother in me wouldn't accept them. I didn't want an angel. And I didn't want her in a better place. I wanted her here in my arms where she belonged.

I slowly began an uncharted journey down a long, painful path toward healing. Every morning I got out of bed and put one foot in front of the other, sometimes tripping over my own feet, sometimes slipping backward.

At times I walked the floors of shopping malls searching for a clue as to what had happened. Where did I think I would find the answer? In a bookstore? In a candle shop? In the children's section of a department store? Did I think someone would emerge from the shadows and slip me a piece of paper explaining why this happened?

No one ever approached me with an explanation; I never got that piece of paper. Walking helped anyway—and losing myself in the crowds.

Parks were good, too. I needed serenity and I went looking for it. I would sit for hours on the soft, green grass and run my fingers through patches of clover, looking for the good-luck ones with four leaves. Any little fragment of peace was welcomed. Then I would try to bottle up that feeling of tranquility and take it home with me, figuring I could keep it on a shelf somewhere for when I needed it.

My first-born, Maria, was seven years old at this time and my son, Christopher, four. When the new school year began, Maria entered third grade and Christopher started kindergarten. I shuddered to think of being home alone without them. So on the first day of school, I took my son by the hand and walked into his kindergarten room with him.

"Can I help you?" I asked his teacher, noticing that she was trying to do ten things at once. "Yes," she replied without hesitation. I immediately took over the task of writing names on nametags.

I soon became a regular in the classroom—sharpening pencils, tying shoelaces, and setting up bulletin boards. I would read stories to the students at story time and found myself jumping headfirst into the book right along with the children. I loved being there. I had found a home.

It wasn't long before the principal approached me, offering me a new position. "I'd like you to teach fifth grade," she said, her nun's veil shadowing the look of horror on my face.

"Teach fifth grade?" I heard my voice echo. "I—I don't think so," I stammered. "I'm not ready." This would be a full-time assignment, and I wasn't sure I could take on such an enormous responsibility at this time in my life. I was petrified. I needed time to think.

I did a lot of soul searching in the next few months. I would see the principal coming toward me from across the playground, and I would hurry in the opposite direction. I didn't have an answer for her yet.

Finally, after much deliberation and prayer, I accepted the

position of fifth grade teacher. My days were filled with lesson plans, classroom exercises, and recess duty. It wasn't long before I knew that I had made the right decision. I loved teaching. And I loved learning. I learned something new every day from my students. I prayed daily that I had touched their lives as they had touched mine.

From time to time I would see a little girl skipping across the playground and suddenly remember a little girl who tugged at my soul one warm summer evening. My heart would skip a beat. Then I would realize how many children I had had the privilege of watching grow into beautiful, amazing adults since then. And my heart was full.

My once seven-year-old daughter is now a teacher and my kindergarten son is a psychologist. I feel an overwhelming sense of pride when I see the good things they are doing with their lives.

Leaving my teaching days behind, I visit my daughter's classroom as a children's author, reading one of my stories to her kindergartners. On my way to Room 23, I pass clumps of clover growing wild in patches of soft, green grass and realize that it's been 32 years since I walked into my son's kindergarten room and read to his class at story time. I feel I've come full circle.

On the days I want to have lunch with my son, I have to travel several freeways to get to the Big City. When I arrive at the quaint, outdoor restaurant where we are to meet, I can hardly wait to see him. Sharing a vegetarian pizza, I see that he is happy—and that makes me happy.

Traveling home, I think of the baby who quietly tiptoed into my life… leaving as quickly as she came. "She's an angel who lives with God in a better place," they said. Those words have come to resonate somewhere in my soul, echoing their truth.

There are still tears now and then when I think of what might have been, but there is also much joy knowing that Angela is a part of my life and always will be. I am grateful to her for coming into my life and leading me down paths that might never have been.

As a teacher and writer, I have found solace and beauty in the many students who have graced me with their presence throughout the years. These children have been my greatest teachers. And I am honored to have been a part of their lives.

And as a mother... I have found solace and beauty in the joyful wonder of my children. They are truly my greatest gifts. I feel honored to share my life with them.

My blessings continue to arrive daily in the light of every new morning. I awaken to the miracle of a brand-new day, welcoming the surprises and possibilities life has to offer me. And I am at peace.

~Lola Di Giulio De Maci

77

Fear

Instead of counting your days, make your days count.
~*Author Unknown*

"Mom, I have cancer." These four words catapulted my son and me on a journey that lasted two years. On that day I felt a wave of paralyzing fear.

Scott was the oldest of my four children. He was 33 years old and a successful assistant principal at Sam Rayburn High School in Pasadena, Texas. He and his wife Carolyn were busy raising four active children. Scott was 6' 2", weighed 200 pounds and had never been sick a day in his life.

A few months earlier a mole on his neck had changed color. "Dr. Warner called," Scott said that spring morning. "It's melanoma." I tried to reassure him, naming all the people I knew who had survived skin cancer. Yet, I felt small tentacles of fear begin to wrap around my chest.

Our next stop was MD Anderson, the famous cancer hospital in Houston. Scott had surgery at the end of May and was scheduled for radiation treatments over the summer recess. "There's an 80 percent chance it won't reoccur," the doctors said. At the end of the summer, all his tests came back negative and Scott was back at school in the fall.

However, in December, Scott discovered a lump on his neck. It was biopsied and the results came back "malignant." We now realized that Scott fell into the 20 percent category. I could feel the tentacles tightening around my chest. He entered the hospital for an aggressive treatment, a combination of interferon and interleukin.

After five months of treatment, he had radical surgery on his neck. The test results were encouraging, only three of the 33 lymph nodes removed were malignant. We were very hopeful.

For the next six months, Scott's follow-up visits went well. Then in October, X-rays revealed a spot on his lung. The spot was removed during surgery and the doctors tried to be optimistic. It was a daily battle to control the fear and panic each setback brought.

In January, he was diagnosed as having had a "disease explosion." The cancer had spread to his lungs, spine and liver and he was given three to six months to live. There were times during this period when I felt like I was having a heart attack. The bands constricting my chest made breathing difficult.

When you watch your child battle cancer, you experience a roller coaster of emotions. There are moments of hope and optimism but a bad test result or even an unusual pain can bring on dread and panic.

Scott was readmitted to the hospital for one last try with chemo-therapy. He died, quite suddenly, just six weeks after his last diagnosis. I was devastated. I had counted on those last few months.

The next morning I was busy notifying people and making funeral arrangements. I remember having this nagging feeling that something was physically wrong with me. It took a moment to realize that the crushing sensation in my chest was gone. The thing every parent fears the most had happened. My son was gone. Of course, the fear had been replaced by unbearable sorrow.

After you lose a child, it is so difficult to go on. The most minimal tasks, combing your hair or taking a shower, become monumental. For months I just sat and stared into space. That spring, the trees began to bloom; flowers began to pop up in my garden. Friendswood was coming back to life but I was dead inside.

During those last weeks, Scott and I often spoke about life and death. Fragments of those conversations kept playing over and over in my mind.

"Don't let this ruin your life, Mom."

"Make sure Dad remodels his workshop."

"Please, take care of my family."

I remember wishing I could have just one more conversation with him. I knew what I would say, but what would Scott say? "I know how much you love me, Mom. So just sit on the couch and cry." No, I knew him better than that. Scott loved life and knew how precious it is. I could almost hear his voice saying, "Get up Mom. Get on with your life. It's too valuable to waste."

That was the day I began to move forward. I signed up for a cake decorating class. Soon I was making cakes for holidays and birthdays. My daughter-in-law told me about a writing class in Houston. I hadn't written in years, but since I was retired I decided it was time to start again. The local college advertised a Life Story Writing class that I joined. There I met women who had also lost their children. The Poet Laureate of Texas was scheduled to speak at our local Barnes & Noble. I attended and joined our local poetry society. I never dreamed that writing essays and poems about Scott could be so therapeutic. Several of those poems have even been published. In addition, each group brought more and more people into my life.

I don't believe you ever recover from the loss of a child. Scott is in my heart and mind every day. However, I do believe you can survive.

Scott fought so valiantly to live and he never gave up. He taught me that life is a gift that should be cherished, not squandered. It has taken years to become the person I am today. The journey has been a difficult, painful process but certainly worth the effort and I know that my son would be proud.

~Barbara Ann Carle

78

Find Your Path

Sometimes in tragedy we find our life's purpose—
the eye sheds a tear to find its focus.
~Robert Brault, www.robertbrault.com

I n May of 1995, I suddenly lost my wife Jody to a very rare illness called a pheochromacytoma. All of this transpired within 24 hours. It felt like a horrible dream.

Robert Frost once said, "There is a time for departure, even when there is no certain place to go." Our two daughters and I had no choice but to take a new direction in our lives. I'm not ashamed to tell you I was terrified. I was always a pretty good father but I needed reinforcements since this was new, scary territory.

I tapped into a spiritual strength I never knew I had. I spoke out loud to God whenever I was alone: in the shower, in the car, at night in bed. I asked to be blessed with divine guidance, courage, strength, and to say and do the right things for my girls. I began meditating daily for about 20 minutes, which I still do to this day.

I visualized doing things together with my girls and I saw them thriving. Those were my daily images—only positive outcomes. I found comfort in books such as Elizabeth Kübler-Ross's *On Death and Dying*, Hope Edelman's *Motherless Daughters* and Bill Cosby's *Fatherhood*.

I learned firsthand what it truly means to be grateful for life and those we love. I worked very hard at balancing what was normal for my girls and not ignoring the death of their mother. Julia, Lauren and

I hugged and cried every day. I made certain that they knew emotionally that we had one another.

If I sensed they were going into a shell, I would try to interact and relate to them by asking them questions about friends, clothes, school, etc. I made it a point to do everything as a family. We went grocery shopping together, out for ice cream, and I had them help make dinner on a regular basis. I wanted them to feel secure and know their dad wasn't going anywhere.

Over time, I had developed insomnia. The sudden absence of Jody in our bed left me awake until late hours of the night, reading, watching TV and just thinking. My heart and soul felt so empty that I wondered if I would ever feel whole again.

After not sleeping for a few weeks I had the urge to be as close to Jody as I could be. And so, every night for weeks, I sat on the floor of Jody's walk-in closet, picked out one of her blouses and wrapped it around my neck and shoulders. Breathing her in, I'd cry myself to sleep. At first I didn't tell the girls about it, but something told me to share it all with them. I think it helped the girls feel okay about their own experiences and sharing them with me.

After a week home, the school counselor and I had agreed that my daughters' lives should get back to normal. So, Lauren and Julia had gone back to school. I remember their first day back was a beautiful sunny day. When I met them at the bus stop, I could tell they were upset, which was to be expected. We walked home in tense silence, and once we entered the safe haven of the house, both girls burst into tears. After a few moments of a much needed emotional release, they shared their day with me.

Amazingly they'd discovered a pair of sisters, one in Lauren's class and the other in Julia's, who had lost their mother to breast cancer one week before our loss. I remembered thinking to myself, "I need to reach out to their father Kevin and let him know he's not alone."

I decided right then to create a support group for fathers who'd lost their wives. And thus began my journey toward becoming a Life Coach.

I started looking at everything differently. I turned down a promotion at work that promised a raise, but more travel, and instead took a lower level position to be closer to home and more available to my girls. My self-reflection eventually led me to completely walk away from corporate America to focus on my Life Coach career.

As my priorities shifted, I became aware of the joy, peace and love that are possible in simple everyday things. My previous notions of what I wanted for my life fell away. I know that when life closes one door, another one always opens. It is my deepest desire to help others find the best path to their open door. If you find the courage to embark on the journey after the loss of a loved one, I know you'll find that open door, for your new path awaits you in your heart and soul, just waiting to be discovered.

~Larry Agresto

79

A New Normal

The best way to predict your future is to create it.
~Peter Drucker

On October 31, 1997 we celebrated our first Halloween with our son Aaron. We all dressed up as clowns and had our picture taken on our front porch. The picture became our holiday card. Year after year, as our family grew to include our daughter Macey, we continued to take a Halloween picture and use it as the basis of our holiday greeting card.

Family and friends came to look forward to each year's card. The four of us enjoyed the tradition we'd established.

In 2005 my father passed away unexpectedly on November 1st. Even though he lived in Florida and I lived in Ohio, we were very close. We spoke and e-mailed daily. Everything I know about sales and business I learned from my father. He was always there to bounce ideas off and to share events and stories. He adored my children and they him. To say I experienced a great loss would be an understatement. That year we didn't send a holiday card.

There is a fog that ensues after the death of a loved one. That fog enveloped me for several months. I am blessed with loving siblings, a caring husband and remarkable children. They helped me navigate the process but a void still existed. The loss of someone close to you creates a hole that cannot be filled easily or quickly.

As we approached Halloween 2006, I found myself unsettled. I could not imagine sitting on my front porch with a smile on my face during the anniversary of my father's passing. However, my children were still young and I felt pulled between a desire to keep some normalcy for them and no interest in posing for the traditional family photo. I wanted to keep Halloween a fun, happy holiday for my kids. I believed it was unfair to burden them with the unhappy memories I had. Childhood should not be about major loss and grieving. My job as their mother is to maintain as much normalcy as possible. There will, unfortunately, be plenty of time for sadness. I knew my father would not want to bring my children any more sadness than he already had.

In early September 2006 I was sharing my dilemma with a friend of mine, Jim. Jim told me a story about a loss he had experienced and shared some insight with me that has proven invaluable. He explained that when you experience tragedy you have to create a "New Normal." You keep what is comfortable and comforting from the past, discard what is uncomfortable, and establish new traditions. I felt a wave of relief come over me. I felt released from the obligation of the photo. I gave away the dilemma and moved forward. I no longer worried about what I would do about a holiday card. If we didn't have one, so be it.

A couple of weeks later I arrived home to find my dog Sparky dressed up in what looked like a house coat. All flowery, it was attached with Velcro. It looked like something an older woman would wear. There she sat, perfectly still on the kitchen floor, as if asking, "How do you like my new look?"

It immediately brought a smile to my face and a laugh to my lips. And this—this I knew was our new holiday greeting card photo.

Each year the perfect photo presents itself as the foundation of our greeting. I have embraced this new tradition. I look forward to discovering that photo opportunity and creating the card that matches it. My children and husband have joined me in this adventure. As always, my family and friends look forward to our holiday greeting.

New? Yes. Normal? Absolutely. This is our New Normal. And it suits us just fine!

~Diane Helbig

80

Sneaking Sodas

God knew I loved you too much to just be your friend,
so He let me be your sister.
~Author Unknown

We were both caffeine junkies and it was a habit our mother abhorred. Her mouth set in a thin, disapproving line, we feared her wrath and learned to sneak them in. We were 28 and 36, my little sister and I. And she was dying.

It was Cherry Pepsi for her and Diet Coke for me. We knew who had the best ice (crushed), the best cups (Styrofoam) and the best fountain sodas (not too carbonated, a little flat and on the sweet side). It became a game. She would shoot me a look that only I could interpret and say something like "I need a drive." We'd both suppress the giggles at two grown women lying to sneak away from our mother for a trip to the drive-through and two cups of sin on ice.

It was a struggle to get her into the car, the right side of her body paralyzed from her brain tumor, and the "good" parts of her too weak to do much. I helped her shuffle and let her lean while I guided her feet, using mine propped between hers. Step, shuffle, step, shuffle. It was a strange kind of dance to get where we wanted. The car always seemed miles from the front door, but the escape was worth it. When she got too sick and too weak to handle the stairs in my house, she stayed with Mom. It ended up being the last few months of her life, and when you're 28 that's not an easy pill to swallow. So we'd run away whenever we had the gumption and the craving for our "fixes." Two troublemakers on a mission.

The steroids she needed to reduce the swelling in her brain kept her awake all night. With death and a broken marriage staring her in the face too, well, neither of us got much rest. So caffeine was a blessing and we reveled in it! But our sneaking out wasn't just for the caffeine, although it was definitely a main staple in our diets. We'd drive through, our cups of rebellion in the holders between us and then we'd drive. This is what we really ran away for.

We'd just drive — no goal, no destination, just us, the road, and our favorite music. We'd hold hands and sing. She couldn't complete a sentence, thanks to her tumor, but she could sing like an angel. Whole songs. Every word. It was precious sister-time that neither of us would ever forget. Sometimes we'd get doughnuts too.

Singing together like the Judds, we'd cruise past the snow-covered mountains of northern Utah and look at dream houses. We'd pick out our favorites and talk about hiring maids so we could shop. When she had the strength, we'd hit the dollar store and painful step by shuffling step, we'd cruise the aisles, hunting for bargains on things she'd never have the time to use. If she wasn't strong enough, we'd just keep driving, talking about our husbands, our friends, and our hometown, 750 miles away. I knew she'd never get back there or to her beloved ocean and I longed to give her the gift of one last trip. I often wonder if there are beaches in heaven. I hope so.

She became weaker and drifted bit by bit, to the Other Side. I watched with agony in my heart, wanted to scream and beg her not to go. She knew deep down, beyond the confusion and almost complete cessation of her speech. She knew, and the closer she got, the more peaceful she was.

She had been given glimpses on two separate occasions and told me it was "marvelous" and "beautiful." I had no doubt and was glad she would be free of the pain and uselessness that was now her body. She couldn't move, couldn't talk, except for a word or two here and there, and she was barely there in those last days. I could no longer take her for drives, but I could sure still sneak in her Cherry Pepsi.

We'd clink our cups together and say "cheers," giggling like kids and innocently tell Mom it was caffeine-free. If she wanted the moon, I'd get it for her.

Two days before she died, I brought her soda and her face lit up when I came in. "Yay!" It was one of her last words. We had this one good day and I just wanted to make her smile, make every single second last. She had a sip or two and then fell asleep in her wheelchair. I looked at my sister, her blond hair now gone, her head bald and scarred, dark baby hair coming in. Her beautiful face was swollen beyond recognition and her right arm dangled dead at her side. It too was hugely swollen. I ached for her. As I had so many hundreds of times, I hid in the bathroom and let the sobs take over, my body shaking from the pain in my spirit. I knew her time was very near.

Two days later, Angel died. I laid my head on her chest and sobbed, but I knew in my heart it was the right time for her. She had completed her time on earth and her body and spirit had endured more than most people ever have to. She had earned her wings.

Time went by and the pain became buried as I worked feverishly to complete my book about her life. We had begun it together during her last year and I completed her legacy a few months after she left.

The day the books came, I stared at the box, tears burning my eyes, knowing what was inside. *Angel's Legacy*. We had done it. I tore open the box and took a breath as the cloud-covered tops stared up at me. I smiled and cried simultaneously. The memories came flooding back as I opened the first copy, gingerly turning the pages and reading my own words, seeing the photos of a lifetime of one person who made a huge difference. I knew it was time to celebrate.

Hopping in the car, I grabbed a copy and hit the road. I stopped off at one store for two things and then another for a balloon. It said, "I miss you." The cemetery is 30 minutes from my house and I cried the whole way there. I cried from sadness, the grief still fresh, and I cried from joy. I had helped her achieve her goal of leaving a legacy. I kept picturing her smile and knew she was pleased that we had done it.

Pulling into the cemetery, I immediately spotted her grave. With an angel emblazoned across a gray marble marker, hers was decorated as beautifully as her life had been. Angels, flowers, pinwheels, wind chimes, all adorned her grave. I grinned at the spectacle. She was loved.

I sat down in front of her grave, tears sliding down my cheeks, my purchases and her book clutched in my hands. I propped the book against her marker and tied the balloon to her Cherry Pepsi. I must have looked like a crazy woman, but I didn't care. I could almost hear her giggles from Heaven. I carefully lifted my soda to hers and silently toasted to her legacy, her life.

I sat there a long time, reveling in the moment, feeling the hugeness of accomplishing a dream we shared. My first book and her last dream come to fruition. Our last sneaked sodas and our last toast. I could feel her with me, warm and comforting like a handmade quilt. I knew we'd be together again and that she knew more joy right then than I could ever dream of.

I stood, grass stains on my knees and gathered the book and my soda. I left hers there, a last sister-day forever saved in my memory. As I pulled away from the cemetery, I felt her hand on mine and began the words to our favorite song, hearing her sweet voice chiming in... just like always.

~Susan Farr-Fahncke

Triumph over Tragedy

Courage is being afraid but going on anyhow.
~Dan Rather

"Get in the car, there's been a bad accident!" my husband, Patrick, shouted at me. After a phone call from my ex-husband to tell me he would be bringing our children home and another one 30 minutes later, from his fiancée asking me if he arrived, Patrick set out to find them.

When he returned for me, his urgency was ominous. We rushed to the hospital, and ran through the sliding doors that lead to the emergency room and up to the first doctor we saw. "Where are the kids from the wreck?" I asked. He pointed in the direction of two closed doors, and as he gestured he said, "There's a little boy in there and his dad is in the next room."

"Where are the girls?" I pleaded, almost too loud, the anxiety growing in my voice. "WHERE ARE THE GIRLS FROM THE CAR WRECK?" I was greeted with a blank stare. He stammered and we were ushered to a small, private waiting room.

It was probably a few minutes later, but felt like a lifetime before the doctor showed up again. He said words that will ring in my ears forever. "I don't know how to tell you this, but your daughters died at the scene of the accident." Katie, Miranda, and Jodi, ages eight, seven, and five, were gone. Jodi's twin, Shane, and their dad, Jay, were clinging to life in separate rooms in the ER. Shane had a broken leg and a concussion. Jay's injuries were more serious and he lost his fight for life a few hours later, the day after his 28th birthday.

A drunk driver stole what I thought was forever mine. I would never look at the world the same way again. Of course I knew that children could die—I read the obituary section in the newspaper. What I didn't know was that something so awful, so tragic, so heart-breaking could happen to me. Thankfully, Shane survived. His broken leg was soon healed, and after a time we found a new normal.

One year went by and my thoughts had turned to how I could use this tragedy to encourage others. I was contacted by Victims' Impact Panel of Oklahoma, Inc. They were conducting an informational meeting in my town and asked me to attend. The representative from VIP was engaging; she had a can-do attitude that was infectious. I did not need much persuasion, I knew from the start that I wanted to share my story to prevent more drunk driving deaths. As I was completing the form to participate, she told me that they needed a speaker the next day at a small school not far from where I live. I agreed to meet her at the school for the program.

I spent that evening preparing what I would say and I spent the drive over to the school the next day reassuring myself that I could indeed give the speech. I arrived at the school gym a little early and spent the time before the program began meeting the other speakers. Soon, students began filing in and sitting on the bleachers. The other speakers and I sat at the table facing them. There was a huge screen behind us for the video that would be shown. I was terribly nervous; I tried every technique I could remember to reduce my anxiety. I would be the last of the three speakers. First, the video, faces of the victims of drunk driving appeared one by one on the screen, along with birthdates and death dates, music was played in the background, tears stung my eyes as I realized I was not alone.

Before I knew it, it was my turn. I rose from my chair and walked to the microphone. Laying my note cards out before me, I wet my lips and began to speak. After I introduced myself, I told them about the day that changed my life. I also told them about the personalities of each of my girls, I wanted the students to know them as real people, not just as names. As I spoke I held a picture of Katie, Miranda, and Jodi that was taken six months before they died. After it was over and I sat down, an amazing feeling washed over me. It felt as if the burden I had been carrying around was lifted and replaced with a feeling of accomplishment. I knew that something I had said changed a life that day. The best part was that I could talk about my children, say their names, and share a memory and no one changed the subject. I could not wait to do it again.

Every time someone from Victims' Impact Panel called I was a willing speaker. I traveled throughout northwest Oklahoma sharing my story at schools and offender programs. Speaking was like an inoculation against bitterness and despair. Anyone who has experienced the death of a child will say it is not something you get over, but something you go through. The hurt never goes away completely, but with the help of the Victims' Impact Panel the wounds in my heart began to heal.

~Brenda Dillon Carr

82

Boughs of Love

We shall draw from the heart of suffering itself
the means of inspiration and survival.
~Winston Churchill

"Why are we decorating this tree?" asked Zach. My five-year-old son held up a sparkling golden ball and carefully placed it on the Douglas fir tree that grew in a corner of our backyard.

"This is a very special tree," I said.

"Because it doesn't die?"

I laughed. "It's true. That's one reason it is special. But mostly it's special because we bought it when it was this small." I held my hand out to show Zachary and his older brother, Chase, that the tree was once less than a foot tall. "We planted it the second Christmas after your oldest brother was born."

They both giggled and Zach pointed to Chase. "You mean Chase?"

"Let's sit down," I suggested. "I want to tell you a story. It's about a boy named Ryan. You didn't know him, but he is your oldest brother."

Astonishment spread across their innocent faces. Had it really been ten years since I had first held my hands against my smooth, round belly dreaming dreams of a soon-to-be-born son?

My first pregnancy had glided through the months with textbook ease. My husband, Mark, and I learned that we were expecting a boy. There were baby showers, nursery plans and all the attending questions. What would he look like? What would he grow up to be? Life took on new meaning, and every stroll in the park or trip to the mall added to the excitement as we envisioned expanding our household along with my expanding belly.

Soon enough, that precious new life did indeed burst on the scene. After a long labor, his smooshed head didn't exactly resemble the cherubic angel of my imagination, but he was perfect enough — ten fingers, ten toes, and deep, soulful blue eyes that I swore from the beginning knew something that I did not.

"What happened to him?" Chase asked. I could sense my sons' growing impatience as I shared stories of Ryan's first winsome smiles and his favorite stuffed mouse. Not unexpectedly, my lashes grew wet, and I drew my boys in close.

"Can you raise your hand?" I asked them both. Chase and Zachary demonstrated with ease the simple task.

"The reason you can raise your hand, or wiggle your toes, or run across the grass is because you want to do those things and your brain sends the message to make your arms or legs move. Our brains even tell us when to breathe." I paused a moment to let this sink in. "Well, Ryan's brain could send a message, but his body wasn't able to answer. This was because he had a rare disease and it is sad, but Ryan wasn't able to move his body like you both, and eventually he wasn't able to breathe air."

"Did he die?" asked Chase.

Chase looked so sad that I wondered if I should continue. I knew it was a lot of information for two young boys full of life to comprehend. It had been difficult for me to comprehend when I first began to understand that all was not right with my son.

I was a first-time mom, but I remember thinking that it was odd that my son did not wiggle much. And his cry. It was so soft — not the squalling reverie that I was sure had been the cries of other babies I knew. Everyone assured me he was just a "good baby." Sweet and passive. All new moms worry, right? So I forced myself to ignore those inner voices that told me that something was wrong.

At around three months Ryan developed a cold that seemed to settle in his lungs, and he emitted coughs so tiny that they sounded like the mew of a just-born kitten. Ryan had developed pneumonia, dangerous enough, but the reasons he developed the infection proved to be much more sobering. It took a few months, but we finally had a definitive answer. Ryan had a genetic neuromuscular disorder called Werdnig-Hoffman disease.

No one really knows what to do when they are handed such news. At that moment my own life became oddly frozen, as if choosing to stop for a latte or take a morning walk were frivolities that I should be denied when I knew my own baby would not a have a normal life, and a brief one at that. We were told to take our baby home and enjoy the time that we would have with him, and although difficult, we decided to take the doctor's advice. Ryan would never reach any of the milestones outlined in the books I'd pored over during pregnancy, but he did have a beautiful spirit, a keen intellect, and a piercing interest in everything that took place around him. He smiled at the costumed trick-or-treaters on Halloween, watched with delight the balloons and festivities at a neighbor's birthday party, and cooed quietly but ecstatically at the simple sight of a butterfly. His joy became my own.

Sometimes I had friends who would say they didn't know how they could handle such a tragedy. Who does? I simply hung on and leaned on the support of friends, family, and the unexpected reserves of strength that were a gift from God. As I gradually came to terms with my son's illness and the realization that I would have to accept a different future than the one I had planned, I made another decision. I made the decision to embrace good things, whether it be the joy of those limited days I would have with Ryan, or something infinitely smaller, be it a quiet jog on a perfect morning, or the sweet peas that were blooming in my garden.

Each person has her own process, her own timeline. For me, the knowledge that I was able to respond to such a blow and continue to live a full and joyful life was a defining moment. Ryan died when he was 14 months old. I now have two sons who will never replace him, but serve as reminders that even though I have lost I have also received. Ryan died shortly before Christmas and we bought the small living fir tree in his memory.

I handed each of my boys another ornament—one, a small frame that held a picture of Ryan, and the other, a tiny wooden crib with a smiling teddy bear. I watched them hang their ornaments carefully, and although they were still such young boys I could see the tenderness in their little hands as they placed them on a branch.

The tree continues to grow along with my boys, and decorating it each Christmas season is one of our most cherished family traditions. Zachary and Chase now stand taller than I do, and the tree points proudly to the heavens, too tall for us to reach its upper branches. It continues to serve as a precious reminder of a boy who is still held dearly in our hearts, and it is also a rising testament to our family's lesson in growth and survival.

~Donna Brothers

Grieving and *Recovery*

Healing in Time

83

The Joshua Tree

Alone with myself
The trees bend to caress me
The shade hugs my heart
~Candy Polgar

Grief is much like water pouring over the rocks in the streams. It needs time to shape a person. I have learned to let grief slowly wash over me, polishing away the hard places and leaving me with the heart of a survivor.

Joshua left us five years ago after taking his life in a lonely attic, miles away from those who loved him. I suppose he thought this would make it easier on me. It didn't. Instead it tortured me that I was not with him as he took his last breath. Although many of the days following his death have run together for me, one day in particular stays with me. It was the day I learned that being a mom does not end after death.

It was muggy and gray when I stepped into the seaside cemetery, which was to be home to my son's body. My legs could barely hold me, and if not for the support of my mom and dad I would not have been able to stand. As I looked around at the headstones, my body experienced the delicate balance between shock and grief. It seemed as if they took turns, one needing me to understand what was going on and the other protecting me from the same.

A tall man with a clipboard approached and began to speak with us about plots and plans as he pointed to the little squares that represented burial plots on his paper. "Are you looking for just one, or several?" he asked. "In which area would you like your son to be buried?" As he spoke, I noticed a tree off in the distance. Before I knew it, I was standing beneath this refuge in my painful storm. The branches leaned over me, both protecting me from the heat and taking me away from the painful conversation I had just left.

I stared, almost mesmerized by the sheer strength and yet vulnerability of this tree. It was so much like me. It was an oak with a large trunk and branches reaching towards the ocean. There were many birds singing and squirrels chasing each other in and out of its leaves. I felt the presence of life and protection all at once and needed Joshua to be buried right where I was standing. I took my sandals off to stand a moment in the thick grass and suddenly knew in my heart that this was the place for my son. If I could not be here to protect him, then this tree would shelter him for me. And then I shouted, "THIS IS THE PLACE FOR MY SON."

They all turned to see a mother standing in the shade of a tree, with her head held high and her body strong, using the very last bit of energy she had, in order to make certain that her last act of caring for her son on earth would be equal to every other decision she had made as his mom. I made certain to stay in this moment for as long as I could, even as the unbearable reality and shock desperately worked against me. "Please, this is the place for my son's body to rest," I said.

The man gazed for a moment at the area, looking around to see if it was possible, and then took another look at the paper in his hands. "I am sorry, we do not have a plot here, and the cemetery does not extend this far," he said, with a look of disappointment.

I must have succumbed to the sweet allure of a momentary break in the pain and left reality behind. The negative words he spoke seemed to almost bounce off me, as I knew in my heart that no matter what, my child would rest here. In a quiet voice, I simply stated again, "This is the place for my son to rest." And between two worlds I waited.

A few minutes later, after pacing, making some phone calls and double-checking the plans on his paper, he walked back towards me and said proudly, "Your son will rest in peace here under this tree." My heart lightened, though there was no room in that moment for joy, for I had just gotten an answer to a question I never wanted to ask. Yet I was proud that even after the life was gone from my son's body, after his soul no longer lingered on this earth, that I could still be Josh's mom. And then I collapsed into the car, with no more energy or life left in me. I gave all that I had that day.

In the years since Joshua's death, this tree has been a true servant to all of those who sit a while with my son. It has protected us from the snow and the rain and even watched over the many flowers that have been placed at his head. It has listened to the wails of a desperate mother and other family as we beg for Josh to come back. There were many times when I would show up late at night, unable to sleep without kissing my son goodnight, and the tree was my only shelter.

This tree has also seen its share of laughter, as Joshua's sisters play cards and sing to him and tell some of the silly jokes he loved. Although this tree has given much of itself, the most remarkable blessing and the one I cherish is that it taught me to honor my grief, to let it take me where I needed to go.

On the fifth anniversary of Joshua's passing, as I visited my son, I noticed that the tree proudly wore a handmade sign carved in wood with a thick strap resting around its trunk. The sign read, "THE JOSHUA TREE."

~Amanda Pool

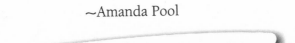

84

A Book of Memories

Grief is itself a medicine.
~William Cowper

oe died on December 22, 2008, at home as he had wished, not in a hospital among strangers. I held his hand and whispered a prayer, "Dear God, take my husband to you peacefully and without fear." I washed his body and dressed him modestly, giving him the dignity in death he had not enjoyed during the last weeks of his life.

I felt his skin cool as I gently removed his fouled garments and bathed him. No longer could I hear the rasping sound of his labored breathing or sense the spark of humanity, the essence of his being. I found satisfaction in this final act of love.

Joe's body was prepared when the mortuary attendants arrived. They urged me to leave the room while they placed him in the body bag. "No need," I said, "That's not my husband, only his earthly remains."

During the first weeks after his death I was numb. I spent my days in a fog and my nights in tears. I talked to Joe when I went to bed. We had always ended the day with "I love you, good night!" to each other as the lights were turned out. I continued my part of that exchange. Perhaps he couldn't respond, but that didn't change my need to repeat our nightly ritual. I trusted his spirit could hear me. I looked at his photo for hours. I opened a bottle of his aftershave to experience his scent. I slept on his side of the bed. I listened to his favorite song, "What a Wonderful World." And in my mind, I repeated his words to me after he was diagnosed with terminal cancer.

"I am going to live until I die."

Later I expanded my monologues. When I arrived home from work, I told him about my day, especially the kindnesses I experienced from associates. Or I discussed challenges I was facing. Joe was always the one who slowed me down when I was tempted to rush headlong into trouble. Even after death I trusted him to show me the way.

Still I had regrets. Our grandson, Ethan, celebrated his first birthday just three days before Joe died. Ethan would never know his grandfather. He would never remember how much Joe loved him, nor would Ethan know how much Joe was loved.

I began to jot down ideas, things I wanted Ethan to know. I crafted a letter with the thoughts that Joe had put into words before he slipped into his final coma. I needed to make a record while the memories were fresh in my mind.

I asked our son John for a copy of the eulogy he had delivered at his father's service. I kept the copy with the letter of Joe's last thoughts. Then I began compiling my memories of our good times together. I packaged each memory in a letter to Ethan.

As I wrote, I realized that I could give my grandson a look at Joe's life, his goodness and his philosophy. Thus began my manuscript, *Letters to Ethan*.

As I wrote each letter, I experienced a sense of overwhelming gratitude for the years Joe and I spent together. Writing my memories was cathartic. My sorrow was replaced by joy. Happiness seeped back into my life. No longer was I empty and alone. I was filled with the same love that had been mine for 34 years of marriage.

I didn't just engage in therapy for my loss; I created something special for Ethan and future grandchildren.

There are times while I am recording these memories that I experience a sense of sorrow. But more often I am filled with Joe's love. I talk to him less frequently, but I feel him with me when I open myself to his presence.

Remembering our love affair, writing about good times, I have moved from the pain of loss to gratitude for what we shared.

~Sharon F. Svitak

85

David

Though the sun is gone, I have a light.
~Kurt Cobain

I was supposed to have gone to a Halloween party the night before in Indianapolis, an hour away from where I lived. But a childhood friend had died in a car accident earlier in the week, and I wasn't in the mood to be around a bunch of people I didn't know. If I had gone to Indianapolis I wouldn't have been checking LiveJournal so early on a Sunday morning, and I wouldn't have stumbled upon a friend of a friend's entry informing me of my cousin's death. I wouldn't have driven across town to my mother's to check her answering machine, and I wouldn't have found out that my aunt had called and left a message that simply said, "Something has happened, and I need to talk to you as soon as possible," her voice cracking throughout. Had I gone to that party I would have had an entire day of normalcy before my life came crashing down around me, stranding me in an impenetrable bubble of grief and anger.

I cried for days, barely able to make it through a single class or shift at work without breaking down. My mother and I helped my aunt plan the service and make phone calls, alerting everyone of my cousin's death. The service was a blur, as was most of the first month after.

The fact that David's death was a suicide made it even more difficult. No one knew what to say because suicide is such a taboo, and the fact that I wanted, needed to talk about what I was feeling, made me realize how few friends I truly had. I worried that I was partly to blame, having made the decision that, since I was tired of being the only person putting any effort into our relationship, I would wait for him to call me. He never did.

When he died, it had been almost three months since our last conversation, and I hated that my stubbornness had kept me from possibly helping him work through whatever it was that led him to make that last decision. I was also mad at him. I was mad that he had done something so selfish. I was mad he had left a six-year-old son without a father. I was mad that I had spent 20 years defending his actions to the rest of the family, and now he had proven them right. I was also mad because I worried that I was overreacting; he was only my cousin, after all, and I hadn't even talked to him in months.

I spent a long time fluctuating between despair and anger. There was not a single day that went by when something didn't trigger a thought of him; sometimes it was a Nirvana song on the radio or my stumbling upon an old letter or picture. I remember when Saddam Hussein was hanged, and my friend's boyfriend tried to show me a clip on YouTube. I broke down, locking myself in the bathroom. After a while though, I could listen to the same songs and read the same letters without focusing solely on the grief; I was able to start viewing them as links to David, things that I could positively associate with him. I realized that although his death was a terrible thing, my memories of him weren't, and I shouldn't let the tragedy of what had happened change my entire relationship with him. It's been over three years, and now I can go days without directly thinking about him, and when I do think of him, it rarely brings me to tears.

However, there are still those days when something will trigger my need to wallow, my need to surround myself with thoughts of him. When that happens, I go to the bottom drawer of my desk and pull out a knotted plastic bag that contains two shirts, both of which still smell like him. I open the bag and breathe.

~Amy Victoria Austin Hert

86

Seven Stages Scrambled

Those who do not know how to weep with their whole heart
don't know how to laugh either.
~Golda Meir

Some say there are seven stages to grief
Others list eleven or more, how exhausting.
Rule breaker am I,
skipping denial and pushing forward to pain.

Friends try to comfort with words
But they are taking my experience and writing their own on top
Like an artist painting oil over watercolor.

I try the usual remedies
Breaking dishes in the garage and beating pillows
But I still have to sweep up the shards and fluff the lumps out.

I walk outside alone on a summer dawn with dewy grass
Breathing deeply, sighing slowly
The pink-grey sunrise only breaks my heart all over again.

And then one nonspecific day
Not marked on any calendar
I felt my mouth quiver into the first trembling of a smile.

Guilt quickly followed.
How dare I be happy?

Joy persisted like trees that grow on rocky cliffs.

It was somewhere between stage five and seven,
Somewhere between the black dress and the day I donated it to
     charity.

Acceptance is not the first and last step
Grief has a will and wildness all its own.
But you will find that very last stage
Begins with a tremulous smile.

A smile that unfurls and brings laughter to your soul.

~Susan Jean LaMaire

87

Auntie Beast

There are things that we don't want to happen but have to accept,
things we don't want to know but have to learn,
and people we can't live without but have to let go.
~Author Unknown

Aunt Janice was the kind of person who melted your heart with her smile, who warmed your entire being with her presence, who touched your soul when you thought nobody else could even get close. Her laughter was the kind that bubbled up, the contagious kind, a deep down, from the gut kind of laugh. She smelled of sweet flowers and something else, something I could never quite identify, but it smelled beautiful nonetheless. Something that I smelled every time she would reach down and whisper in my ear, secrets spent in soft, breathy undertones that were meant just for me. With her golden mane of hair and emerald eyes that dared anyone to mess with her, she was dazzling, understated, the epitome of beauty. How ironic it is, I think, years later, that I spent the entirety of my life calling her "Auntie Beast."

Auntie Beast was my father's youngest sister, the youngest of five children, the beloved aunt of ten nieces and nephews. It hardly matters now where the name Beast came from. What's important is that it was, that it still is, an affectionate nickname that reverberates throughout our family constantly. We talk about Auntie Beast's collectables, her outlandish outfits, and her crazy, cat-lady tendencies. We talk about her loves, her desires, her wishes, her dreams. And sometimes we talk about what she would have been like if she were still alive today.

When I was in grade ten, I learned that Aunt Beast was sick, and that she had been for some time. Not the kind of sick that I knew, not a cold or the flu or an upset stomach. Aunt Beast was depressed. I was 15, a hormonal teenager, and I didn't understand. Okay, she was depressed. So what? I got a 65 on my math test and had a huge fight with my best friend. I was depressed, too. After all, that's what my parents meant, wasn't it?

"Aunt Janice is sick. She has depression."

"Yeah," I thought. "Welcome to the club."

For two years I downplayed my aunt's illness, not to her or to anyone else in my family, but to myself. Surely, since I was younger, and I could pick myself up in tough times and move on with my life, couldn't everybody? Every time I saw Aunt Beast, she never looked sick, never acted sick, always profoundly expressed her love for me and constantly confirmed, despite my attempts to get her to confess otherwise, that there was nothing wrong with her.

"How are you, Aunt Beast?"

"Oh, I'm fine, sweetheart."

"Fine? Are you sure?"

"Oh, yes. I'm as Frazzled, Insecure, Neurotic, and Emotional as they come. I'm FINE."

The two of us laughed at her clever acronym, dismissing it as we always did, because by then I was used to her version of contentment, as puzzling as it could be. I left it alone then, because if she said she was okay, then I figured that she must be okay. She was always smiling and laughing and telling me that she loved me. Her definition of the word "fine" never fazed me. I was so much in denial that I always looked at the whole, the "fine" Aunt Beast, instead of taking apart the pieces and seeing what was really there.

I never got the chance to really look at those pieces of her soul. Auntie Beast died in November of my senior year of high school, at her home by the lake. She had committed suicide.

The days following her death were a blur. I know I was in shock.

My dad and his sisters tried to come to some kind of understanding, tried to piece together why it might have happened. I asked him if he had any idea, if he knew she was suffering, why we didn't do anything to help her.

"We knew she was sad. We knew she was depressed. We didn't think that she was going to do this."

And while I knew that she didn't lay it out for us, that I couldn't have solved her problems for her, I still felt guilty. I felt guilty for not being there, for not understanding. Mostly I felt guilty for being so naïve. I chose to look the other way when Aunt Beast said she was "fine." I didn't want to look any closer, to believe anything other than that she was strong and healthy and beautiful, and that she always would be.

With time that guilt subsided, and I know now that I can't blame myself for Auntie Beast's death. I know that she knows that I loved her with all my heart, that I love her still, that I will love her always. But I wish I had paid more attention, that I had looked at the pieces of her problem, of her depression, that I had taken it seriously. I miss her every single day of my life, but the pain is sporadic now instead of a constant ache. Her loves, her hopes, her wishes, her dreams... she will always be a part of me. I can still hear her voice, whispering in soft secrets, just for me....

"How are you, sweetheart?"

"Oh, I'm fine, Auntie Beast."

"Fine? Are you sure?"

On second thought... I'm good.

~Carly Commerford

88

Stickers

He spake well who said that graves are the footprints of angels.
~Henry Wadsworth Longfellow

On a very cold March night, my sister Joey was in a car accident. She was driving and no one else was in the car with her. When she rounded a curve going too fast, she lost control, hit a tree, and died instantly. She was 18 and I was 26.

Needless to say, the months that followed were very difficult for my mother and me. My mom and her second husband, Joey's father, had been divorced for a few years, so they grieved separately. My mother and I grieved together. Our family was so supportive—my mom's sister Penny and her children, my husband, my father and his wife, and many other relatives far and near. We had friends, new and old, who were there for us, too. Without them I can't say we would have come as far as we did in such a short period of time. Every time we turned around, someone was there encouraging us, especially my mom, to keep going.

Soon however, the visitors tapered off, the mail contained more bills and junk than sympathy cards, and we had to go back to work. It was then that we were forced to confront our faith. What else could we do? True, we had each other along with all of the wonderful people who had sustained us through the past few weeks. But if Joey was gone forever, what reason did we have to keep going? All of our future plans involved her. Every day we faced the thought, "Is this how God intends us to live the rest of our lives?" We just couldn't wrap our minds around the fact that she was gone.

A few months later, when her birthday was getting close, we organized a small party with my aunt and cousin. Before we lost Joey we would have thought it silly for someone to have a party for someone who was gone, but not anymore. How could we possibly let the day go by without acknowledging it? We had a cake and even put a candle on it. The four of us sang a tearful "Happy Birthday" and I attempted to say a prayer afterwards, something I desperately wanted to do. It was hard, but I managed to say what I wanted to: "Dear God, please help us have faith that Joey is with you. If we are sure of this we can go on knowing we will see her again one day."

More time passed and the days became warm. My mom felt the urge to clean, reorganize and change. Joey's clothes, shoes and other teenage belongings had sat untouched for many months, and we both knew it would do us good to go through them. We put aside her clothes and shoes to donate. My mom brought one of Joey's favorite stuffed animals to a little boy in my kindergarten class who desperately needed to feel loved. When she handed him the teddy bear, his face lit up and so did hers.

Then we came to a box filled with stuff Joey had packed from her father's house. It had been sitting in the closet for almost a year waiting for her to go through it, and now the job was ours. It would have been easy to just set it on the curb to be picked up with the garbage; we knew it was mostly junk. But we didn't want to risk not retrieving that one picture of her we might not have, that note she wrote to her best friend during class, or any number of other things the box might hold.

Not surprisingly, there were more stuffed animals. She loved animals of all kinds and would have had as many live ones as cuddly stuffed ones if our mom had let her. There were spiral notebooks with names of her friends and who they all loved written in curly lettering. A small jewelry box held several pairs of earrings. There were sketches of the horse she had owned and trained for several years and her name, "Dolly," written next to some of them. And there were stickers—lots of them. Sticker books weren't as popular when she was young as when I was growing up, but she and her friends collected them nonetheless. We found letters with stickers on them, stickers with drawings around them, and notebooks decorated with stickers.

It was then that I saw something shiny. I looked closer and saw that it too was a sticker. Not just one, but two exactly alike. They were big, probably two inches wide by three inches tall and were still on their original slippery paper. The shiny part I had seen was the background, which was silver. My first thought was that they were probably stickers Joey chose at the doctor's or dentist's office. When I realized they had words on them, I picked one up to examine it closer. "I'm an angel," the words said, written on a ribbon that flowed across a white dress. Wearing the dress was a young girl adorned with wings and a halo and holding a harp. "These two stickers are for us," I said to my mom, handing the other one to her. I felt this with all of my heart.

Even now after all these years, I can look at my sticker and feel the same way I felt that day. I have it in a frame, silver to match its background. Even though I pass by it several times a day, I don't always notice it. I don't need to; I have known since the minute I found it that I would see Joey again one day. For now I need to keep going.

~Jane Barron

89

White Boxes

In a soulmate we find not company but a completed solitude.
~Robert Brault, www.robertbrault.com

T wo simple, white boxes define my whole life. Four long years ago, these small items came through my front door, and still cause my breath to stop when I think back to their arrival.

There is a John Lennon song that says, "Life is what happens to you when you're busy making other plans." Just months before the unimaginable, we were on cloud nine.

After many years of hunting for our perfect home, the place of our dreams materialized for my husband Duane and me. We called it our Miracle House as it came into our lives the exact moment we needed it. We felt like teenagers, intoxicated at having a property that could be a retreat for friends, family, and occasional clients. It would house both our offices so we could work from home. Our postage stamp-sized piece of real estate was on a little jewel of a lake, so small it didn't have a name.

After we moved in, Duane often said, "We are simply the stewards watching over this place."

He didn't feel anyone could literally own something so magical. He carefully selected the right spot to place unique garden bells he'd made from recycled materials and proudly hung on a six-foot tall cedar frame. Their deep resonating range of sound would stop you in your tracks. The soft and tranquil sound blended with offerings of Mother Nature: Blue Heron, circles of carp, bull frogs and owls serenading one another across the water at night. Entertainment was at our back door. We were in awe that life on the edge of the city could be this good.

The house itself overflowed with possibility, standing proudly over the water, a petite Titanic beginning its famous cruise. Looking through large French doors and windows, one viewed a long deck running the length of the house with various bird feeders hanging in large trees at its helm. A lower deck contained by wrought iron fencing to support the voyage to another world, lead to an even lower third tier with a small dock, just big enough for accessing a little boat on the water and further lounging. We joked we'd never leave this place; we'd have to be carried out, feet first on a stretcher.

Thanks to my husband, the vessel inside had 4,000 square feet of fresh paint, rich shades of butter, terra cotta, copper and turquoise in rooms begging to express themselves. The breathtaking views offered a glimpse into the sacred, watery otherworld. We filled spaces with farm tables, antiques, paintings, plants, hand-knotted rugs, books, music, and Duane's writing. Trays of candles, glass bowls of nature's offerings, vases of flowers graced the tables. The house was a work of art in comfort, colors, contrasts, and textures.

We shaped these spaces while honoring the kaleidoscopic views, working together as if joined at the hip. It was always hard to leave, even for errands. Completing this new place became our mission so we could expand our creative consulting offerings to the world, oblivious to what lay ahead.

Just six months after we moved in, unpacking almost complete, in the middle of a typical Saturday, life was normal one minute, but then with absolutely no warning, everything changed. The ship that was my life began to sink.

It was not really any different than the story of the Titanic, where people onboard were full of adventure and life. Suddenly the ship hit an iceberg. Bam! The party was over.

Our disaster happened on the kitchen floor, where my husband's head landed with an unbelievably hard thud on gleaming wood. He'd been making jokes just five minutes before. Then, he was in the kitchen starting dinner. He was never sick. This could not be happening.

Within ten minutes, the kitchen was turned into an emergency room. Paramedics were ripping off my husband's shirt as they performed mouth-to-mouth resuscitation, and using defibrillator paddles to restart his heart. I rushed, looking for his health insurance card thinking, "Thank God we have this." After minutes of unsuccessful resuscitations, my hands were shaking as I handed over the insurance card to the paramedic. The paramedic said, "That insurance card won't be necessary ma'am," as they carried him out to the ambulance on a stretcher. The next few days were a blur trying to figure out his funeral service. So much happened that I could only go through the motions.

Like the Titanic, my great voyage ended. Our life sank. Within 48 hours, he was cremated, and I was buried. Buried in the aftermath of not knowing where to turn, how to run a sinking ship, how to stay afloat while the one I cared about most was now gone. Later his precious, well-built body came back to me in a little white box draped in a burgundy velvet bag. That's all it was, one small, white linen box with his ashes in it.

Sometimes that's how life happens to you when you are busy making other plans.

After the funeral, the assistant funeral director dropped by our house. I had left prayer candles; he returned them in an identical white linen box.

"I have never before assisted in a funeral where it was so incredibly peaceful among family and friends, and I have been involved in this work for a long time. Believe me, what makes this business stressful is unpleasant tension and arguing during services," he said, as we stood outside on the upper deck. Then he looked out toward the little lake and said, "This sure is a special place and it feels so very peaceful here."

Duane's bell went off with a big gentle, deep chime as if his kind-hearted, appreciative spirit was present, saying "Thank you." It was that powerful "om" sound that vibrated through the day lily bed, put to rest for the winter, vibrated further out in waves through the microscopic world Duane loved.

Now, I believe he comes here in spirit, chiming garden bells, flickering house lights. Each chime reminds me to be in the present as I create visions vital to my own life. Numb while packing, I allow our relationship to continue its transformation, our dream and its glory. I say goodbye for now, saluting the mysteries of life, knowing timing is divine. Life could cease instantly, only to return in a simple, small white linen box that really takes no room in physical space, but encompasses the whole universe in my aching, yet trusting, heart.

~Jo Anne Flaming

90

Winging It

*Men are made stronger on realization that the helping hand they need
is at the end of their own arm.*
~Sidney J. Phillip

W ho could resist falling for a fellow who figures a flawless tryst involves ambling through the aisles of Trader
Joe's in search of snail shells? Who sends compliments
to the chef at the strip mall Chinese eatery for dishing up a savory
platter of General Tso's chicken? Who brags he served eggs Benedict
to friends and family for New Year's Eve brunch for 20 years running?
Obviously not me.

I couldn't help falling in love with Ken on our first date when we
hit the winery trail between Napa and Calistoga, and he explained to
me why he'd choose a Chenin Blanc to accompany lobster ravioli.

Heretofore, I'd figured wine came in three varieties: red, white
and dessert. I'd never even heard of varietals. I'd never known anyone
who made ravioli except Chef Boyardee, and I figured his repertoire
was limited to cheese and beef. Both my father and my first husband
were meat and potato men, so I'd never been exposed to or learned
much fancy cooking.

"Where did you learn so much about food and wine?" I asked,
my head abuzz. I was dizzy not so much from the few ounces we'd
sampled at the vineyards, but from my new suitor's worldly wit and
wisdom.

"I grew up in Modesto," he said. "I went to school with kids whose families owned wineries. For years my mom ran a restaurant, so I took an early interest in how food was prepared."

"That's impressive," I said. "I worked as a counter girl at Owl Drug as a teenager, but all I learned to make were hamburgers and Denver omelettes. I put together good meatloaves and stews, but that's it."

"Don't worry. I love meatloaf, so long as it isn't covered with tomato sauce. But after we get married, I'll cook dinner if you just promise to clean up afterwards."

"That's a deal," I responded, dreamily envisioning future feasts prepared by the man who apparently had just agreed to be my spouse.

So there we were, a pair of sixty-somethings, thrown together through an Internet dating service, meeting in person after months of cross country courting via phone and e-mail, already agreeing to wed, and making the house rules.

Those rules worked, too. Ken relished retirement. He'd sleep until noon, putter around, play with our Akita puppy and then prepare elegant suppers that he'd serve on trays in the downstairs den. We'd munch while we watched *Jeopardy!*

"I can't get over how you know so many of these answers," he'd say.

"Been a bookworm all my life, and have a good memory," I'd reply, pleased.

I'd reached the height of my career, so I'd rise before dawn, catch the Metro into the capital, work in front of a computer all day, and return at dusk, tired and ravenous. Ken's suppers were so delicious that most nights I had to restrain myself from licking the plate.

Then one evening he asked if I liked hot wings. He'd cultivated this specialty when he worked swing shift as a poker room manager in Reno in the late '70s. All the people who got off work at 2 a.m. wanted to party a bit before heading home. So Ken, who loved playing host, invited the gang to his place. He bought one of the original FryDaddys and concentrated on perfecting his hot wing recipe.

"I always ask how hot people want them," he said. "I don't want to take the skin off somebody's grandmother's tongue."

"Count me mild," I said, thinking how lucky I was to be married to such a thoughtful man.

I watched while he prepared the chicken wings, shaking them in a big Tupperware with Tabasco and melted butter, and getting them well coated before dipping them into the fryer.

Maybe I'd never master his lobster ravioli or his wild rice stuffed tenderloin, but this was a dish I thought I could handle. A few weeks later I volunteered to take over the cooking that night. I suggested he stay downstairs in the den and I'd surprise him.

Within minutes I'd manage to scald the butter, nick my index finger separating the flats from the drums, and splatter cooking oil on my new suede shoes. When the celery I pulled out of the veggie bin sagged limply in my hand, I burst into tears.

"Baby, what's going on?"

I whirled around. I hadn't heard him coming up the stairs.

"I'm never going to be able to cook anything decent," I sobbed.

Ken took me in his arms. "Your meatloaf's magnificent, not a drop of tomato sauce in it. You make a good grilled cheese sandwich, and there's nothing wrong with your Denver omelettes."

"But I can't make hot wings."

"Oh, baby. Don't worry. I'll walk you through it. Just start over, and I'll sit here and tell you what to do."

So he did, even down to helping me resurrect the dismal wilted celery. He also suggested that I sprinkle cornstarch on the oil stains on my shoes. That worked, too.

Over the nine years of our marriage Ken taught me a few of his other specialties, and my cooking improved. So did my disposition, since I learned that he appreciated the simple foods I could prepare well. And that most of all, he appreciated me.

He taught me so much more… how to swirl and sniff wine before sipping, how to play gin rummy, and how to stop worrying about not doing everything right. He also taught me that accepting love can be just as rewarding as giving it.

A few weeks ago I browsed the poultry bins at the supermarket and discovered that chicken wings were on sale.

"Oh, great," I thought. "I'll get a couple of packages for the freezer so that Ken can prepare them this summer."

Then, as I reached for a second tray, I remembered. My husband had died last summer after a long valiant struggle with cancer. He isn't here now, in the country home where we finally retired, to cook chicken wings… or any other delicacies. I started to return the tray of wings to the bin.

"Wait a minute," I reminded myself. "My loving husband taught me to make these." I put them back in my cart.

In September it's my turn to host my book group. The hostess always provides refreshments, and we sip some wine as we discuss our current selection. I plan to serve hot wings as an appetizer.

I may look as if I'm winging it, but I won't be. Ken will be off stage in the wings, coaching me. He'll remind me to add extra crumbled blue cheese to the dressing, to steep the celery in ice water for an hour to ensure its crispness, to add a pinch of celery seed and a dash of garlic salt to the sauce.

Who could resist still loving the man who laughed aloud and shook his head when I asked which wine goes best with hot wings? Who claimed that there's more to life than wine and roses? Certainly not me! When the book group convenes this September, the ladies will be drinking lager… like it or not.

~Terri Elders

91

Cyber Blessings

Dare to reach out your hand into the darkness,
to pull another hand into the light.
~Norman B. Rice

When my son died, I found that reading books on loss and grieving helped me to a certain extent. But for the most part, reading about the "steps" in grieving made me anxious and questioning where I should be and what I should be feeling. Whether or not it was a typical reaction, I developed an insatiable need to talk about my son to anyone who would listen. I needed an outlet, but did not want to be social. It was hard enough breaking down on my own without the embarrassment of breaking down in public.

I was using my husband's computer years before my son Donnie's death and would visit various forums and talk with people who shared some of my interests. Subsequently, three weeks after we buried our son, I was sitting at his computer wondering if there might be help out there for the grieving mother. I found a "Loss of a Child" forum, and posted a message stating my desire to talk to other mothers who were feeling similar pain.

A woman who was vacationing in Nags Head, North Carolina read my post. She had been toying with the idea of starting a group where moms who lost children could e-mail each other every day. I signed up right away, and was able to talk to approximately ten moms that first year who had the same broken hearts as I.

When I first started receiving replies from the moms, I could not wait to get on my computer every morning! I even remember nights when I could not sleep, and I would get up to check my e-mail account. I would nearly always have mail, and I fully recognized what a blessing it was going to be to have this place where I could bring up any aspect of my son's death and funeral and release some of my perpetual anguish. My husband soon got me my own computer, since I was taking over his every hour of the day.

What a blessing this group turned out to be. Most of us, after ten years, are still close friends.

Some of us are able to get together in a hometown of one of the moms every year. When you are a mom who loses a child, you feel a strong connection to your child even after death, as if the umbilical cord had never been severed. How could we not want to talk about them to others, and help keep their memories alive in this way?

We also began making donations to various facilities or institutions on our children's birthdays. Blankets went to hospitals and Ronald McDonald Houses, books went to school libraries and reading programs for preschoolers, toys went to daycare programs, medical supplies to the school nurses' offices, clothing to school "care closets," many of us learning to sew baby blankets for the first time! We all chipped in for each donation in honor of all of our children. And our donations continue today.

I am so very thankful for the "blessing" of these friends in my life. We've cried together over our tear-stained keyboards in our individual homes, and shed tears together in person when we are able to get together. There is nothing in the world like a "real" hug from another mom with the same broken heart as you. We have come to know each other as family and now seem to do more laughing together than shedding tears. Each child holds a special place in our hearts, and we believe without a doubt that they are all friends on the Other Side.

~Beverly F. Walker

92

Sliding into My Father's Shoes

He didn't tell me how to live; he lived, and let me watch him do it.
~Clarence Budington Kelland

"Do you want any of this stuff before I send it off to Goodwill?" I looked over at the shirts my mother had just piled on the dining room table. My dad's shirts. Stacked on a table that had just been moved back to its usual place in front of the windows overlooking the slope of the front lawn. The hospital bed that he had occupied for six weeks and died in had been picked up yesterday.

What could I possibly do with my father's clothes?

Wandering over, I started pulling out familiar pieces. The tie-dyed shirt the grandkids had made him with help from an adventurous aunt. It bordered on obnoxious, but it would make a great nightshirt. The red striped polo shirt. I didn't "do" red—black was more my look—but it was so familiar, I couldn't stand the thought of it heading to a donation box. The red and black insulated hunting plaid would be perfect for farm chores—if I ever got a farm.

"Sure, I'll take a few." Translated, that meant at least five.

I hauled the clothes home. First thing, I washed them, then washed them again. I couldn't stand the scent of flowery detergent any more—still can't to this day. Its smell brought back cancer and hospital beds and Dad fading away in front of me. But getting rid of the scent allowed me to actually wear the clothes. And actually wearing the clothes allowed me to come to grips with Dad not being around anymore.

I don't remember much of my relationship with my dad when I was a teenager. We didn't fight—we just didn't talk much. He was always there, each and every time I needed him, but ours wasn't some daddy-daughter connection immortalized in stories and songs.

I grew up, went off to college, then to grad school, then to work. Each time, more geographical space grew between us. Our relationship stayed the same though. He was always there when I needed him.

Like most teenagers, and later as an arrogant young adult, I swore I never would be like him—teacher, farmer, good guy that he was. I was going for the big time—scientist, travel, money. But I discovered a funny thing on the way to my jet-setting job.

It didn't make me happy.

I wanted roots and good clean dirt and people who knew my name. I wanted all the things that Dad had been. So I moved back to my home state, became a stay-at-home mom, and my husband and I plotted our course to our own farm. We fought our way to actually owning those ten acres in the country the fall after Dad died. The problem was, when we got it, Dad wasn't there to see it.

His clothes were though.

I wore the tie-dyed shirt to bed just like I planned. It draped wild and vibrant around me. My last sight at night and my first in the morning was a swirl of colors. Even when it was raining, that shirt lit up my country kitchen like a mini-sun. My little girls snuggled into my lap and we remembered just how much fun they had making the shirt in the first place. Sitting on the porch steps, I could pull it down over my knees, listen to the birdsong and drink coffee. I had the perfect nightshirt. It felt like Dad was around.

On an afternoon when I felt particularly beat, I wore the red striped polo. I was on my way to a wellness fair and just wore what was folded on the top of the laundry basket. A denim skirt and my dad's shirt. Listless and miserable, I drifted through the booths trying to stay low-profile. An energetic woman stood in front of one of the tables. Heaven help me. She was the personal style consultant, and she had focused in on me. I wanted to peel off, run away, get off her radar, but the stream of people pushed me right to her.

"That is a perfect color for you," she said, gesturing to my shirt.

"It is?" I was stunned.

"Absolutely. It's perfect with your hair. But not just any red. This red—the old faded barn-type red. That's what you want."

I floated off from the encounter. Faded barn red—an old farmer's older shirt—and it was one of my perfect colors.

That fall, cold weather rolled in. Hand in hand with our farm came the inevitable daily chores. My secret weapon to ward off the chill? Dad's insulated plaid hunting shirt. I wore it layered over sweatshirts to muck out stalls and to daydream of being a child again and seeing Dad head down to the barn. That was the fall I started teaching, just once a week, at our church.

It took me almost two years to quit wearing Dad's clothes (although truth be told, they still sit folded on my closet shelf). I hadn't just slid into his shirts, I had slid into his shoes. I had become the farmer, the teacher. Every day, I struggle to be the good person he was. Dad is still there for me—wrapped around me. Just like always.

Not more than a month ago, I went to the funeral of a childhood classmate's mother.

"I'd recognize you anywhere," she said. "You look just like your dad."

In my distant past, when I was young and less than wise, that remark would have wounded me. Now I just smiled and said, "Thanks. I'm glad to hear it."

I look like my dad, whether I'm wearing his clothes or not. He's still around.

~Theresa Woltanski

Grieving and Recovery

Signs from Beyond

93

The Blessing of a Dream

Happiness is a function of accepting what is.
~Werner Erhard

My son fell asleep at the wheel around one in the morning. He passed away before the sun rose to bless the day. As anyone knows who experiences such a loss, your world is turned upside down and you are changed forever.

At first I was sure I would never smile again and never find joy in the simple blessings of everyday life. When I did begin to experience joy, I would feel guilty about it. How could I feel happy after experiencing the death of my child?

Very disturbing dreams in the early months left me tossing and turning, sweating and waking up with a gasp. I dreamed of plane crashes, cars in flames, and falling off the edge of bridges. Terrifying dreams that made no sense, but spoke of my inner anguish. Then one night about six months after the tragedy of my son's death, I had a dream that changed everything.

In my dream, I was seated in an audience of listeners and my son was playing guitar on a stage. My son was a classical guitarist with his master's degree in music. He had done many recitals in his college years, and my husband and I had been there for most of them. Now, in my dream, he was performing, seated between two other guitarists on the stage before me. I heard and felt the music drawing me closer and closer to him. It was as if I was floating! My only desire in the dream was to get as close to him as I could. I felt myself rising and nearing the stage, and then I stopped in the front row. The heavenly music continued, and I saw my son reach to turn the page on the music stand in front of him. This portion of my dream was ironic, because he never used music sheets at a recital—he practiced until he knew the pieces by heart!

As my son reached to turn his sheet music, it fell. Every last piece floated into the air and onto the floor around him. The music stopped. The performers on either side of him also stopped playing, and a hush fell over the entire auditorium as I reached out, wanting to gather up his music and make things right for him.

But suddenly he stopped me. He looked me right in the eyes. The message conveyed to me in that dream, even though he never said a word, was, "It's okay, Mom. The music is supposed to stop now. This is the way it's supposed to be!"

I felt such a peace come over me in that dream. I don't know why or how it happened, but I woke up feeling that peace still permeating my entire being. And it stayed with me for a long, long time.

I believe that there are so many things in this lifetime we will never understand. So many "whys" that we scream towards the heavens, demanding answers. But we won't get the answers. Very often instead, perhaps in dreams, we are blessed with peace—the peace that passeth all understanding!

~Beverly F. Walker

94

Another Miami Moon

In the night of death, hope sees a star, and listening love can hear
the rustle of a wing.
~Robert Ingersoll

It's 5:30 p.m. on a Monday, the peak of Miami rush hour, and my car is speeding up the ramp from U.S. 1 onto I-95 heading north to my parents' home in Hollywood, Florida. My speeding abruptly turns into bumper-to-bumper crawling. A dangerous game of lane weaving gains me a few yards on competing drivers, who unlike me, have all the time in the world to get where they're going. Can't they tell I don't? Can't they sense my urgency, see my pleading eyes, the strain on my face? If only God would part the Red Sea of creeping taillights with a screaming emergency vehicle I could slip behind and follow.

My sister, a nurse, had called unexpectedly. She was down from Daytona, staying with Mom and Dad for a while. "You'd better get here," she said in an ominous tone. I had just been there yesterday for a nice Sunday visit and everything seemed stable. Still, I grabbed my keys and flew down the stairs from my third floor South Miami apartment, not waiting for the elevator. This had to be a false alarm. It was too soon. I wasn't ready.

Hunching over the steering wheel, I raise desperate eyes to heaven. What I see through the blur of tears and my dusty windshield startles me. In the darkening sky, a brilliant full moon is gently rising, casting what feels almost like a protective glow upon Miami's motorized masses. The sudden sight of it loosens my inner knots, and reminds me of the tradition I started years back when travel became my passion. "Even when we're separated by so many miles, sometimes continents," I said to my parents, "we share the same moon. Wherever we are, when we spot the full moon, let's think of each other, sending love and energy across the distance. That'll make us feel closer."

With that memory, I sit stuck in traffic. There's nothing to do but stare at the moon. It stares back, lulling me into a stupor with its steady, hypnotic eye. The next instant my awareness shifts. I'm keenly alert... and I know with certainty. A wave of calm peace washes over me. I surrender, float in it. Traffic no longer matters. Now, I too, have all the time in the world. No need to drive in an insane hurry to get to Hollywood. It's too late. I rest my head on the seatback and look out at the cars around me with eyes no longer frantic. The other drivers remain unseeing and oblivious, probably even to the moon.

But now, Dad's with me. He's telling me not to worry about being late. He's letting me know this time he's the traveler who couldn't wait to leave on his own journey. His way is traffic-free. He's taken a short detour to meet me here before passing on. He says that for us, yesterday was goodbye, but wants me to understand that on his road or mine, we're not apart. He knows I'll catch the humor and meaning of his choosing a moonlit night to go—so he won't get lost in the dark, but mostly as proof he's keeping our full moon tradition.

Amid earthbound souls inching forward on the highway, I stop and go, cry and laugh, sending love and energy to one who soars on a higher way.

~Jude Bagatti

Angels Slobber Too

Some pursue happiness, others create it.
~Author Unknown

O ne morning I had been married to my best friend, Mart, for 20 years, and the next I was a 43-year-old widow. I felt lost and wondered how I was supposed to continue living, and then an angel in disguise appeared to help me.

I don't remember where I had been on the day that I discovered the path to my own personal angel. But I do recall realizing on my way home that I had not eaten in a long time. I stopped at a burger joint and bought a newspaper on my way in so I would have something to do while I ate alone. I still don't know why I was looking through the classifieds. I never read them before. Mart would peruse them almost every day for a good deal on something we really didn't need. I normally just read the front page and the entertainment section. But on this fateful day, I ate food I had no taste for and idly flipped through the classifieds. In just a few minutes my eyes filled with tears. There, in big bold letters, was the answer to a prayer that I had not yet uttered: "Rare—Clumber Spaniel for Sale."

For over ten years Mart and I had haphazardly looked for a Clumber Spaniel. But we could never find one, or we couldn't afford the price, or it just wasn't a good time for a new puppy. But now, here was my Clumber Spaniel, right in front of me. I immediately called the listed number. I learned that the puppy was seven months old, approximately 60 pounds, and had to be sold because the family had just adopted a baby who was allergic to him. I agreed to meet the owner the next day in a bookstore parking lot on the other side of town. And in that parking lot, I caught sight of the first angel I had ever seen!

From the back of an SUV, peering out of a dog kennel, he looked into my eyes as slobber hung from his huge jowls. Hmmmm... definitely not most people's idea of a first angel sighting. However, in my mind's eye, I could almost see his beautiful angel wings hidden under the thick and shedding white fur on his muscular back. As the two of us looked into one another's eyes, I somehow knew, deep in my soul, that this dog and I were meant to be together. I paid the previous owner and loaded my new angel into the back of my Jeep and we headed home.

However, just a couple of miles down the road I had to wonder if I might have been mistaken. A stench unlike any I had ever smelled filled the interior of the Jeep. With outside temperatures in the low 30s it didn't take long for the Jeep to completely fog up with his musk! A few more miles and I found myself driving down the interstate with the heater on high and all the windows open, desperately trying to clear my nose. Even my eyes were watering from the smell! I kept thinking that perhaps this wasn't the angel I had envisioned, because surely nothing from heaven could smell this bad.

Twenty windy and cold miles later we paid a surprise visit to the vet. She quickly diagnosed infected glands and said I would have to help her clear them since she had no vet tech on Saturdays. I'll tell you right now, angel or not, I don't think I would ever agree to do that again. I don't know what she did, but as I firmly held his sturdy body, a stench was unleashed that rivaled that of a stockyard auction! Whatever she did fixed the problem because on the rest of the way home, my angel no longer emitted his foul smell. What a relief! But there was still another challenge ahead of me.

At home, there were two very spoiled girls who I doubted would view this new addition as the angel I believed him to be. Abbey, a 14-year-old English Cocker Spaniel and Casey, a 12-year-old West Highland Whitey ruled the house. I feared that they might be too set in their ways to accept a new member of the family. But I had to make it work because deep in my heart I knew that Mart had sent this dog to me. So with a hopeful heart and sweaty palms, I introduced him to my two old spoiled girls through the backyard fence.

Typical excited dog sniffing took place and then some barking from the old girls ensued. My angel calmly took it all in, his tail wagging in a funny little circular way. Strange, I never knew angels could wag their entire behinds. Things appeared to be going well, so I opened the gate and let him join the girls.

Within a few hours it was like he had always been there with us. Known as King Solomon in his first life, he quickly adopted his new name, Sully. He brought life back into the house. In the evening, when other families were settling in to eat dinner or watch television, I would curl up on the couch, feeling the loss of Mart as strongly as I did on that first day. But Sully would come put a slobbery face on my lap and look up at me with those two beautiful light brown eyes and I couldn't stop myself from smiling. Other times he would be so intent on scratching an itch he would literally fall over in the middle of the floor. It's impossible not to laugh at a 70-pound dog when he just falls over!

His sheer joy at seeing me come home from work every day and the way his tail wagged in a complete circle added joy to my life. Not known for being very outspoken, it is pure joy to hear the occasional WOO-WOO bark Clumbers are known for. And "Clumber" describes the movements of this breed perfectly. Watching him clumber across the yard and tumble head over heels trying to not overrun the toy I've thrown for him makes me laugh so hard I worry the neighbors will think I have lost my mind.

On the other hand, there have been days when I thought I could just shoot him. For example, there was the day I came home to discover that he had eaten part of the linoleum in the laundry room. Then there was the phase of pulling all the toilet paper off the roll and shredding it throughout the house. And apparently, television remote controls can be mistaken for rawhide bones. That's all in addition to the daily antics that many of my friends find repulsive, but that I have learned to accept as just another part of living with a Clumber angel.

He sleeps at my bedroom door and snores so loudly that he sometimes wakes me up and I have to get up and roll him over! He snorts like a pig when he's excited. White fur covers my furniture, carpet, basically everything in the house, including me. But hey, lint brushes aren't that expensive and I should vacuum more often anyway. Worse than the fur, my angel feels an instinctive need to share his slobber with everyone who enters the house. And it doesn't matter how he shares it. Pant legs, shoes, and sleeves are apparently great places to deposit a little Clumber love, but hands and faces are the best! Most people just don't seem to understand his need to share with them, but they can't see his angel wings like I can. And every single day he makes me laugh and brings joy to my broken heart.

Almost a year later, I still have bad days along with the good. Marty is in my every thought every second of every day. But through it all, I have a 70-pound Clumber Spaniel angel, sent to me from my beloved husband, who helps me realize that life is short and that some slobber in your life is okay, as long as it comes from a funny, furry angel.

~Kelly Van Etten

Traveling On

For death is no more than a turning of us over from time to eternity.
~William Penn

My mother's mom passed away in early November of 2004. She'd traveled down to Florida to attend the elegant wedding of her great-niece, and it had been the first time in years she'd been able to make the long trip from her Chicago home. Everyone was shocked when a few short days after the wedding my grandmother's heart stopped beating. Although it had been an abrupt shift from merriment to mourning, we were grateful to have had that final evening of celebration to share with her.

In the thirty days that followed her death, my family and I were delivered another devastating blow. My other grandmother, my father's mother, became very ill.

I hadn't been to visit since the death of my other grandmother, partly because it would force me to recognize her own mortality. To atone for my cowardice, I agreed to stay with her that night in the nursing home. She hadn't wanted to be in a hospital; she'd made it clear that when her time came she'd wanted to go in peace.

The only times I permitted my eyes to close during the night were when I needed to wipe my tears away. Eventually the sun rose behind the December clouds, but I barely noticed.

A young woman from hospice arrived hours later, lifting the depressive atmosphere with her good spirit and jokes. She was the first person to put a smile on my face when she told me stories about the trouble my lively grandmother had brewed up only weeks before. It was when she was applying eye shadow to her closed lids that the woman leaned down and spoke softly into her ear. "What are you waiting for, sweetie? Why are you fighting so hard to hold on? It's going to be okay...."

It was that moment I realized that I still clung to a spark of hope that my grandma would fight her way out of this illness like she had all of the others. My tears became a river.

My mother came later that morning and sent me home to get some sleep, but only a few hours passed before I was up again and heading back to the nursing home. My sister had also come that afternoon and the three of us were alternating between making jokes and experiencing fits of sorrow. A nurse sat quietly in the corner, respectfully not disturbing us.

That evening my grandmother finally gave up her fight. My sister and I each held one of her hands and told her we loved her over and over as she struggled for her last breath. I don't know what she had been holding on for, and I doubt I ever will.

We held each other and cried as more nurses came in and took her body away. Reality has a tendency to come crashing in at awful times, and before they left they warned us to take anything of sentimental value. The looters would be out when word spread about her death.

Slowly we collected her belongings, allowing ourselves time to feel her lingering presence. Although we doubted anyone would want to steal them, we started to peel away the family pictures that covered the walls. As I moved her bed to get to some hard-to-reach photos, my mother let out a cry that made me jump.

"Oh my gosh! Do you smell that?"

Confused, I took a deep breath. The only thing I could detect was the stale aroma of mothballs and medicine. As I opened my mouth to ask what in the world she was talking about, the invisible cloud enveloped me too, with the most beautiful fragrance a person could imagine. I thought a bottle of perfume might have broken when I'd moved the bed, but we searched and searched. We never found the source.

The fragrance eventually faded for each of us. I was the first to lose it; my mother was next. My sister, who had been closest to my grandmother, told me later that it had lingered with her until we walked down the corridor, leaving the empty room behind us.

That evening I sat alone in my car and cried. When my eyes cleared enough to safely see the road, I turned the key and prepared to head home. The radio was already on, and I heard the beginning melody of Lynyrd Skynyrd's "Free Bird." I kept the car parked and cried the tears I didn't know I had left as the words acquired new meaning. Things wouldn't have been the same if she'd stayed, and there were things I couldn't change. It was her time to travel on to the other places she had to see. Before I left the parking lot that night, my grandmother had let me know that now she was as free as a bird.

Skynyrd's song on the radio may have been a coincidence, if one believes in those. But that beautiful perfume won't ever be forgotten or explained. There aren't many things I can say I know for sure, but my grandmother did settle one question for me that night. Death isn't an ending. It's a transition, and a new beginning.

~Rebecca Degtjarjov

97

Beyond the Cocoon

Unable are the loved to die. For love is immortality.
~Emily Dickinson

For years, my mom, Marie, dreamed of being published. She wrote and submitted articles, stories, jokes—you name it—in hopes of seeing her words in print and a check in the mailbox. She was a former teacher turned stay-at-home mom who always put her family before herself, but deep inside she had a longing to work and contribute monetarily.

Unfortunately, Mom passed away from complications caused by her cancer treatments. And, so too, it seemed, did her dream.

Or so I thought.

You see, from where Mom now stands, dreams always come true. She just enlisted me, her son, a writer, to prove that to all of you.

So here's her last story, but one that never ends. The story of Mom's love.

It was the day after the funeral. My sisters were bringing the last of the flowers to Mom's graveside. The weather cooperated, as it often does in sad times, with gray skies, cold and rain. As my older sisters gazed at the mound of flowers, tears in their eyes and aches in their hearts, they both silently asked Mom to let them know she was all right. Almost on cue, and in spite of the pouring rain, a solitary white butterfly arose from the mound and fluttered effortlessly past their noses and out of sight.

Mary and Pat looked at one another and felt that chill you get when you know something extraordinary just happened, as seemingly insignificant as it might have seemed. When they came back to our childhood home, they related the story to my dad, myself and my brother Tom and sister Liz. Inside, I was jealous. I wished Mom had given me a sign too.

I walked outdoors with this thought and sat on the bench that only two months earlier I had assembled for their 45th anniversary. I cried uncontrollably as any son would who had lost his mother. But when I opened my eyes, a strange thing happened. A beautiful yellowish-white butterfly brushed past my face almost on cue, just as my sisters had related in their experience. In my case, however, I got up to follow the butterfly.

It fluttered left, then right, then up and down. It seemed to dance in front of me, almost coaxing me to follow. We rounded the corner to the side of the house when suddenly I was led into a small swarm of white butterflies! They all danced and fluttered around me and then whooshed away toward the front of my neighbor's house, then over the roof until they disappeared.

I had a feeling about this continuing butterfly phenomenon but, through the days of grief that followed, had neither the will nor the strength to look into its significance.

Of course, Mom would not allow me to brush it off.

I went home to my wife and son but was regaled with further butterfly incidents during phone conversations with my oldest sisters—one story, in particular having to do with my mom's first grandchild, Taryn. She is the oldest of two born to my sister Liz.

About a week after Mom's passing, Liz went to visit our dad and two oldest sisters, who were still helping him around the house. Upon arrival, Taryn jumped out of the car and was greeted by a white butterfly landing on her head! At this point, we all decided to finally confront the phenomenon head-on and did a little research on the meaning of white butterflies. We discovered that the Japanese believe they are the spirits of the dead, while the Chinese and many Christians believe they are the souls of the departed, flying free.

This revelation only confirmed the feeling we all had. Mom was letting us know that she was still with us and that she was okay.

A few weeks passed with no other butterfly sightings. The numbing pain of Mom's passing was still as fresh as the dirt on her grave.

A month after Mom's passing, on her 74th birthday, my father and I went out to the cemetery to bring her flowers. We paused, said a prayer, held each other and cried. When we finally composed ourselves, we began walking toward the cemetery maintenance garage to get water for our flower vases. Suddenly and from out of nowhere, a spectacularly large and colorful monarch butterfly whizzed between my dad and me and bounced joyfully in the light breeze.

We'd experienced the white butterflies but never a colorful monarch. That's when I looked at my dad with conviction and said, "Mom dressed up for her birthday."

Which she always did.

Mom, thanks for staying close, and congratulations on having your story published. I always knew you could do it.

~Michael J. Cunningham

98

A Message from Dad

*She was no longer wrestling with the grief, but could sit down with it as a
lasting companion and make it a sharer in her thoughts.*
~George Eliot

M y 86-year-old father was dying of heart failure. My sister, brother and I wanted to care for him at home as long as possible so he could be with the family that loved him so much. During the last year of Dad's life, we gave all our energy to our father. It was the most difficult time of our lives.

After Dad's death I was devastated. Although I'd comforted friends who had lost someone close, nothing prepared me for the way I felt after his death. I had lost not just a beloved parent, but also a teacher and a friend who was always there to offer love and support. He shared my joys and hurts, accomplishments and milestones, and he had a generous heart, a playful side, and never lost his sense of humor. I missed him terribly.

Certain reminders were just too much to bear, and I battled emotional turmoil for months. Gradually, things began to get better, but the wound was still deep. One day, about six months after he died, I got a message from a stranger. Dad found a way to tell me he was still here. And with it, acceptance and peace finally came.

A World War II veteran, Dad had many medical problems, any one of which could cause many people to lose more than their sense of humor, but not him. He had a talent for finding humor in everything, and for making people laugh. He also liked to flirt. Once, during a trip to the grocery store years after my mother died, he asked a cashier who was in a bad mood to come home with him. "I'll make you smile, honey," he said laughing. At first I found this embarrassing but didn't let on. But then, I was laughing with him.

I have vivid memories as a teenager of Dad singing songs in the morning. How I loved to wake to the sound of his voice and the aroma of fresh, percolated coffee. "Up, up, up! Rise and shine! It's a beautiful day!"

Eventually, Dad's health began to deteriorate. He was diabetic, and his legs were gradually becoming weaker. He started to have difficulty walking and he had to start using a cane. Then came the walker. Shortly after, a wheelchair became his mobility. But he didn't lose his sense of humor. He would still climb stairs slowly, whistling all the way.

Every summer, my sister and I would help Dad with the garden that he loved so much, and spend many days sitting with him outside, admiring his beautiful flowers. Summers always ended too soon.

In the months that followed his death, I was overwhelmed with sadness. I took many walks in the woods with my dog, Remington. The quiet solitude and beauty of nature comforted me. One warm afternoon, as I strolled, I began to cry. I prayed for a sign that Dad was all right. Just then an elderly man walked towards me, singing "My Wild Irish Rose," a song that Dad had sung often during the years!

As he got closer, I told him that I enjoyed his singing, and we chatted for a few moments. His presence comforted me enormously. I felt at ease talking to him. He told me he was 86 years old and offered some advice on exercise and diet for a long, healthy life.

"You're a nice lady," he said. "What's your name?"

When I told him, a big smile lit his face. "What's your name?" I asked.

"Just call me George," he replied. I was stunned.

Before we parted, he mentioned that he had a son, also named George, a daughter who was 60 years old, and a sister named Virginia. "My daughter is separated from her husband," he said. The similarities amazed me. I had a brother named George. My half sister, Linda, was 60 years old and also separated from her husband. My dad also had a sister named Virginia.

A few moments later, I heard a voice calling my name—the same way Dad had called out to me many times when we were in different aisles at the grocery store. I turned around and there was George running towards me.

"What's wrong?" I asked.

"I forgot to ask you if you needed any money or anything," he said. "All you have to do is ask."

I tried to hide my tears as I told him that I really didn't need anything. "But thank you so much for the offer," I said, recalling the same exact words I heard so often from Dad over the years.

"Well, okay, Linda," he said. "But if you do, I'm here to help you." I reminded him that my name was Kathy, not Linda. "I know that," he said, smiling, as he walked away. A few seconds later, I looked over my shoulder, and he had vanished.

Suddenly, I had a "feeling." As tears ran down my face, I knew that Dad had found a way to tell me he was never far from my side. I haven't seen "George" since that day, but I do believe that it wasn't just a coincidence. He was sent to comfort me. Dad found a way to tell me he was still here.

~Kathryn Radeff

99

The Sign

The angels are always near to those who are grieving,
to whisper to them that their loved ones are safe in the hand of God.
~The Angels' Little Instruction Book *by Eileen Elias Freeman*

Valentine's Day was always special in our house. Dad would return from work bearing an armload of sweetheart roses for Mom and a small box of chocolates for me. My younger brothers, who thought the flowers-and-candy ritual was too mushy to bear, managed to find delight in whatever heart-shaped bakery goods Mom provided. After dinner we would sit on the family room floor, shaking a flurry of dime-store valentines from hand-decorated boxes we'd fashioned at school. We ran our hands through the piles, searching for cards with sweets attached. Only after the candy hearts and foiled chocolates had been retrieved would we bother to read our classmates' sentiments. Our rituals were simple and predictable. We took comfort in that.

Even after my brothers and I grew up and began our own families and traditions, Mom could count on those street-vendor roses, still wrapped in damp newspaper. They weren't as fancy as the floral shop variety, but they were hand-delivered by the man of her dreams. None of us, in our comfortable little world, could have predicted that Dad would be only 56 years old when he brought home his last bunch of roses. Cancer took him swiftly and left our family with a few short months to say our goodbyes. In that time, Mom begged

Dad to send a sign once he was "settled in" and watching over us. He promised he would.

Nearly three years passed and Mom watched diligently for something. Nothing came. Nothing, anyway, that prompted her to confidently say, "Now that's a sign!" There had been a Thanksgiving evening when she stood washing dishes and felt the weight of a hand on her shoulder so surely that she had turned around to see who it was. She briefly played with the idea that it was Dad, but convinced herself it was probably her imagination. "Holidays are the hardest," she often confided to me. "That's when I feel most alone."

If holidays were hard, I imagined, Valentine's Day must be the hardest. My brothers must have felt the same way because we all tried our best to distract Mom with gifts, cards and restaurant meals. Nothing ever felt adequate. Last year, Mom insisted we enjoy Valentine's Day with our own families. She spent the afternoon shopping with her sister, who had also lost her husband at a young age. The two chose a simple diner for their evening meal, one that wasn't likely to be filled with couples on the most romantic day of the year.

Over meatloaf and country fried steak, the two widows playfully badmouthed their late husbands for leaving them alone. They suspected perhaps the men were having so much fun in the afterlife that they had forgotten about the women who still missed them very much. Lost in their commiseration, they didn't notice a stranger who quietly approached their table. The gentleman gave six roses to each of them, then mysteriously walked out of the restaurant.

"Red roses," marveled my aunt. "Herm always gave me red roses."

"They must know we're mad at them," Mom joked. But they were both washed with an inner calm that had for so long eluded them. The flowers were, it must be told, pathetically wilted. "Oh, well," laughed Mom. "Dead roses from dead husbands. It seems rather appropriate." The next morning, Mom took the roses to the cemetery and put them on Dad's grave. She thanked him for the long-awaited sign.

Holidays are still hard. But thanks to a miracle delivered by a

Valentine's angel, we believe that Dad is okay and watching over us. And that makes every day a little easier.

~Lisa Naeger Shea

100

To Fly with Herons

*Sadness flies on the wings of the morning
and out of the heart of darkness comes the light.*
~Jean Giraudoux

T he ringing of the telephone rudely interrupted my first sip of coffee. The night before had provided little rest, and I was feeling puffy-eyed and groggy. I looked at my husband. Which of us was going to answer? I picked up the receiver, greeted the caller, and heard the voice on the other end giving me information I did not want. I listened, made a few replies, and hung up the phone.

"They just took Jennifer off the ventilator," I whispered to my husband. "It won't be long."

We looked at each other and felt our connection to the living world, to our two young sons who sat on the couch watching cartoons, to our beautiful, young friend in a hospital bed 20 minutes away. Then we felt the heat of tears, as we had for days, but now they felt changed, a different kind of tears: aching, instead of hopeful.

Jennifer lived her life with cystic fibrosis. She was an incredible example of how to live a loving, kind, caring, nurturing, fun, humor-filled life—with or without a debilitating, breath-snatching disease. Tiny and adorable, with a huge, Pepsodent smile, she uplifted those around her. And now, at age 30, she was leaving us.

The morning wore on, the hands of the clock seeming to be

mired in glue—slowly, so slowly the seconds turned to minutes. I made a few calls, checked in with friends, had the same conversation with all.

"I need to do something," I said to my husband. "But I can't figure out if I should go running or go to church."

He gave a funny, but sad, little laugh.

"What will make you feel better?"

"Well," I replied, "I don't feel like I can put any make-up on right now, so the run is probably the better idea. I'm going to go look for my heron."

The Great Blue Heron is an incredibly majestic, enigmatic bird. During my solitary runs along the banks on the Tualatin River, I often see a Great Blue (sometimes two of them), on the other side, seeming to hover on the edge, white-capped water rushing by. The stature and grace of the Great Blue has always held an allure for me. A friend of mine feels the same way; we have talked about what we see as a spiritual quality that emanates from a heron in repose, or even more strongly—in flight.

The sun darted in and out from behind the clouds as I gained my rhythm along the sidewalk. It seemed that even the sky could not decide how it was feeling on this Sunday morning. My cadence evened out, and my breathing settled into its comfort zone. How easy, just to take a breath when it was necessary. Such an irony on this day when my friend could no longer take any more breaths of her own.

Late in May, Oregon is lush, verdant, and in full bloom. Camellia blossoms littered the stretch of road I followed. From somewhere to my left the smell of daphne was lifted on the breeze. Azaleas and rhododendrons lined my course as I approached the path leading down to the river. The water was high, and I could hear it from the crest of the hill. I checked my watch as I descended the path, a subconscious part of my running pattern—how many minutes out, how many to get back home. 11:24 a.m. A man with his two black Labs passed me on my descent and I gave a halfhearted smile.

Thoughts began to haphazardly fill my already bruised and tired mind. They crashed and collided in a cacophony of noise and sound with no rhythm, rhyme, or melody. I ran and cried. Cried and ran. Stopped to stomp my feet and sob a few inappropriate expletives. What will friends do without her optimistic outlook, her deep faith? How would her parents go on with only memories of their lovely daughter? How does a man find the words to tell his kindergartner and preschooler how much they are loved, even thought they have been left? What about evenings drinking lemon drops and playing *Pictionary*, and days splashing at the fountain, laughing and sharing stories of our sunscreen-covered children? We need more time; we need more experiences; we just need more....

Then I saw it. Across the expanse of sun-dappled water, the Great Blue Heron sat, as if ready to answer all of my unanswerable questions. My bottomless well of tears seemed to dry for just a moment. I slowed my steps and wiped the sweat off my brow. Leafy green branches moved to hide the heron and expose it in the next second, like a trick being played on the eyes. But it was no trick. There it was in all its long-necked, silvery-blue glory, looking across the water at me, taking in my pain with patience and stillness. As I took a deep, lung-filling breath, the silvery figure glanced away, then back at me, before the flu-fluup, flu-fluup, flu-fluup of those mighty wings commenced. It took off low across the water, gaining altitude slowly, but surely, with purpose, before arcing gracefully over the treetops and out of my line of sight. The clouds broke open and a golden cast shone over the river. I looked at my watch—11:31. I took off back up the hill, not sure what would greet me at home.

The early afternoon was spent cocooned on the couch, the wind picking up force outside, the rain falling. We sat under blankets listening to Josh Groban sing to us that a breath away is not far from where you are, and Bette Midler harmonizing that God is watching us from a distance.

Later in the day, a friend called to say that Jennifer's spirit left her earthly body at 11:30. I already knew it. I was there to see it happen. Not at her bedside, holding her small, well-manicured hand. But at the edge of the water, as she took off, gaining altitude slowly, but surely, with purpose, before arcing gracefully over the treetops and out of my line of sight.

~Antonia C. Everts

In Their Heavens

Hope is grief's best music.
~Author Unknown

In the past several years, three people with whom I shared a close bond have died. The first was my 42-year-old brother, the second a 51-year-old close friend, and the third and most recent a 50-year-old friend from high school. With each passing I was confronted anew with questions to which I still have no answers: the existence of God and the likelihood of life after death.

I have not grown to be a spiritual man. I think the good Sisters of Mercy may have beaten the Lord out of me years ago, but neither am I firm in my conviction that we are not guided by a force greater than ourselves. I suppose that I fall into the "crisis Catholic" category. If there's a crisis in my life, I'm transformed into a devout Catholic. Needless to say, the death of my high school friend John did give me pause and caused me to reflect once again on the reality of mortality and the prospect of an afterlife. It is with this in mind that I share the following, for in what I am about to tell you I have found a measure of comfort, and I hope you do also.

My brother Larry passed away suddenly six years ago. He went to work one morning and never returned home. He suffered a major heart attack and died, as it is said, before he hit the floor. We were devastated at having lost him at so young an age and our grief was at times overwhelming. As the days and then weeks passed by I began to wonder if Larry had found peace.

One night, several weeks after his death, I had a dream. I was in what I perceived to be a large theater. I could hear the buzz of the crowd and sensed that the house was packed, but I could see no one, for the theater was lit with the most brilliant white light you could imagine. And then I saw Larry, and he looked as he did on the day he was married. Twenty-six years old, in the best physical condition of his life and a look of absolute happiness and serenity on his face. He looked at me and said, "Joe, it's all right. Everything is okay." Larry loved to act and was in several plays in high school and studied drama in college. I believe that what I dreamed that night was Larry's version of heaven, that he was on stage and at peace.

Five months after Larry's death, my 51-year-old friend was involved in a car accident and died on Christmas Eve. This was hard; at times it seemed harder even than Larry's death. His name was Stafford, and if you had met him you would have been reminded of Bob Dylan. Staff wasn't the most responsible guy and he could be a bit self-centered, but he was creative, funny, non-judgmental, loyal, and I counted him as one of my best friends. He was a talented guitar player and a fair photographer. He always aspired to be a rock star or an actor. He was never quite sure how this was going to happen, but he was convinced that someday his break would come.

Several weeks after Staff died I dreamt of him. This dream was brief and no words were spoken. I looked up and saw him in the prime of his life. He was dressed in a wool sport coat and cap, and he looked so cool. An entourage surrounded him and hung on his every word. He looked in my direction and gave me a nod of his head as if to say, "I'm where I belong and where I always knew I would be." Staff was in his heaven.

Which brings me to two weeks ago. I'm in the stands at Yankee Stadium. I'm in a field level seat halfway down the line in right field. John, my friend who most recently died, is on the mound and throws his last pitch to strike out the batter, and for some reason I get the feeling he struck out the first two also. The stadium is sold out and it erupts as he bounces toward the dugout.

I swear to God he was 19 again, and in this dream he moved just like he did when we were young. He walked with that same swagger, not cocky but confident. He had that beautiful smile on his face, that sly, knowing smile that I remember as being a bit higher on one side than the other, and his head was slightly down and was tilted so that his hair fell across half his forehead. I watched him walk off the field and my dream was over before he reached the first base line. He never acknowledged my presence but I could see him as clear as day, and he was beaming.

I am fortunate to have these dreams. I wake remembering them vividly and they leave me with a good feeling. I'm skeptical that they are anything other than pleasant dreams, but I do still send the occasional donation to Holy Family, recite the occasional Hail Mary and occasionally look skyward and smile. Just in case.

~Joseph J. Kruger

Meet Our Contributors

Sami Aaron is a software developer in the Kansas City area and is developing a program that will teach people how to "green up" their events while managing all the planning details. Sami teaches yoga breathing and meditation workshops to offer her healing journey to others. Contact her at samiaaron@beingontosomething.org.

Cate Adelman currently lives in the Midwest and serves as an advocate for people with disabilities. She has completed a Bachelors degree from NLU, and religious studies with the Servants of the Holy Heart of Mary. Her passions include issues of peace and justice, the arts, and the spiritual journey.

Larry Agresto is a Life and Business Coach and the founder of Peak Performance Coaching. He is also a writer, author and speaker. His work and writings focus on "breakthrough changes" in life and business.

Jude Bagatti likes challenges and has pursued passions as diverse as photography, hiking, writing, acting, triathloning and adventurous world travel. A master gardener and massage/Reiki therapist, she holds BA and JD degrees from the University of Miami. Her nature photo/poetry book, *Fauna, Flora & Fantasy*, was published in 2010. E-mail her at heyjudebagatti@msn.com.

Teresa Curley Barczak retired from AT&T in 2007 and devotes her time to writing, reading, cooking and spending time with family and friends. Teresa enjoys traveling, gardening, and volunteering for her church. She plans on completing a collection of short stories. E-mail her at tabarczak@bellsouth.net.

Jane Barron received her Bachelor of Science, with honors, in Elementary and Early Childhood Education from the University of Alabama in 1994. She taught elementary school until 2002 and is now a full-time mom, author, and owner of a small gift business. E-mail her at jbarron9@bellsouth.net.

Brenda Black, an award-winning author, Christian speaker, pastor's wife and mother of two sons, has written over 1,500 published works, including three books. The country girl lives near rural Deepwater, MO, and delights in beautiful music, family, friends and a good laugh. Visit www.thewordsout-brendablack.com to learn more about the author.

Bob Brody lives in Forest Hills, NY, with his wife and two children, Michael and Caroline. He is an executive and essayist whose pieces have appeared in *The New York Times*, *Smithsonian* and *Reader's Digest*, among other publications.

Donna Brothers received her BA in Communications from California Polytechnic University. She worked for CBS Television for several years before receiving teaching credentials in Language Arts and Special Education. She has published a short story in *Woman's World* magazine and enjoys photography, scrapbooking, and hiking. E-mail her at djeanbrothers@gmail.com.

Ann Brown currently resides in Southern Indiana where she is the director and instructor for a non-profit Suzuki violin program. She also performs regularly as a violinist with the Owensboro Symphony Orchestra in Owensboro, KY. After spending twelve summers working in Glacier National Park, she now returns each summer for several weeks of hiking and swimming.

Barbara Ann Carle is a personal essay writer and poet. Her essays have been published in *Chicken Soup for the Chocolate Lover's Soul* and several anthologies. Her poetry has been published in several magazines. She is the mother of four; grandmother of six. Barbara lives in Friendswood, TX, with her husband.

Brenda Dillon Carr loves caring for her husband, Patrick, and children, Landry, Kelley, Carissa, and Aliceyn. Her oldest son, Shane Dillon, lives nearby and visits often. She continues to speak for the Victims' Impact Panel of Oklahoma and is available to speak at your church or women's event. E-mail her at brenda.carr@suddenlink.net.

Candace Carteen has written dozens of short stories. In 2007 her best friend, cheerleader and husband died, leaving her a widow and single mom. She is helping her son understand that life sometimes gives you horrible blows, but you acknowledge them and move forward. E-mail her at scribe@ae-mail4u.com.

Paige Cerulli received a Bachelor of Arts degree in English and Music from Westfield State College in 2010. She is also a certified equine massage therapist. Paige enjoys playing her flute, writing and riding her horse. E-mail her at PaigeCerulli@gmail.com.

David Chalfin is a television and film editor in Los Angeles by way of New York where he was born and raised. A graduate of the University of Pennsylvania, he has always referred to himself as a non-practicing writer—until now. He owes his creative spirit to his father, and his ability to pursue it to his doting Jewish mother. E-mail him at dchalf@aol.com.

Elynne Chaplik-Aleskow, Founding General Manager of WYCC-TV/PBS and Distinguished Professor Emeritus of Wright College in Chicago, is an author, public speaker, adult storyteller and award-winning educator and broadcaster. Her nonfiction stories and essays have been published in numerous anthologies and magazines. Her husband Richard is her muse. Visit http://LookAroundMe.blogspot.com.

Carly Commerford is an aspiring writer with hopes of completing her own book someday. Raised in Thorold, Ontario, Carly currently attends Queen's University where she is studying to become a teacher. Carly would like to thank her Aunt Janice for her endless love and inspiration. E-mail her at carlycommerford@gmail.com.

Harriet Cooper is a freelance writer who specializes in writing creative nonfiction, humor and articles. Her topics often include health, exercise, diet, cats, family and the environment. A frequent contributor to *Chicken Soup for the Soul*, her work has also appeared in newspapers, magazines, newsletters, anthologies, websites and radio.

Mandi Cooper Cumpton is a mother of two girls, Shelby and Katy. Mandi is an RN, with an oncology certification. She is married to a Louisiana State Trooper, Keith. She and her family live in Quitman, LA. E-mail her at shelbyaleeyasmom@yahoo.com.

Michael Cunningham graduated from St. John Fisher College in 1984. A marketing copywriter, he has also written two screenplays, *Driver Ed* and *Swing Vote* (2nd place in the 2001 Scriptapalooza screenwriting competition). A former standup comedian, Mike enjoys family, friends, creating music and film. E-mail him at mrsea@frontiernet.net.

Priscilla Dann-Courtney is a freelance writer and clinical psychologist living in Boulder, CO, with her husband and three children. Her book, *Room to Grow*, is a collection of personal essays previously published in national newspapers and magazines. Her passions include family, friends, yoga, running, skiing and baking.

Aleesah Darlison lives in Sydney (Australia) with her husband and three children. She writes picture books and novels for children and reviews books for *The Sun-Herald*. The true story appearing in this anthology deals with her mother-in-law's two-year battle with lung cancer. Learn more about Aleesah at www.aleesahdarlison.com.

Brenda Dawson is a sixty-three-year-old mother of four and grandmother of seven beautiful grandchildren. Recently retired from a twenty-year service in Dietary and Nursing Resident Care, she now splits her time between Michigan and Florida — finally a "Snow-Bird." Brenda is also active in her church.

Rebecca Degtjarjov is a military wife who travels the world. She, her husband, and their rowdy Anatolian Shepherd currently reside in Northern California, where Rebecca works in retail. E-mail her at rebeccadegtjarjov@yahoo.com.

Lola Di Giulio De Maci is a contributor to several *Chicken Soup for the Soul* books. Her grown children and former students inspire her children's stories, some appearing in the *Los Angeles Times*. Lola has a Master of Arts in education and English and continues writing from her sunny loft overlooking the San Bernardino Mountains. E-mail her at LDeMaci@aol.com.

Sheri Gammon Dewling, a former software executive, runs a small consulting business, while raising two young children with her husband in Cornell Village, Markham, Canada. Sheri aspires to turn her life lessons into stories that will inspire others. You can reach Sheri via e-mail at sheri@justmomsense.com.

Kathy Dickie completed her Human Resource Management and Business Administration education at the University of Calgary, SAIT and BCIT. She lives in Vancouver, B.C. and works as a coordinator in Business Development for an Alberta-headquartered utility company. Kathy enjoys travelling, quilting and documenting ancestry research.

Terri Elders, LCSW, lives near Colville, WA, with her two dogs and three cats. Her stories have appeared in numerous magazines and anthology collections, including several editions of *Chicken Soup for the Soul*. E-mail her at telders@hotmail.com or follow her at http://atouchoftarragon.blogspot.com.

Antonia Everts lives in Oregon with her family and loves the Pacific Northwest weather. She has a Bachelor's degree in Recreation Administration and teaches gymnastics to children. Antonia is an avid runner and baker and is currently working on a novel about life with dogs. E-mail her at antoniaeverts@yahoo.com.

Barbara Farland of New Hope, MN, operates an independent business communications and creative writing practice. Her latest works appear in *Christmas Traditions: True Stories That Celebrate the Spirit of the Season*, *A Cup of Comfort for Fathers* and *Hugs Bible Reflections for Women*. Visit her website at www.barbarafarland.com.

Susan Farr-Fahncke is the founder of 2TheHeart.com, where you can find more of her writing and sign up for an online writing workshop! She is also the founder of the amazing volunteer group, Angels2TheHeart, the author of *Angel's Legacy*, and contributor to over sixty books, including many in the *Chicken Soup for the Soul* series. Visit her at www.2TheHeart.com.

Jo Anne Flaming is the Creative Founder of Queen Beedom. She can be found buzzing about as an innovative writer, speaker and facilitator, inspiring her clients to reinvent their tired, boring lives into their "sweet life," emerging from their royalty within. Find her blog at www.QueenBeedom.com or e-mail her at Joanne@QueenBeedom.com.

Jenny Force is an occupational therapist in Columbus, OH. She enjoys traveling, reading, writing, and spending time with family and friends. Jenny would like to say thank you to her husband Rob for all his endless love, support, and laughter.

University of Pennsylvania graduate **Sally Schwartz Friedman** has been an essayist for over three decades, sharing the sounds of her life. Her husband, three daughters and seven grandchildren provide those sounds. Her work has appeared in *The New York Times*, *The Philadelphia Inquirer*, *AARP Magazine*, and numerous national and regional publications. E-mail at pinegander@aol.com.

Melissa Frye graduated from nursing school in 2004 and has since received her Bachelor of Science degree in Nursing. She will earn her Master's degree in early 2012. She is currently a Labor and Delivery nurse in southern Arizona. She enjoys traveling, football, and spending time with her husband and little boy. E-mail her at frye_mel@yahoo.com.

Cindy Golchuk lives near Las Vegas with her husband and not so angelic grandson, Zack, and two dogs that rule her house with iron paws. Her passion runs deep when it comes to writing, whether it be inspirational nonfiction or placing the finishing touches on her three manuscripts. E-mail her at golchuk@embarqmail.com.

Libby Grandy lives in Claremont, CA, with her husband, Fred. She has published magazine articles and is currently marketing her novels: a mystery and a women's fiction trilogy. Libby belongs to the California Writers Club and facilitates a weekly critique group. Visit her website at www.libbygrandy.com or e-mail her at quillvision@aol.com.

Jan Grover lives in Houston, TX, and writes, drawing upon her experiences to help other grieving parents in their loss process. She is the author of *Forever Connected… A Guided Journal For A Parent Who Has Suffered The Loss Of A Child*. E-mail her at jan.grover@sbcglobal.net or visit www.lazybpress.com.

Brigitte Hales received a Bachelor's degree from Vassar College and an MFA in Screenwriting from the American Film Institute. After five years in the film business, she took a hiatus to give birth to her first child and her first novel. She has great hopes for both. E-mail her at brhales@att.net.

The writing bug bit **Thomas P. Haynes** during his mid-life crisis. A native Arizonian he uses life experiences to dominate his tales, enhanced by his vivid imagination. Between writing classes, conferences and writing groups Thomas has worked at perfecting his craft. E-mail him at tpjh721@yahoo.com.

Diane Helbig is a business development coach, author of *Lemonade Stand Selling*, and the host of the Accelerate Your Business Growth BlogTalkRadio show. She works with small business owners, entrepreneurs, and salespeople. E-mail her at diane@seizethisdaycoaching.com.

Amy Hert graduated from Indiana University in May 2009 with a Bachelor of Science degree in Education, concentrated in English. She works as a substitute teacher and spends her free time reading and traveling. She has been writing since childhood and is excited to see her first piece published (for real-real).

John Hitchcock grew up in the Adirondack Mountains of New York State and started his teaching career in central New York. He now lives in Southern California, still teaches science, enjoys golf, fly fishing, writing and maintaining his website, www.education-for-excellence.com.

David Hull has been a teacher for over twenty years and writes a monthly column for a local newspaper. He also enjoys gardening, reading and spending time with his family. E-mail him at Davidhull59@aol.com.

Amy Schoenfeld Hunt is a professional freelance writer and the author of three published books, as well as a costumed historical interpreter at an outdoor museum that depicts life in the 19th century.

She lives in Milwaukee, WI, with her husband and three daughters. She loves to hear from readers. E-mail at AimeeClaire@aol.com.

Craig Idlebrook is a freelance reporter and essayist in New England. He has written for over thirty publications including *Mothering*, *Mother Earth News* and *Funny Times*. When not writing he takes his daughter to as many different libraries as possible. E-mail him at craigidlebrook2@yahoo.com.

Jennie Ivey lives in Cookeville, TN. She is a newspaper columnist and the author of numerous works of fiction and nonfiction, including stories in several *Chicken Soup for the Soul* collections.

Peg Kehret is the award-winning author of more than fifty books for children, including *Ghost Dog Secrets* and *Small Steps: The Year I Got Polio*. Her books are known for their emphasis on family, friends, and kindness to animals. Learn more at www.pegkehret.com.

Jean Kinsey resides in Brooks, KY. Her hobbies include reading, writing, and traveling. Jean teaches Sunday school and enjoys her seven grandchildren. She has multiple stories in variable anthologies and periodicals and hopes to find a publisher for her novel. E-mail her at kystorywriter@yahoo.com.

Allison Knight-Khan received her M.A. in English Literature from the University of Waterloo. She teaches high school students with autism in Marietta, GA. Allison enjoys gardening and hiking with her children. She writes historical time travel novels for children. E-mail her at allisonakhan@yahoo.com.

Ruth Knox has loved writing ever since she could first hold a pencil. She believes in the power of the written word to unite people. Currently living in Boise, ID, this grandmother just learned to ride a bike. Ruth is now working on her first novel. E-mail her at ruthknox@live.com.

Joseph Kruger was born in Auburn, NY, and received his master of education from Nazareth College in 1996. He is a middle school special education administrator in upstate New York. He enjoys traveling throughout the United States and spending time with his children and granddaughter.

Susan LaMaire lives in Parsippany, NJ, with her husband Brian. She has been published in *Chicken Soup for the Soul: Tough Times, Tough People* and *Chicken Soup for the Soul: All in the Family*. She is working on a collection of humorous short stories. E-mail her at hunkoftin8@ yahoo.com.

Bobbie Jensen Lippman is a prolific professional writer who lives in Seal Rock, OR. Bobbie's work has been published nationally and internationally. She writes a human interest column for the *Newport* (Oregon) *News-Times*, in addition to a radio program which is available as a podcast on www.knptam.com. She can be contacted via e-mail at bobbisbeat@aol.com.

Barbara LoMonaco received her BS from the University of Southern California and has an elementary teaching credential. Barbara has worked for Chicken Soup for the Soul since 1998 as an editor and webmaster. She is a co-author of *Chicken Soup for the Mother and Son Soul* and *Chicken Soup for the Soul: My Resolution*.

Rob Loughran has 200-plus articles and nineteen books in print. Check out www.lulu.com/rloughranjokes for his *Funny, Funny Kidz Jokebook*. Rob lives in Windsor, CA.

Cheryl MacDonald has written, co-authored or edited nearly forty books on Canadian history as well as numerous articles and essays. When she's not researching or writing, she can usually be found talking about history or at a War of 1812 re-enactment. E-mail Cheryl at heronwood@execulink.com.

Sandra E. Maddox lives in Newport Coast, CA, with her husband, Ron. She is active in service at Saddleback Church in Lake Forest, CA. Sandra leads Treasured, a mentoring ministry to mothers of pre-school children, and has written a children's book with co-author Peggy Matthews Rose. E-mail her at semaddox@cox.net.

Bridget McNamara-Fenesy received her BA from the University of Notre Dame, and her JD from the University of Denver. She works as an independent business consultant when she is not pursuing her passion of writing. She enjoys travel, gardening, and spending time with her husband and daughter. E-mail Bridget at bridgetmcnamara@comcast.net.

Shaylene McPhee graduated in Fashion Design Technology in 2007 and became a licensed cosmetologist in 2009. She loves art in all its forms and enjoys writing, playing music, painting and photography. She aspires to write a novel in the future. E-mail her at shaylenesays@yahoo.com.

Claire Mix composes children's music and is a documentary film-maker. She has two books being published by Screaming Dreams Publishing in 2011. She is writing a young adult book based on her mother's experiences as a volunteer in the Japanese American Internment Camps of WWII. E-mail her at thesolo@sbcglobal.net.

Highland Mulu is an American Samoan who belongs to six children: five boys and one girl. He still lives close to his childhood home of Independence, MO, and works in the IT field. Highland enjoys playing and composing music. He continues to write inspirational stories of his childhood. E-mail him at Highland.mulu@gmail.com.

Scott Newport, inspired by the short and profound life of his son Evan, began writing in 2002 to help himself cope. He quickly discovered that his writing also helped other families facing similar challenges. This is his third publication in the *Chicken Soup for the Soul* series. Scott lives in Michigan.

Laura O'Connor earned her nursing degree, with honors, at the Pennsylvania College of Technology in 2010. She resides in north central Pennsylvania with her fiancé and two children. Laura enjoys the outdoors, reading, writing, and spending time with family. E-mail her at ocolau55@yahoo.com.

LaVerne Otis lives in Southern California where she loves writing, photography, bird watching, gardening and spending time with family. LaVerne is recently retired and is taking classes at a local community college. She has been published in *Chicken Soup for the Soul* books and various magazines. E-mail her at lotiswrites@msn.com.

Freelance writer by day, fiction writer by night, **Susan Palmquist** is the author of four novels. Her work and short stories have appeared in *Arthritis Today*, *Health*, *Woman's World* and *American Profile* and in both the UK and US. Two of her short stories will appear in upcoming anthologies. Find out more about Susan and her work at www. susanpalmquist.com.

Laraine Paquette and her husband, Ken, have a language school in the Boston area. Besides teaching English, she does children's entertainment (story-telling, magic, face-painting and balloon sculpture.) She is a mother of six and a grandmother of eleven. She holds a BA in English. E-mail her at lpaquette@learneslnow.com.

Saralee Perel is an award-winning columnist/novelist and multiple contributor to *Chicken Soup for the Soul*. Her book, *The Dog Who Walked Me*, is about her dog who became her caregiver after Saralee's spinal cord injury, the initial devastation of her marriage, and her cat who kept her sane. Contact her at sperel@saraleeperel.com or www. saraleeperel.com.

LeDayne McLeese Polaski is the Program Coordinator of the Baptist Peace Fellowship of North America which works around the world for peace rooted in justice. She lives in Charlotte, NC, with her husband Tom and daughter Kate. E-mail her at ledayne@bpfna.org.

Amanda Pool lives with her husband and children in Massachusetts. She is a stay-at-home mom who spends her time writing and advocating for suicide prevention. Recently she has completed the Out of the Darkness Walk to prevent suicide in Boston. She created and maintains a Facebook fan page called "Life Is A Highway" to help others cope with the loss after a suicide.

Kathryn Radeff has over twenty-five years experience as a professional writer and educator. She teaches writing workshops in Western New York and South Florida, and enjoys empowering aspiring writers to follow their dreams! She loves to travel and spend free time with her dog, Remington. E-mail her at kradeff1@msn.com.

Jacqueline Rivkin lives in New York and has a Masters degree from The Columbia University Graduate School of Journalism. Her work has appeared in several publications including *Newsday*, *Self* and *The Philadelphia Inquirer* on topics ranging from retirement planning to chocolate. Since the death of her husband in 2009, she has been experimenting with personal essay writing.

Sallie A. Rodman lives in Los Alamitos, CA, with her husband Paul and has three grown children. Her work has appeared in numerous *Chicken Soup for the Soul* anthologies and various magazines. Sallie feels that she learned many life lessons when coping with the death of her beloved mother. E-mail at sa.rodman@verizon.net.

Liza Rosenberg is an Israel-based freelance writer and blogger, writing about subjects that include current events, fertility, parenting and loss. She also writes poetry, has a serious coffee habit and harbors a penchant for dark chocolate. Married and mom to a six-year-old son, her website address is http://lizarosenberg.com.

Carolyn Roy-Bornstein is a pediatrician and writer whose essays, book reviews, clinical reports and short stories have appeared in numerous medical and literary journals. You can read her work at her website, www.carolynroybornstein.com, or e-mail her at carolynroybornstein@gmail.com.

Suzanne F. Ruff is the author of the recently published book, *The Reluctant Donor*, described by critics as a "beautifully written, gut-wrenching memoir."Along with a closet filled with black and white clothes, Suzanne lives with her husband, Bill.

Heather Schichtel is a freelance writer and special needs advocate. All of the inspiration for the story in this book came from her sweet daughter who is missed every day. She thanks her husband, family and an incredible group of friends for constant love and support. You can follow Heather at www.samsmom-heathers.blogspot.com.

In addition to authoring twenty-six published romance novels, **Candace Schuler** also writes case studies, white papers, grant pro-posals, press releases, marketing collateral, and more. She shares her life with her husband of thirty-seven years and two seventy-pound Dobermans who think they are lap dogs. Visit her website at www. CandaceSchuler.com.

Lisa Naeger Shea works in corporate communications and writes from her home in St. Louis, MO, which she shares with her husband, three daughters and precocious puppy. Lisa earned her Bachelor of Science in Education and Writing Certificate at the University of Missouri. E-mail her at lisa.shea@sbcglobal.net.

Pat Snyder, a recovering attorney and humor columnist from Columbus, OH, writes and speaks about life balance. She recently published her first book, *The Dog Ate My Planner: Tales and Tips from an Overbooked Life*. Learn more about Pat at www.PatSnyderOnline.com.

Lorna Stafford launched her "writing" career at age seven copying the Bible by hand. She didn't get far but soon began writing more original material. A public relations professional, newspaper columnist, feature writer, and author of several almost finished novels, she still loves the written word.

Joyce Stark has retired from local government in Northeast Scotland. She does freelance writing, currently concentrating on travel articles about her road journeys thru the USA. She plans to explore all fifty states, and has only five to go. E-mail her at joric.stark@virgin.net.

Sharon Svitak is recently widowed and now retired from her position as the Finance Department Office Manager of a local municipality. She writes regularly and is the newsletter editor for "Write Around the Valley," a monthly publication of the Tri-Valley Branch of California Writers Club. E-mail her at svitak5@comcast.net.

Lisa Tehan received her Bachelor of Arts from Purdue University and her Master of Science from Indiana University. She plans to go back to school (again!) for nursing because of her experiences with David. She lives in Indiana with her wonderful husband AJ and their two crazy dogs.

Kelly Van Etten spent twenty-two years in the Air Force and now works in Air Force Emergency Management as a civilian. She is also a senior at The University of Oklahoma pursuing a bachelor's degree in Administrative Leadership. Kelly enjoys traveling, swimming, gardening, and her four dogs. E-mail her at kellyinok@yahoo.com.

Sarah Wagner lives in West Virginia with her husband and two young sons. Her work has appeared in *The Front Porch, Celebrations:*

Love Notes to Mothers, and *A Cup of Comfort for Cat Lovers*. You can find her online at www.sarahwagner.domynoes.net.

Bettie Wailes tutors, writes, and runs in Winter Park, FL. She is working on a memoir about her experience as a back-of-the-pack runner, including her relationship to Paul, her biggest cheerleader. E-mail her at Bettie.Wailes@gmail.com.

Beverly F. Walker lives in Greenbrier, TN, with her retired husband. She enjoys writing, photography, and scrapbooking pictures of her grandchildren. She has stories in many *Chicken Soup for the Soul* books, and in *Angel Cats: Divine Messengers of Comfort*.

Meaghan Elizabeth Ward is a high school senior. In her free time, she enjoys reading, writing, drawing, kayaking, horseback riding, and spending time with her family. She dreams of one day becoming a full-time novelist and sharing stories that will truly honor God. Check out her blog at www.thepatriotscall.blogspot.com.

A retired hospice RN from north central Pennsylvania, **Jeanne Wilhelm** has experienced the grief journey to renewed joy in life. Newly wed in August 2010, her darling husband, children, grandchildren and volunteer work fill her days. She writes to encourage and share hope. E-mail her at ptlwilhelm@yahoo.com.

Diane Wilson is a voracious reader and an aspiring author. Having taken a college course in Expressive Writing, Diane has received the inspiration for her stories from her wonderful family and her life experiences. E-mail her at doe@cogeco.ca.

Ferida Wolff writes books for children and adults. Her essays appear in newspapers, magazines and online. She speaks at schools, women's groups, and writer's conferences. She also writes a nature blog—www.feridasbackyard.blogspot.com. Visit her website at www.feridawolff.com.

Theresa Woltanski started writing young adult and adult fiction after a stint in the scientific world writing reports and journal articles. She is the author of several novels. She lives on a farmette in Michigan with her husband, children, a too-big garden, and a number of obsessive-compulsive animals.

Verna Wood's story, "Cancer's Gift" appeared in *Chicken Soup for the Soul: A Tribute to Moms*. She is in the process of writing a book about some of the tragedies she has endured. She hopes it will help women going through the same things. E-mail her at renossnowflake@ wichitaonline.net.

Meet Our Authors

Jack Canfield is the co-creator of the *Chicken Soup for the Soul* series, which *Time* magazine has called "the publishing phenomenon of the decade." Jack is also the co-author of many other bestselling books.

Jack is the CEO of the Canfield Training Group in Santa Barbara, California, and founder of the Foundation for Self-Esteem in Culver City, California. He has conducted intensive personal and professional development seminars on the principles of success for more than a million people in twenty-three countries, has spoken to hundreds of thousands of people at more than 1,000 corporations, universities, professional conferences and conventions, and has been seen by millions more on national television shows.

Jack has received many awards and honors, including three honorary doctorates and a Guinness World Records Certificate for having seven books from the *Chicken Soup for the Soul* series appearing on the New York Times bestseller list on May 24, 1998.

You can reach Jack at www.jackcanfield.com.

Mark Victor Hansen is the co-founder of Chicken Soup for the Soul, along with Jack Canfield. He is a sought-after keynote speaker, bestselling author, and marketing maven. Mark's powerful messages of possibility, opportunity, and action have created powerful change in thousands of organizations and millions of individuals worldwide.

Mark is a prolific writer with many bestselling books in addition to the *Chicken Soup for the Soul* series. Mark has had a profound influence in the field of human potential through his library of audios, videos, and articles in the areas of big thinking, sales achievement, wealth building, publishing success, and personal and professional development. He is also the founder of the MEGA Seminar Series.

Mark has received numerous awards that honor his entrepreneurial spirit, philanthropic heart, and business acumen. He is a lifetime member of the Horatio Alger Association of Distinguished Americans.

You can reach Mark at www.markvictorhansen.com.

Amy Newmark is the publisher and editor-in-chief of *Chicken Soup for the Soul*, after a thirty-year career as a writer, speaker, financial analyst, and business executive in the worlds of finance and telecommunications. Amy is a *magna cum laude* graduate of Harvard College, where she majored in Portuguese, minored in French, and traveled extensively. She and her husband have four grown children.

After a long career writing books on telecommunications, voluminous financial reports, business plans, and corporate press releases, Chicken Soup for the Soul is a breath of fresh air for Amy. She has fallen in love with Chicken Soup for the Soul and its life-changing books, and really enjoys putting these books together for Chicken Soup's wonderful readers. She has co-authored more than three dozen *Chicken Soup for the Soul* books and has edited another two dozen.

You can reach Amy through the webmaster@chickensoupforthesoul.com.

Thank You

We owe huge thanks to all of our contributors. We know that you poured your hearts and souls into the thousands of stories and poems that you shared with us, and ultimately with each other. We appreciate your willingness to open up your lives to other Chicken Soup for the Soul readers and help them through their own losses with your words of wisdom and your personal memories. Writing these stories was a selfless act of sharing, and we hope that putting your thoughts on paper was helpful to you as well and contributed to your healing.

We could only publish a small percentage of the stories that were submitted, but we read every single one and even the ones that do not appear in the book had an influence on us and on the final manuscript. Reading these stories was an emotional experience for us, as we shared in your pain and grief, and tried to imagine what it would be like to be in your shoes, so we owe special thanks to our editor Barbara LoMonaco, who read every submission to this book and narrowed the list down to about 300 semi-finalists. Our assistant publisher, D'ette Corona, worked with all the contributors as kindly and competently as always, obtaining their approvals for our edits and the quotations we carefully chose to begin each story. And editors Kristiana Glavin and Madeline Clapps performed their normal masterful proofreading.

We also owe a very special thanks to our creative director and book producer, Brian Taylor at Pneuma Books, for his brilliant vision for our covers and interiors. Finally, none of this would be possible without the business and creative leadership of our CEO, Bill Rouhana, and our president, Bob Jacobs.

Improving Your Life
Every Day

Real people sharing real stories—for seventeen years. Now, Chicken Soup for the Soul has gone beyond the bookstore to become a world leader in life improvement. Through books, movies, DVDs, online resources and other partnerships, we bring hope, courage, inspiration and love to hundreds of millions of people around the world. Chicken Soup for the Soul's writers and readers belong to a one-of-a-kind global community, sharing advice, support, guidance, comfort, and knowledge.

Chicken Soup for the Soul stories have been translated into more than forty languages and can be found in more than one hundred countries. Every day, millions of people experience a Chicken Soup for the Soul story in a book, magazine, newspaper or online. As we share our life experiences through these stories, we offer hope, comfort and inspiration to one another. The stories travel from person to person, and from country to country, helping to improve lives everywhere.

Share with Us

We all have had Chicken Soup for the Soul moments in our lives. If you would like to share your story or poem with millions of people around the world, go to chickensoup.com and click on "Submit Your Story." You may be able to help another reader, and become a published author at the same time. Some of our past contributors have launched writing and speaking careers from the publication of their stories in our books!

Our submission volume has been increasing steadily—the quality and quantity of your submissions has been fabulous. We only accept story submissions via our website. They are no longer accepted via mail or fax.

To contact us regarding other matters, please send us an e-mail through webmaster@chickensoupforthesoul.com, or fax or write us at:

Chicken Soup for the Soul
P.O. Box 700
Cos Cob, CT 06807-0700
Fax: 203-861-7194

One more note from your friends at Chicken Soup for the Soul: Occasionally, we receive an unsolicited book manuscript from one of our readers, and we would like to respectfully inform you that we do not accept unsolicited manuscripts and we must discard the ones that appear.